Generation to Generation

THE GUILFORD FAMILY THERAPY SERIES
Alan S. Gurman, Editor

Generation to Generation

FAMILY PROCESS IN
CHURCH AND SYNAGOGUE

Edwin H. Friedman

THE GUILFORD PRESS
New York London

© 1985 The Guilford Press
A Division of Guilford Publications, Inc.
200 Park Avenue South, New York, N.Y. 10003

Printed in the United States of America

Library of Congress Cataloging in Publication Data
Friedman, Edwin H.
  Generation to generation.
  (The Guilford family therapy series)
  Includes index.
  1. Family—Religious life.   2. Family—Religious life (Judaism)   3. Family—Psychological aspects.   4. Psychology, Religious.   I. Title
II. Series.
BL625.6.F75   1985   261.8'3585   84-19347
ISBN 0-89862-059-7

To all my families

CONTENTS

CONTENTS

Section IV. The Personal Families of the Clergy

Generation to Generation

Introduction

For decades I have listened to the anguished tales of ministers, rabbis, priests, and nuns as they relate their experiences about entanglements with members of their congregations, conflicts within their religious hierarchies, and ambivalence toward their relatives. The extraordinary similarity of these stories, despite their different contexts, has led me to two conclusions. One is that the family is the true ecumenical experience of all humankind. The second is that what most unites all spiritual leaders is not a set of beliefs or practices but the factors that contribute to our stress.

It is the thesis of this book that all clergymen and clergywomen, irrespective of faith, are simultaneously involved in three distinct families whose emotional forces interlock: the families within the congrega- ✓ tion, our congregations, and our own. Because the emotional process in all of these systems is identical, unresolved issues in any one of them can produce symptoms in the others, and increased understanding of any one creates more effective functioning in all three.

This integrated perspective of our personal and professional life turns crisis into opportunity and moves in the direction of lessening our stress. From a family systems point of view, stress is less the result ✓ of some quantitative notion such as "overwork" and more the effect of our position in the triangle of our families. It is always possible to handle more stress when we are doing it for ourselves than when we have taken it on for a relationship, no less than for a set of conflicting connections.

Employing the models and approaches of the relatively new field of family therapy, this work will demonstrate how the same understanding of family life that can aid us in our pastoral role also has important ramifications for the way we function in our congregations, for our position in our own personal families, nuclear and extended, and for the entire range of our emotional being. (For Catholic clergy, the rectory or religious order often functions exactly like a nuclear family.)

BEYOND PASTORAL COUNSELING

This is not the usual book on "pastoral counseling." While those who wish to improve their counseling skills will find much in these pages to enrich their repertoire, my intent goes well beyond a cookbook of recipes for each family "mix." The concepts of family process bring together in one perspective counseling, administration, officiating, preaching, personal growth, and leadership. Such a perspective has the effect of reintegration rather than disintegration, and, just as important, the family model offers something beyond an approach to problem solving. It presents an organic way of thinking that unifies our families and ourselves with the forces of Creation.

We can learn, for example, a great deal about what is happening in families within the congregation during terminal illness, divorce, or other end-stage family situations, by applying the family model to a congregation's responses (and our own) when *we* separate. From the other direction, the same model offers a complete strategy for how to leave or enter a new post in a manner that is least injurious to both partners by observing what happens in the families making up our congregations, and in our own, during similar separation periods.

Other reciprocal learning processes exist with regard to caring for elders. The family model offers a similar insight concerning leadership within a congregation and leadership within a personal family. It thus integrates our pastoral efforts with parents and with the way we ourselves function in our churches and synagogues. In fact, family theory suggests that *leadership is itself a therapeutic modality*. This view of leadership is so basic to what follows that it is worth elaboration. Not only does it underpin many of the counseling approaches to be described, but it also supplies the major factor that differentiates the clergy as family counselors from all other members of the helping professions.

EXPERTISE VERSUS SELF-DEFINITION

Leadership has inherent power because effecting a change in relationship systems is facilitated more fundamentally by how leaders function within their families than by the quantity of their expertise. What is vital to changing any kind of "family" is not knowledge of technique or even of pathology but, rather, the capacity of the family leader to define his or her own goals and values while trying to maintain a nonanxious presence within the system. Also, when it comes to change in families, clarity may be more important than empathy. This concept of leadership should not be confused with role modeling. It is an organic concept rooted in the nature of family process. The message pathways between any family and its "head" are embedded in the structure of the organism; they are far more direct than conscious communication, and too basic to be explained adequately by the concept of the unconscious.

The notion that self-definition is a more important agent of change than expertise unifies our healing power with that which promotes our own health (literally, our wholeness). There is an intrinsic relationship between our capacity to put families together and our ability to put ourselves together. This is why in some respects this book is aimed less at healing than at the healer. It is not easy, however, to preserve this perspective on leadership because both congregational and personal families tend to reverse the priorities of expertise and self-definition, particularly when they become anxious. This is equally true of their demands in our general ministries and in our counseling efforts.

MULTIPLE EXPERTISE

In our general ministries, as we all know, society's emphasis on expertise rather than on self-definition has forced us to think about our existence in terms of specialities and subspecialities of teaching, preaching, counseling, administrating, fund-raising, organizing, socializing, and politicizing, and trying to do each equally well. The resulting fragmentation dissipates our power into discontinuous directions and crazy-quilt patterns. Worse, the patterns themselves are so inextricably interwoven that whenever we are stretched in one direction the fabric of our lives is simultaneously tugged in another. But the specialization is not the disease. The sickness is in the way society wants us to cope with our specialities: by becoming expert, by assuming that our effectiveness lies in walking an unending treadmill of always trying to learn all we can, despite the fact that we live in a world where even the best specialists can no longer cover more than a corner of their field. If we must conceive of leadership in terms of expertise rather than self-definition, none of us will ever feel adequately prepared. The disintegration of self that threatens all clergy today is due less to the structure of our lives than to the way we are expected to organize our thinking. And yet, because family theory locates the power of change in those who assume the *position* of family leaders, it offers a way of thinking about all our various roles that is at once less enervating and more integrative. Because this view of leadership focuses on the self-definition of the leader as the unifying matrix of his or her existence, it veers away from thinking in terms of roles.

COUNSELING EXPERTISE

But if all of the above is generally true, it is particularly true with respect to counseling. Society's way of thinking inevitably determines our thinking; once again the focus is on expertise (in pathology and technique) rather than on self-definition, and once again, it is this very perspective that deflects us from the real source of our own power. Here especially the family model offers a way of thinking that potentiates the power inherent in our position.

The world of psychotherapy has become specialized *ad absurdum*. It is possible today to become expert in thousands of emotional problems that range from:

- agoraphobia to xenophobia
- living with preschoolers to living with aging parents
- coping with single parenting to coping with stepchildren
- personality disorder to schizophrenia
- impotence to promiscuity
- abuse of substances to child abuse
- creativity to catatonia

And all of the aforementioned cross-referenced to "women's issues."

Not only that, it is possible to specialize further by taking any one of many different approaches from Freud, Sullivan, *et al.*; family theories; therapies of art, dance, and milieu; training in sensitivity; training by means of biofeedback and hypnosis; and the like.

Nor does the specialization end there. One can narrow his or her focus further by deciding to concentrate on any of the above problems with any of the above approaches from the particular point of view of any given member of a family and from any specific ethnic or socioeconomic group.

Were it necessary for counselors to have all that information, no one could promote healing at all. In the world of psychotherapy, the focus on pathology has almost become pathologic because healers have been turned into pathologists. But, as we all know from our experience with the higher criticism of Biblical texts, complexity should not be confused with profundity. The fact that a whole can be broken down

4

into its component parts does not necessarily guarantee better understanding.

This emphasis on pathology and, therefore, expertise inhibits the power of pastoral counseling in two different ways: in the nature of healing, and in the nature of our profession.

First, with regard to the nature of healing, it is not clear at all that knowledge of pathology is even necessary to promote healing. In the real world of family life there may be no such thing as "abuse," "single parenting," "hyperactivity," or maybe even "cancer." In reality, one is always dealing with the diagnosed condition plus the family's own response to that condition (see Chapter 2). Thinking about families in terms of diagnostic categories leads both the family and its counselor to view pathological conditions as so many slices of life, even as the laboratory pathologist observes different slices of tissue. Cells that function one way in the laboratory, however, can function differently within the living organism. And family members who function one way in textbook case histories will function differently in real life depending on other differentiating factors such as motivation and resiliency. Ultimately, healing and survival depend on existential categories: on vision, for example, on hope, on the imaginative capacity, on the ability to transcend the anxiety of those about us, and on a response to challenge that treats crisis as opportunity for growth (all attributes of, or best promoted by, leadership). Without these personal factors knowledge of pathology may be quite irrelevant and often their presence makes such information unnecessary. This deemphasis on pathology should not be confused with faith healing. Faith healing may be any kind of healing that puts faith in the functioning of the healer (no matter what his or her degree) rather than in the family's own natural resources.

Second, with regard to the nature of pastoral counseling, the family model strongly suggests that no other member of society is in a better position to foster these existential encouragements to healing than the clergy because of the unique entrée into family systems our community position has given us. Ministers, rabbis, priests, and nuns have an entrée into the multigenerational processes of families that is just not available to any other members of the helping professions no matter what their training or skill. This entrée gives us unusual therapeutic potential.

There are many reasons for this special position, all connected to the nature of family process itself. One is the multigenerational forces behind our respective traditions. A second is our involvement in families during rites of passage. As will be discussed later (Chapter 7) these rites are the most advantageous moments for entering and changing any family system. Life-cycle events are "hinges of time" on which doors can open or close for generations. A third, more subtle, factor is the length of time over which we become intimate with families (sometimes it spans more than a generation), as well as the wide variety of noncounseling experiences we share with them. On the one hand, this type of entrée enables us to observe families endure major crises and change without resorting to professional expertise. On the other, the same unusual entrée enables us to become acquainted with families that are not overly disturbed by the very factors usually blamed for the troubles other families are experiencing—differences in background, possessive mothers, or alcoholic fathers. We are therefore in a unique position to appreciate, and therefore promote, the healing power of natural family resources and to realize that like bacteria, viruses, and carcinogens, emotional pathogens cannot undo a family alone. The fourth factor contributing to the clergy's unusual entrée into families is that we are often their leaders.

These four aspects of our therapeutic position do not come together in the same way for any other type of counselor. Members of the other helping professions may be able to teach us the tools of their trade, but with rare exceptions they cannot comprehend our position—either its healing potential or the problems of the emotional interlock of our various families (not to mention its insight crossovers); and they rarely have the kind of personal experience that would enable them to appreciate how leadership itself can be a therapeutic modality.

THE FAMILY MODEL AND RELIGION

The family model not only has the capacity to potentiate natural aspects of our healing position, it does so without doing violence to religion's metaphor. This is an important caution today as religious leaders of all faiths eagerly seek to benefit from new knowledge. There is, however, a fundamental difference between benefitting from new approaches and buying wholesale into another conceptual system's paradigm. The first approach increases understanding; the second is simply conversion.

Because we are positioned within all of our families, the family model, rather than having the appearance of a graft, seems to be more in organic harmony with religion in that it is less likely to lead us away from our professional roots and further strengthens our traditional position. Actually, the family model places pastoral counseling in the service of heightening spirituality rather than creating one more burdensome subspeciality. The emotional processes in a family always have the power to subvert or override its religious values. The emotional system of any family, parishioner or congregational, can always "jam" the spiritual messages it is receiving. Thus, to whatever extent we can use our unique access to families to foster emotional healing, we are always at every moment preparing the way for other, more spiritual experiences to come later. Indeed, because of this intricate connection between the emotional processes of a family and its spirituality, the family model creates a perspective for heightening the religiosity of many occasions simply by the way we involve family members.

AUTHOR'S EXPERIENCE

The ideas and examples contained here are based on a quarter century of continuous experience in the Washington, D.C., metropolitan area where I have served ever since I was ordained as both congregational rabbi and family therapist with a broadly nonsectarian practice. This experience came to include the teaching and supervising of family counselors from all the helping professions, as well as members of the clergy from all the major denominational groups. The latter function has included counseling clergy families with respect to their own problems, and the "coaching" of clergymen and clergywomen with regard to their congregations and their community of faith.

My own personal experiences both with my family and my congregation have also influenced this work. (See Chapter 12 on my family of origin and Chapters 9 and 10 on my congregation.) It is more than a matter of practicing what I preach, however. What I have written about here has been the central focus of my life for more than two decades. It was impossible that my ideas would not have carried over into my own personal and professional life, or that my personal experiences would not have influenced the development of my thinking.

A NOTE ON STRUCTURE

Finally, two comments are in order about the structure and contents of this book. In two different ways they mirror the very processes I am about to describe. First, the book is not filled with quotations from Scripture or other Holy Works. This is so in part because it is ecumenical by nature, and I have left it to each reader to supply the appropriate words from his or her religious traditions. But the omission of religious texts also results from the aforementioned emphasis on self-definition rather than on technique. I do not believe that what makes pastoral counseling pastoral is whether we have packaged our psychology in Scripture.

Consistent with the family model, I believe that the efficacy of the pastoral approach resides in our position in the emotional processes of our community and how we function within that position, in all aspects of our "family leadership" and not just while we are counseling. It has always seemed to me, therefore, that what makes pastoral counseling "pastoral" is whether we, the pastors, have listened to Scripture! If so, then to the extent we function and grow within the context of our own souls (a lifetime project) and abet the emergence of our own selves (by a willingness to face life's challenges and oneself), our spirituality and our tradition will spring naturally from our being.

The second way in which this book mirrors the process it describes is that the various chapters form the same kind of spiral feedback process that occurs in families. In the effort to understand any family, we might begin with one relationship and, then, after exploring all the others, ultimately return again to the first in order to deepen our initial understanding. Thus, the reader could really begin with any chapter, as long as he or she completed the cycle. The organic connection between the chapters means that reading any one in isolation from the others can give it the wrong slant. The three different sections of this work are devoted to three different clerical families that more than parallel one another. As with the various types of families they describe, they reinforce a better understanding of one another.

The deepest appreciation of emotional process, for example, shows up in the chapter on physical illness (Chapter 5); the clearest delineation of effective parenting is in the chapter on congregational leadership (Chapter 9); the most powerful evidence for the natural therapeutic power of religion is in the chapter on life-cycle officiating (Chapter 7); and the most encompassing explanation of emotional process in divorce, death, and leaving home is in the chapter on separating from a congregation (Chapter 10).

Each of these chapters feeds back to a deeper understanding of those that preceded it, and yet each only has that retroactive power because the others came first. The reader is invited, therefore, not only to explore a book on family process in church and synagogue, but also to encounter the very nature of that process itself.

FAMILY THEORY

1

The Idea of a Family

Several weeks before her wedding, a bride (1) came in to see her minister. The young woman looked tired and was exceedingly nervous. She had been dreaming about other men. Consciously, at least, she loved her fiancé (2), though she did feel frustrated by the fact that he was not taking stronger stands with his former wife (3) regarding their daughter (4). (See Figure 1-1). The other woman's hostility toward her also perplexed the bride because they had never met. Adding to her burden at the moment was increasing indecision over whether to have children. The bride told her pastor that she was beginning to have doubts about her capacity to do anything, and was afraid there might be something "deeply" wrong with her.

Trained in a family approach, the minister did not treat her depression as if it were her own. He suggested that she resist the temptation to analyze her dreams. He proposed that she consider them a symptom of her relationship with her fiancé, for whom she had begun to take too much responsibility, and that she give her bridegroom back his anxiety by reporting her fantasies directly to him and by saying, for example, "You know, honey, I have been having the weirdest dreams recently. I wonder if you have any thoughts on where they could be coming from?"

The bride was then coached to get out of the "triangle" between her future husband and his former wife by establishing a direct relationship with the other woman, perhaps with a note something like this:

Dear Joan,

As you know, John and I are about to be married. Though we have never met, I thought I should introduce myself since I will be sharing in the responsibility of your daughter when she comes to visit from time to time.

11

John has told me how important Jeannie is to you. I hope that you will feel free to communicate your standards or concerns directly to me, so that I can help raise her in accordance with your goals and wishes.

Sincerely,

Finally, because issues related to the reproductive cycle are often connected to unresolved issues with one's mother (5), the minister suggested that the bride invite her own "bossy" mother to lunch and reverse her tendency to shy away from leaning on her mother "at all costs," by presenting her mother with the childbearing conflict.

Two weeks later at the rehearsal dinner, the bride looked radiant and mentioned that she hadn't slept so well in years. In addition, her mother, not always this minister's favorite parishioner, was absolutely gushing in praise over "their longstanding relationship." And John's former wife caused none of the expected trouble about their daughter coming to the ceremony.

Several months later, John's former wife again began to make excessive demands. Instead of getting caught in the middle, however, by sympathetically listening to her new husband's laments, the new wife took a stand about what she was willing to put up with in their relationship. This time it was the bridegroom who called the minister to discuss his difficulty sleeping. With the problem now located where it belonged, the minister helped the bridegroom rework his relationship with his own mother (6), whom he tried never to upset, and thereby become better able to take stands with his former spouse. That relationship then ceased to be a source of harassment in the new marriage.

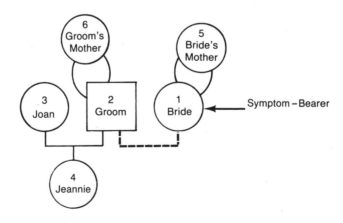

The strategies of healing employed by this minister focused on the overall relationship system of the family rather than the psychodynamics of its members. It is based on new ways of thinking about personal difficulties and is known as *family therapy*. This approach deemphasizes the notion that our conflicts and anxieties are due primarily to the makeup of our personalities, and suggests, instead, that our individual problems have more to do with our relational networks, the makeup of *others'* personalities, where we stand within the relational systems, and how we function within that position. It understands the symptom bearer to be only the "identified" patient and the person's problem to be symptomatic of something askew in the family itself. The theory can be extended to any relational system from a business partnership to a religious institution, where a problem in the "flock" can show up in the burnout of its "shepherd."

This chapter will introduce five basic concepts of family theory, describe how the family model differs from the individual model, and show the range of its application for the families of the clergy. In keeping with the approach, we will begin with a short history of its origins.

HISTORICAL PERSPECTIVE

Family therapy is the child of two mid-20th-century revolutions: one in the way we think about ourselves and one in the way we think about the world about us; like any offspring, it is a combination of the two.

A MODERN REFORMATION

The first revolution, which has been somewhat like a reformation, is the extraordinary upheaval that has been occurring in the world of psychotherapy since World War II. Today there are probably more than 200 therapeutic modalities. Back in the early 1940s psychotherapy was practically synonomous with psychoanalysis. Freud, Jung, Adler, and Rank all had their differences, but they belonged to the "true tradition," so to speak. Thus, when B. F. Skinner began to publicize his unorthodox ideas in the late '40s, that behavior patterns were fixed by the reinforcements that occurred *after* the behavior, rather than elicited by what was in a person's head *before*, his views were immediately branded apostasy. *Walden II* was no less than a theological treatise tacked on the academic doors, and it set the stage for the kind of irreconcilable conflict for man's soul (Greek: *psyche*) that had not been seen on this planet for 500 years. Insight versus behavior replaced faith versus works, and excommunication became a matter of whose practice was excluded from the health insurance plans.

The aftermath of this recent reformation has been a myriad of denominations and sects arguing about words and rites. Each, in an effort to define its own identity, began by ambivalently attacking and borrowing from the "mother church" (psychoanalysis). Each developed its own view of man, sin, and atonement; each had its own holy works, priesthoods, saints, sacred societies, devils, rites and exorcism, and heretics. (Generally everyone sees everyone else as a heretic.) Some of the approaches emphasize dependency on the spiritual leader, some seem to be saying "every man his own therapist." Some emphasize rites or methods, others awakening. Some (Esalen) are more charismatic, while some (Primal Scream) are tinged with apocalypse. Even with T.A. (Transactional Analysis) one can be "high church" or "low church." Today, apostles proliferate everywhere, often interpreting the same masters differently. And, as the founders of many of these movements pass on, eyewitness accounts of their words and deeds, written by their closest disciples, come to light. Finally, to complete the analogy, a counterreformation has already begun, as psychoanalysts publish ideas today that would have been totally anathema only a few decades ago.

From this perspective, family therapy (including its own schisms and sects) is one more denomination, one more approach to the ways human beings think about their nature and seek salvation from their emotional difficulties. From another perspective, however, family therapists are of a different faith entirely. For unlike almost all the other schools of psychotherapy, the family approach is also the by-product of another revolution that has been going on in humankind's thinking. This second revolution has to do with the way we order the world about us. It is called *systems thinking*, and is the response of the human mind to the challenge of the information explosion that has been steadily expanding during the past half century.

SYSTEMS THINKING

Since computers were introduced in the '50s, the speed with which they can perform functions has doubled at least every other year, and their size has been reduced proportionately to the increase in their memory capacity. The process feeds upon itself as the various fields of human endeavor cross-pollinate their findings.

Our brains have been avalanched by this blizzard of data. But the sheer volume of information is only one aspect of the problem. More significant is the fact that the increasing quantities have reached new thresholds of complexity, so that even the old ways of making sense out of information have become inadequate. Computers may aid in the collecting, storing, and sorting of information, but it is still necessary for the human mind to think meaningfully about what is "at hand."

Systems thinking began in response to this dimension of the information problem. It deals with data in a new way. It focuses less on content and more on the *process* that governs the data; less on the cause-and-effect connections that link bits of information and more on the principles of organization that give data meaning. One of the most important ramifications of this approach for individuals who must organize and make sense out of a great deal of information (such as members of the clergy) is that it no longer becomes necessary to "know all about something" in order to comprehend it; the approach also helps establish new criteria for what information is important.

The most outstanding characteristic of systems thinking is its departure from traditional notions of linear cause and effect. In linear thinking, cause and effect is a billiard ball concept: A causes B; B causes C; C causes D; D causes E. (See Figure 1-2.) Multiple causation (Figure 1-3), where $A + B + C + D = E$, is also linear thinking.

Systems thinking (Figure 1-4) at first resembles multiple causation but there is a significant difference. While A, B, C, and D again come together to "cause" E, they are not independent forces themselves. They are interdependent with one another. Each part of the system (including the effect itself, "E") is connected to, or can have its own effect upon, every other part. Each component, therefore, rather than having its own discrete identity or input, operates as part of a larger whole. *The components do not function according to their "nature" but according to their position in the network.*

It is the *structure* ABCDE that becomes the unit of study. To take one part out of the whole and analyze its "nature" will give misleading results, first, because *each part will function differently outside the system*, and second, because even its functioning inside the system will be different depending on *where it is placed in relation to the others*. In fact, the very notion of "effect" becomes relative. It is simply that part of the structure (system) that one has decided to focus upon.

Thinking systemically has always been natural to chess champions. It opens new ways for understanding history. Only the most unsophisticated football fans reserve their praise for the ball carrier alone, or blame the quarterback every time he gets "sacked." In meteorology it has long been recognized that for a tornado to come into existence, the temperature, the barometric pressure, and the humidity all must reach certain thresholds in the atmosphere at exactly the same time. Systems thinking can even be applied to genetics, where recent evidence from microbiology has shown that the same gene can function differently depending on its relationship to other genes.

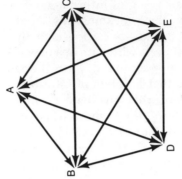

FIGURE 1-4. Systems thinking.

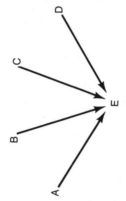

FIGURE 1-3. Multiple causation.

FIGURE 1-2. Linear causation.

Systems Thinking and the Family

When nonlinear thinking is applied to family process it produces similar formulations. It understands emotional phenomena in terms of interdependent variables. For example:

- The "atmosphere" necessary for physical symptoms to erupt in a family may only occur when more than one condition, some physical and some emotional, are both present simultaneously.
- Mother–child relationships must be understood not only in terms of their mutual influence upon one another, but also in terms of the emotional field in which they are both situated.
- The same mother–child relationship will have a different character depending on how father is functioning, not just on how he relates to the child, or to mother, but by the *extent to which* his presence throughout that nuclear system tends to be reactive, distant, or nonanxious.
- Even trauma can be conceived in terms of systems rather than linear cause and effect by saying that psychological or physiological trauma resides in the response of the family to a shock. It is the emotional system of the family that either sets up the precondition for the quantity of damage a shock can promote, or extends the effects of that shock by its continued reaction to the event. A shocking event, therefore, will leave traumatic residue *to the extent* some other variables (such as guilt) are present. Neither shock nor guilt can "cause" it alone.

Family theory maintains that such focus on the systemic forces of emotional process rather than on the content of specific symptoms is just as applicable whether the family problem surfaces as anorexia, senility, bad school habits, obesity, alcoholism, adultery, or chronic lower back pain. As will be seen, the elimination of linear cause-and-effect thinking has important consequences for diagnosis (and blaming), for prediction, and for evaluating change.

Systems Thinking and Change

Systems thinking also creates different strategies for inducing change. As is the nature of new tools, their creation contributes to their evolution. When sophisticated electronic equipment became too complex to take apart if they dysfunctioned, an approach to "healing" developed that came to be called "black box theory." Instead of trying to analyze the infinite variety of A–Z connections in a system, it once again treats the structure as a whole and tries to correct problems not

17

by eliminating or fixing the "bad part," but by inserting new input designed to cancel out what has gone wrong.

In other words, the "sick" part does not have to be removed or corrected if other components in the system can be made to function differently or to change their relationships with one another. In such a view, "sick" becomes a matter of definition rather than essence. The characterization of "sick" depends less on the nature of the dysfunctional element and more on how the whole of which it is a part is functioning, as well as how that whole responds to its own "ill" member. (See Chapter 2 for the role of feedback in maintaining chronic conditions.)

Black box theory may seem soul-less at first, but it leads to a highly moral approach to change. For if a human relationship system is so inextricably connected that the functioning of any member can best be understood in terms of the presence of the *others*, then the most successful way to bring change to all our families is not by concentrating on the input of others; indeed, that very effort will become incorporated into the system. The possibilities of change are maximized rather when we concentrate on modifying *our own* way of functioning, our own input, into the family "black box." As we shall see, the concept of responsibility for our own "input" is applicable to efforts to change in a personal or a congregational family. It is the rationale for the "coaching" approach to counseling that will be described later, and it lays the basis for a powerful style of leadership in both professional and personal families that will be called leadership through self-differentiation.

In sum, the contribution of the systems revolution to family therapy is a way of thinking characterized by:

1. Focus on (emotional) process rather than symptomatic content.
2. Seeing effects as integral parts of structures rather than as an end point in linear chains of cause.
3. Eliminating symptoms by modifying structure rather than by trying to change the dysfunctional part directly.
4. Predicting how a given part is likely to function not by analyzing its nature but by observing its position in the system. This has enormous ramification for approaches to premarital counseling that focus on the position of the bride and groom in their respective families of origin rather than concentrating on the fit of their own personalities (see Chapter 3).

Circling back to the opening example: The woman's minister did not focus on the content of her dreams or her depression, either of which could be seen as symptomatic of her position in the family. Instead, he applied certain systemic principles, to be explained shortly, about emotional triangles, in particular, the fact that if we get caught in the middle of an unresolved issue between two others, we will wind up with the stress in their relationship. Then, rather than trying to change the bride's nature, the minister suggested changes in the way the bride was functioning, having her bring new input into the system in order to shift the stress and increase her partner's motivation to change.

In short, he located the problem in the *structure* of the system rather than in the nature of the symptomatic member. Family therapy does this by describing the person with the symptom as the *identified patient*. The logic of this theory suggests that this way of thinking can be applied to any symptom, emotional or physical, and it fits equally well with all family members (parents, grandparents, spouse, or child) and in any culture (black or white, Jewish or Christian, Western or Oriental). This fact is extremely important. Because it is transcultural, the theory may be rooted in protoplasm itself; nothing could be more fundamental to the characteristics of ecumenicity.

FAMILY SYSTEMS THEORY: FIVE BASIC CONCEPTS

Here are five basic, interrelated concepts that distinguish the family model from the individual model. They are the aforementioned idea of the *identified patient*, the concept of *homeostasis* (balance), *differentiation of self*, *the extended family field*, and *emotional triangles*. Each will be discussed in terms of its place in family theory and its importance for the families of the clergy. Not all schools of family therapy emphasize these five concepts to the same extent or with the same terminology. The choice reflects my own theoretical orientation within the family movement, and the fact that, taken together, they form a useful matrix for understanding the similarities and the crossovers among the clergy's three families.

THE IDENTIFIED PATIENT

The concept of the identified patient, as stated earlier, is that the family member with the obvious symptom is to be seen not as the "sick one" but as the one in whom the family's stress or pathology has surfaced. In a child it could take the form of excessive bedwetting, hyperactivity, school failures, drugs, obesity, or juvenile diabetes; in a spouse its form could be excessive drinking, depression, chronic ailments, a heart condition or perhaps even cancer; in an aged member of the family it could show up as confusion, senility, or agitated and random behavior. In a congregational family it could surface as the drinking, burnout, or sexual acting out of the "family leader."

19

The purpose of using the phrase *identified patient* is to avoid isolating the "problemed" family member from the overall relationship system of the family. Some have said that this is a break with the medical model used in individual theories of behavior. That is only partially correct. To the extent that the medical model employs diagnosis of individuals (diabetic, cardiac, hemophiliac), the concept certainly appears to be a break with that model, which when applied to emotional conditions uses terms like "hysteric," "manic–depressive," "obsessive," "alcoholic," or "hyperactive." However, to the extent the medical model suggests an organic way of thinking, the *identified patient* concept *is* harmonious with that model, and in some ways, as in the notion of referred pain, is simply an extension of it.

The Family as the Unit of Treatment

Physicians obviously do not assume that the part of a human organism that is in pain, or failing to function properly, is necessarily the cause of its own distress. The color of the skin can be related to a problem in the liver; a pain in the jaw could be referred from angina. In addition, problems in any organ can be related to excessive overfunctioning, underfunctioning, or disfunctioning of another. For example, the failure of the kidneys to reduce salt content ultimately could increase stress on the heart. The failure of the pancreas to regulate its production of insulin could lead to stress on the kidneys. When it comes to the human organism, medicine has long realized that focusing on symptoms alone, or on a dysfunctional part in isolation from the rest of the body, will only bring short-term relief.

And so it is, says family theory, with the organism known as the human family. When one part of that organism is treated in isolation from its interconnections with another, as though the problem were solely its own, fundamental change is not likely. The symptom is apt to recycle, in the same or different form, in the same or a different member. Trying to "cure" a person in isolation from his or her family, says family theory, is as misdirected, and ultimately ineffective, as transplanting a healthy organ into a body whose imbalanced chemistry will destroy the new one as it did the old. It is easy to forget that the same "family" of organs that rejects a transplant contributed to the originally diseased part becoming "foreign."

In a family emotional system, when an unresolved problem is isolated in one of its members and fixed there by diagnosis, it enables the rest of the family to "purify" itself by locating the source of its "disease" in the disease of the *identified patient*. By keeping the focus on one of its members, the family, personal or congregational, can deny the very issues that contributed to making one of its members symptomatic, even if it ultimately harms the entire family. This notion will be explored more in depth in the discussion of *homeostasis*. It is mentioned here, however, because it is exactly this process of displacement that the coinage of the term *identified patient* was designed to prevent.

The Family Projection Process

Some have equated the family process of alienation by labeling with scapegoating, and it does have much in common with scapegoating phenomena. The position of blacks in the United States can be conceptualized by family theorists as symptomatic of unresolved issues between whites, and a similar analogy can be made about the position of any small nation among larger powers. The term *scapegoating*, however, suggests far more conscious awareness than is usually present when this process occurs in families. The creation of an identified patient is often as mindless as the body's rejection of one of its own parts. A more important reason for not calling this labeling process scapegoating is that pathology can also surface as a "superpositive" symptom of a strikingly high achiever, for example, or an overly responsible sister. Such family members are just as likely to be overly stressed, particularly at times of crisis, because their position in the system allows them little freedom to function differently. As with the human body, severe overfunctioning, as well as severe dysfunctioning, is itself evidence of a problem in a system and will, in turn, promote problems elsewhere, whether the system is a family or a congregation.

An example of this type of overfunctioning especially familiar to clergy is found in men or women who get "cold feet" before a wedding. The apparent "cowardice" is almost always symptomatic of their position in their families of origin. In my experience, every male I have ever seen, and some females, who backed out after a wedding date was set, was in a position of "standard bearer" in his or her family of origin. The standard bearer usually is the oldest male, or the only one to carry on the family name, or anyone (male or female) who has replaced a significant progenitor two or even three generations back. Such individuals have great difficulty giving emotion or time to their marriage or their children. Success has the compelling drive of ghosts behind it. They have too much to do in the short span of a lifetime. In addition, failure is more significant because it is not only themselves or even their own generation that they will have failed. Individuals, for example, who commit suicide after business failures often occupy the standard bearer position. If it had been only their own failure, they might have been able to "live with themselves." Such family members are caught in a multigenerational cul-de-sac in which history is their destiny. Something similar is frequently found in the family history of

21

members of the clergy and will be illustrated further in Section IV. For the moment, that multigeneration identifying process can be put in the form of a question: Which of your ancestors really ordained you?

Ramifications for Counseling

The concept of the *identified patient* has two important practical ramifications for counseling that also help distinguish the family method from approaches based on the individual model. With the latter, by the nature of the case, the counselor works primarily with the problemed person, perhaps also seeing other members of the family to give them support or for additional insight into the identified member. With a family systems model, however, it is possible to work with a nonsymptomatic member of the family instead! There are situations where the symptomatic member is so unmotivated that it is probably advisable not to give them an opportunity to sabotage progress of the counseling. (Insight only works with people who are motivated to change.)

As will be seen later, this effort to defocus the symptomatic family member is really to focus on leadership and is the basis for the coaching model to be described throughout this work. With an organic systems model, the criterion of whom to counsel is no longer who has the symptom, but *who has the greatest capacity to bring change to the system*. That may or may not be the member with the identifiable symptom. To return to the previous medical analogy, an approach that leaves the symptomatic member out of the counseling eventually may become concerned with how other parts of the organism being examined relate to still other parts. As will be illustrated in coming chapters, it is possible to relieve a symptom in a child by leaving him or her out of the counseling altogether; the process can also be aided by focusing instead on mother's relationship with her own mother. It is possible to relieve a symptom in one spouse by seeing the other spouse alone; the process can also be facilitated by reconnecting that partner to his or her own extended family. Similarly, in congregational families it is possible to tone down, if not resolve completely, severe congregation–clergy disputes by defocusing the congregational issue and focusing the key parties on unresolved issues in other important relationships in their lives.

The second important practical ramification of the *identified patient* concept is that counseling based on the family model is not distinguished from individual model counseling with respect to how many people are seen at one time. *The difference has to do with where the focus is placed*, in a person or in the system. A major consequence of this distinction is that *family therapy* should not be confused with what has been traditionally understood as "family counseling." In the latter, family members are seen in order to help them cope with a problem in another family member. But that only reinforces the labeling process. Family therapy, instead of simply trying to calm the family, tends to treat crisis as an opportunity for bringing change to the entire emotional system, with the result that everyone, and not just the *identified patient*, personally benefits and grows.

To refer to the opening example once more, had the minister focused on the identified bride alone, not only would the system have remained unchanged and created more symptoms later (in the bride's health or perhaps in divorce), other members of the family would also have lost out because of the stillborn opportunity. They never would have benefited from the overall healthier atmosphere that resulted when the minister refused to "conspire" in the identifying process. The unresolved conflicts and attachments in that family eventually could have resulted in emotional or physical health problems in other members. It was a system in search of a symptom. The concept of the *identified patient*, therefore, is not only freeing for the symptomatic family member, it places a healing power in the hands of the counselor, a power that is far wider in range. No one is better situated to take advantage of that position than the clergy.

HOMEOSTASIS (BALANCE)

As stated, family systems thinking locates a family's problem in the nature of the system rather than in the nature of its parts. A key to that relocation is the concept of homeostasis: the tendency of any set of relationships to strive perpetually, in self-corrective ways, to preserve the organizing principles of its existence. Theories based on the individual model tend to conceptualize the "illness" of a family in terms of the character traits of individual members, and the ways in which their various personal problems mesh. The family model, on the other hand, conceptualizes a system's problems in terms of an imbalance that must have occurred in the network of its various relationships, no matter what the nature of the individual personalities.

Family theory assumes that no matter what the various members' quirks or idiosyncrasies, if the system exists and has a name, it had to have achieved some kind of balance in order to permit the continuity necessary for maintaining its identity. The basic question family theory always asks, therefore, is not do these types of personalities fit, but, rather, what has happened to the fit that was there? Why has the symptom surfaced now? This is not a static concept, but a dynamic one, as when a thermostat controls the temperature balance, not at a fixed point, but within a range. Similarly, the fact that the balance in a family system has gone beyond the range of its own thermostat is not always bad. If only some families could be less stable!

The concept of homeostasis can help explain why a given relationship system, family or congregation, has become troubled. It sheds light on which family member becomes, or is likely to become, symptomatic (the *identified patient*). It elucidates the resistance families have to change. It guides in the creation of strategies for change. And it helps develop criteria for distinguishing real change from the recycling of a symptom.

Symptom and Position

The most important ramification of homeostasis for family theory is its emphasis on position rather than personality when explaining the emergence of a symptom. For example, imagine a set of conduits connected in an asymmetrical pattern. Let us assume that one of the pipes becomes blocked, causing the pressure in the rest of the system to increase. Eventually, if the added pressure cannot be redistributed, in order for the system to stay stable, one pipe or another will have to spring a leak. But the pipe so "chosen" will not necessarily be the one that was structurally the weakest. It will be rather that conduit whose *position* in the overall system caused it to pick up most of the pressure. This is exactly what can happen in a family when a death, a geographical move, a divorce, or a sudden cutoff results in added pressure (focus) on another member. And the process can appear to be just as automatic.

The concept of homeostasis also helps explain a system's resistance to change. This time our set of pipes is in a house. Underneath every sink is the well-known vertical looped cylinder. The purpose of that pipe, called a trap, is to prevent noxious gasses from entering the system. Every time it fills up or "chokes" on the influx, it saves the house and ultimately the entire network. But now let us animate those pipes. Suppose one of those traps under a sink decided to straighten itself out. We may well imagine the increased anxiety in the others, some of which might well "go through the roof." And it would seem right to conjecture that they would do everything they could to pressure that newly autonomous pipe not to straighten itself out, or, if that were too late, to bend it back in shape (out of shape?) again.

There are family members who seem to function as the anxiety trap for their system, and who regularly go to their form of "plumber" to be disgorged so that they can protect the rest of their system again. It would be nice to think that humans function on a higher level. But take a family with an ineffective mother; she lectures and threatens rather than taking stands on what she is willing to do. The husband, however, depends on her to be adaptive in their marital relationship. As much as he (as parent) would like his child to "get better," if he senses that the change in his adaptive wife necessary for continued growth in their child will disturb the balance of his marriage, he will often quit the counseling process. Sometimes he will decide suddenly that they can't afford it any more. There are husbands who even have gotten themselves transferred in order to preserve the homeostasis of their marriage.

In work systems, the stabilizing effect of an identified patient and the resistance from the togetherness at all costs help explain why even the most ruthless corporations (no less churches and synagogues) often will tolerate and adapt to trouble-making complainers and downright incompetents, whereas the creative thinker who disturbs the balance of things will be ignored, if not let go. Such homeostatically induced sabotage is a major obstacle to change in any emotional system, family or congregation. Ironically, the same qualities that allow for "familiness" (that is, stability) in the first place, are precisely what hinder change (that is, less stability) when the family system is too fixed.

Two Kinds of Interdependency

Not all systems are connected in so interdependent a fashion, of course. The reactivity of family members to one another is not always as automatic. Sets of electrical connections help illustrate this point. It is possible to connect electrical systems in what is known as "series" or "parallel." When a system of electrical components is connected in series, the outlets are related in such a way that the source of energy runs directly through each part (Figure 1-5). In such a system, if one connection goes bad, they will all go out.

But it is also possible to connect electrical components in what is called parallel (Figure 1-6). In this type of system, each outlet has its own independent connection to the main source of energy, and the functioning of each component is less dependent upon the functioning of the other members of its network.

With human networks, also, some are connected more in series, and some more in parallel. In the former, when one marital partner is depressed, so is the other, or conversely, automatically compensates. When one becomes energized by anxiety, so does everyone else. For the same reasons, in such families trouble seems to come in clusters. Often such systems can have a lot of togetherness, but the "circuit-breaker" effect of self, necessary for a system to survive crisis, is missing. It has less togetherness than stuck-togetherness.

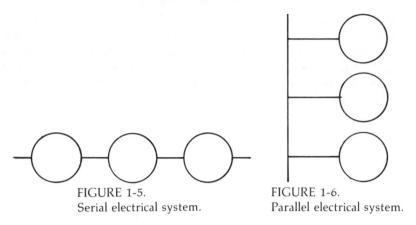

FIGURE 1-5.
Serial electrical system.

FIGURE 1-6.
Parallel electrical system.

On the other hand, to the extent any family is connected in parallel, while the members may appear to be less closely connected, they are also capable of handling more stress precisely because there is less automatic interdependency. They generally are less anxious about change in the system, and the effect of their being less reactive is that when any family member does dysfunction, he or she is enabled to heal more easily.

No human family is connected totally in series or in parallel, but all can be placed on a continuum between the two extremes, with most families closer to the "series" end. (During crisis, all families tend to slide in that direction.) The major variable that determines where any nuclear family falls on such a continuum is the degree of emotional distance between the spouses and their own extended families. Where there is great distance, the cutoff tends to make emotional forces in the nuclear family system implosive, with the result that the reactivity of its members becomes more automatic. Where there is not enough distance, the parents create a "series" connection between their families of origin and their marriage.

There is one other aspect of the concept of homeostasis worth noting because it has particular implications for the position of the clergy among their various families. With few exceptions, a nonfamily emotional system rarely achieves the same level of emotional interdependency as a personal family. The one nonfamily emotional system that comes closest to a personal family's intensity is a church or synagogue, in part because it is made up of families, and in part because so much of the force of religion is realized within the family. What this means for the clergy is that we are constantly caught between counteracting forces of two separate but interlocking homeostatic systems, each of which is difficult enough to keep on an even keel much less to keep afloat when they are influencing one another!

DIFFERENTIATION OF SELF

But if systems are self-corrective, why does or how can change occur at all? If we are trying to help a family change, what resources are available within the family for helping it overcome its own homeostatic resistance? Analogies to inanimate systems can only show us a way of thinking. With organic or animate systems there are the added factors of will and of mind (though lower biological forms of life can create symbioses that are completely homeostatic, and in human families, when there is little self-differentiation, the symbiosis in a marriage or a parent–child relationship can resemble the fusion in lower forms of cellular life). Generally, the human components of a family system have the capacity for some self-differentiation, the capacity for some awareness of their own position in the relationship system, how it is affected by balancing forces, and how changes in each individual's functioning can in turn influence that homeostasis.

One way of trying to preserve the value of a systems orientation, yet not let it become totally deterministic, has been developed by Murray Bowen of Georgetown Medical School, one of the founding fathers of family therapy. He has suggested that a key variable in the degree to which any family can change fundamentally is the amount of self-differentiation that existed in previous generations in the extended families of both partners. This multigenerational notion is worth examining for a moment, not only because it helps explain the "individual" factors in creating or overcoming homeostatic resistance, but also because it provides a theoretical framework for strategies of healing and leadership.

Scale of Differentiation

What Bowen has hypothesized is a scale of differentiation. Differentiation means the capacity of a family member to define his or her own life's goals and values apart from surrounding togetherness pressures, to say "I" when others are demanding "you" and "we." It includes the capacity to maintain a (relatively) nonanxious presence in the midst of anxious systems, to take maximum responsibility for one's own destiny and emotional being. It can be measured somewhat by the breadth of one's repertoire of responses when confronted with crisis. The concept should not be confused with autonomy or narcissism, however. Differentiation means the capacity to be an "I" while remaining connected.

Bowen suggests that all members of the human family are placed on a continuum. Where one falls on the scale, according to the theory, is determined in large part by where our parents, their parents, etc., were on the scale, with various children in each generation being

27

slightly more or less mature than their parents and tending to marry individuals with similar ranges. (This is a far more important factor in marital compatibility than cultural or other similarities.) Over several generations, different limbs on a family tree would be ascending or descending in relation to maturity. Families composed of individuals toward the bottom of the scale are not necessarily sicker, nor do they necessarily have more problems, nor are they necessarily less competent in the work world. They would, however, be far less equipped to deal with crisis, and by the nature of the case, would respond more quickly to redress the balance if the homeostasis of the family were disturbed, particularly if the disturbance were caused by another member trying to achieve a higher level of differentiation (maturity).

Such a scale might be used to describe homeostatic forces in any partnership, husband and wife, or clergyman and congregation (Figure 1-7). It can also illuminate the problems of achieving change, the homeostatic resistance to change, and the leadership quality needed to persist in the face of such resistance. A hypothetical couple at 100 on the scale would have their relationship A–B marked by infinite elasticity. Each could move toward or away from the other in separate, disengaged movements. If the husband said he was going to the movies, his wife would not be insulted if she were not invited. In fact, she could state, "I would like to go along." Or, if he asked her to go along she could feel free to say no and he could still go. There would be a maximum of "I" statements defining position rather than blaming, "you," statements that hold the other responsible for their own condition or destiny. At times, the partners might appear to be disconnected.

FIGURE 1-7. Scale of differentiation.

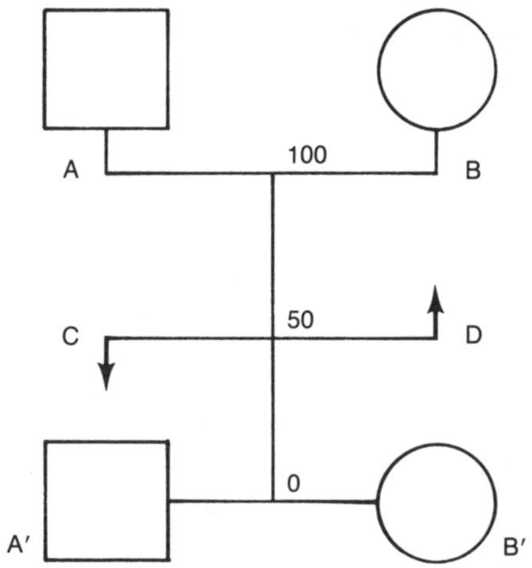

But there is nothing internally wrong with the way they are connected, nothing to keep them from being close one minute or separating another minute, with minimum tugging on each other.

At the opposite end of the scale (to which we are all closer) is a couple diagrammed as though they were fused to the ends of a stick (A'–B'). Whatever either does automatically moves the other. There is no thinking of self, only *we* and *us* and the blaming *you*. The nature of the relationship might appear close. They might appear to be together, but they are really *stuck together*. They will wind up either perpetually in conflict, because they are so reactive to one another, or they will have a homey togetherness achieved through the total sacrifice of their own selves. In the latter case, their marriage might last 50 years, but their kids are likely to dysfunction all over America because, coming out of such an ill-defined system, they carry with them little capacity for autonomy in any emotional system.

Given a couple at the middle of the scale (C–D), if either partner tries to move up, it is predictable that the other will respond in a compensatory move downward, usually in seductive or sabotaging ways to rebalance the togetherness. (Marriage counseling itself could be defined as trying to help couples move up the scale.) The farther down the scale any family is located to start with, the more automatically this principle will operate, and the more difficult it will be to find a family member who can maintain the kind of nonanxious presence needed to keep the family on a course for change. Anxious systems are less likely to allow for differentiated leaders, while leaderless systems are more likely to be anxious.

While it may sound unsympathetic, it will be shown that supporting the strengths in the family (as manifested in the differentiating member) by coaching that person to stay on a committed course can bring more fundamental healing to the entire family than can focusing on the family's weaknesses (as manifested in the dysfunctional or recalcitrant member). This does not mean coaching the leader to leave; on the contrary, that usually is neither differentiation nor a promotion of change. It is the maintaining of self-differentiation while remaining a part of the family that optimizes the opportunities for fundamental change. This emphasis on supporting family strengths, rather than shoring up family weakness, is also the basis for the leadership model. (See Chapter 9.)

Leadership and the Scale

The scale of differentiation also can be used as a means of unifying leadership in the congregational family with counseling families in the congregation because exactly the same homeostatic process is involved in the reactions of congregations to growth in their religious leaders. Here one also encounters henpecking comments: "Rabbi, your sermons need better preparation"; "Minister, why didn't you visit so-and-so at the hospital?"; "Father, we can never find you when we want you." All of these can be understood as sabotaging efforts to keep their "partner" close. In this respect, the scale helps explain which families in a congregation tend to gravitate toward one another, how various members of a congregation tend to relate to their spiritual leader, as well as why in all faith groups some congregational "families" are perceived as "pills" or "plums." It also explains one of the crossover networks between emotional process in families within the congregation and emotional process in the congregation itself. Families that function lower down on the scale are more likely to produce members who are quick to adore or be easily hurt by their clergy. They are more likely to deify (or crucify) their leaders.

Actually, there is a very accurate test any religious leader can use to obtain a reading on where the members of his congregation tend to cluster along this scale of differentiation. All we have to do is give a talk in which we carefully differentiate ourselves—define clearly what we believe and where we stand on issues, in a way that is totally devoid of "shoulds" and "musts." The response of the congregational family, no matter what the faith, will always range along the following spectrum. Those who function emotionally toward the "better differentiated" end will respond *by defining themselves*: "Father, I agree"; "I disagree"; "I believe"; etc.; or, "Ms. Jones, I like what you said, though I am not sure I can agree with you on. . . ." Those at the "less well-differentiated" end will respond not by defining themselves but by continuing *to define their clergyman or clergywoman*: "Father, how can you say that when . . ."; "Ms. Smith, how do you reconcile this with what you said the other day when you . . ."; "Rabbi, sometimes I wonder if you are even Jewish."

These responses can be extraordinarily important information in understanding and predicting how parishioners will function in crises in their own families, particularly during major life-cycle events, or during crises within the congregational family, particularly when there is a sudden loss of membership. In Chapter 9, when the resistance problems all leaders face are discussed, it will be seen that those who respond in the least differentiated manner are precisely those who sabotage progress when their leaders are functioning best. (One can also use this test with one's own children and any other partner, of course.)

One other dimension of Bowen's scale of differentiation is worth noting. It comes up four-square on the side of personal responsibility because it does not blame forces outside the family for problems inside the family. Today there is much important discussion among concerned people about schools, neighborhoods, etc., and their effect on families. But the focus on how society affects the family, rather than on how the family affects the family, can be self-defeating. Cults, for example, do not destroy families as much as stuck-togetherness attitudes in families create candidates for cults. When parents focus on societal influence it actually serves to increase their anxiety even though it helps them avoid personal responsibility. On the other hand, parents who accept the fact that their children are less likely to be influenced by other systems to the extent that they are comfortable in their own, while they might find the idea more painful at first, are given a means of approaching the problem that is quite within their power, and that can, in turn, contribute to their own self-respect.

EXTENDED FAMILY FIELD

A fourth notion that deserves introductory discussion is the concept of the extended family field. It will be explained in more detail in other chapters. The term refers to our family of origin, that is, our original nuclear family (parents and siblings) plus our other relatives (grandparents, aunts, uncles, cousins, etc.). The only members of the extended family that individual theory tends to consider important are one's parents, and their influence tends to be relegated to their impact in the past. In contrast, family theory sees the entire network of the extended family system as important, and the influence of that network is considered to be significant in the here and now as well. In addition, the concept suggests that parents themselves are someone's children, even when they are adults, and that they are still part of their own sibling systems, even after marriage.

The importance of emphasizing the contemporary relevance of the extended family field is that one "can go home again." Gaining a better understanding of the emotional processes still at work with regard to our family of origin, and modifying our response to them, can aid significantly in the resolution of emotional problems in our immediate family (marriage or parenting) or of leadership problems in a church or synagogue. In Chapter 12 it will be seen that crises of faith among the clergy also can be resolved by taking them back to their families of origin.

In addition, specific patterns of behavior, perceptions, and thinking, as well as specific issues, for example, sex, money, territory, drinking, separation, health, have an uncanny way of reappearing. When family members are able to see beyond the horizons of their own nuclear family area of trouble and observe the transmission of such issues from generation to generation, they often can obtain more distance from their immediate problems and, as a result, become freer to make changes. As will be seen, family trees are always trees of knowledge and often they are also trees of life.

Here are two examples of how multigenerational transmission can be charted on genograms to help family members gain more distance from their immediate lives.

The Figurine on a Ship's Prow: A 40-year-old woman (represented by circle number 40 in Figure 1-8) with four daughters said she was the "baby maker" of her family. She saw herself as the "figurine on the prow of a ship." Though well educated, she had never been able to get going with a career. She had become involved in several short-term affairs. The woman wished to get on with her "own" life and was unable to understand what kept her so stuck, despite her intelligence, her desire, and her efforts.

A family history showed, first, that though all the other members of her generation, her siblings and first cousins, were of reproductive age, she was the only one reproducing. Second, her mother had given up a promising career as an attorney when she married (just after her own brother had died). She also seemed content just to reproduce. In addition, both the woman's brother and her only male cousin had married women who could not conceive. They were named for their dead uncle! Grandmother also was the only one to conceive among her siblings; one brother had died early, and the other, though very successful in business, had never left home. Further investigation back another generation showed a catastrophe that had started the shock wave that was still being felt in the next two generations.

Observing family transmission over the generations can also be helpful in making predictions. This is particularly useful in premarital counseling. (See Figure 1-9).

Like Mother, Like Daughter: A history of the bride's side showed three consecutive generations in which a marriage broke up upon the birth of the first child (always a daughter). This couple can be told that their marriage might have some rough sledding after their first child is born, particularly if it is a girl. However, if the bride is willing to investigate the process further by learning about the family, from her mother and grandmother, she might be able to differentiate herself out of the cycle of multigenerational transmission.

Differentiation and Family of Origin

The most significant aspect of the extended family field is the role it can play in the process of self-differentiation. The position we occupy

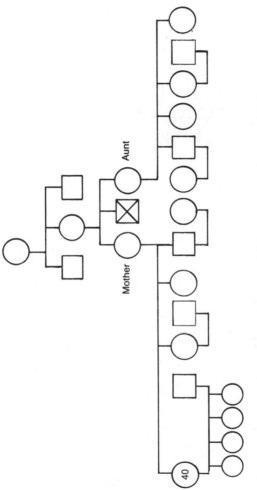

FIGURE 1-8. Genogram I: Multigenerational transmission.

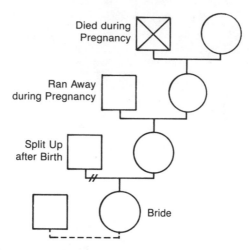

FIGURE 1-9. Genogram II: Multigenerational transmission.

in our families of origin is the only thing we can never share or give to another while we are still alive. It is the source of our uniqueness, and, hence, the basic parameter for our emotional potential as well as our difficulties. This unique position can dilute or nourish natural strengths; it can be a dragging weight that slows our progress through-out life, or an additive that enriches the mixture of our propelling fuel. The more we understand that position, therefore, and the more we can learn to occupy it with grace and "savvy," rather than fleeing from it or unwittingly allowing it to program our destiny, the more effectively we can function in any other area of our life.

In marriage, such awareness of the power of the extended family field can enable a partner to take more responsibility for, and make changes in his or her contributions to, marital problems that are chronic; in parenting, this knowledge can enable a father or mother to be more aware of, and thus diminish uptightness about, various chil-dren; and in all matters of faith and responsibility it can enable any religious leader to maximize commitment as a conscious act of self rather than duty.

For the clergy and their families there is an added bonus: No one on this earth, no counselor or even family physician, is in quite the same position for coming into contact with the multigenerational pro-cesses. They show up in a multitude of ways at rites of passage; they endure in our memories as we have different kinds of intimate contact with the same family over many years; they surface in family health crises, or problems associated with aged members. We can even see them in the emotional processes of our churches and synagogues, in the way such institutions become part of a given congregant's or parishioner's extended family, with all the consequences that holds for emotional intensity in both systems. As will be shown in Section III, the problems in the emotional system of the congregational family also can be understood by setting them in the framework of its own extended family (the hierarchy) and by tracing its own multigenerational transmission down through the years.

The thinking that surrounds the individual model tends to see the extended family field almost exclusively as the source of difficulties or pathology. The family becomes something to learn to deal with so that it won't get you. The model tends to focus on what is sick or weak in the family, what to avoid or keep at a distance. It therefore encourages individuals with problems to see their family of origin only as a source of their weakness and not as also a source of their strengths.

The family systems model, on the other hand, enables individuals to seek relationships with their family of origin; the problem with parents, after all, is that they had parents. As I will describe, the counseling approaches that encourage extended family contact are not simply techniques for bringing about change; they are, in effect, angles of reentry into the world that shaped the "ground of our being."

EMOTIONAL TRIANGLE

The fifth construct useful in understanding personal and congregational families is the concept of the emotional triangle. It offers a way of operationalizing the previous four concepts in both counseling and administrative functioning. The concept is also basic to understanding the depth and complexity of the interlocking emotional processes that link the three families of the clergy. It also provides strategies that promote survival within this "system of systems."

An emotional triangle is formed by any three persons or issues. In the case example that introduced this chapter, the bride was in a triangle with her fiancé and his former wife; her fiancé was in a triangle with both of these women. The bride was also in a triangle between her mother and the issue of becoming a mother herself, and the groom was also in a triangle between his own mother and his first wife (or with all women). Had the families of origin of both bride and groom belonged to the congregation, then the minister would have been in a triangle between those two families' various triangles.

The basic law of emotional triangles is that when any two parts of a system become uncomfortable with one another, they will "triangle in" or focus upon a third person, or issue, as a way of stabilizing their own relationship with one another. A person may be said to be "triangled" if he or she gets caught in the middle as the focus of such an unresolved issue. Conversely, when individuals try to change the relationship of two others (two people, or a person and his or her symptom or belief), they "triangle" themselves into that relationship (and often stabilize the very situation they are trying to change).

Typical emotional triangles found in families are mother–father–child; a parent and any two children; a parent, his or her child, and his or her own parents; a parent, a child, and a symptom in the child (doing badly in school, drugs, stealing, sexual acting out, allergies); one spouse, the other, and the other's dysfunction (drinking, gambling, an affair, depression).

A triangle basic to all work systems is any position of responsibility, someone you oversee, and the person who oversees you. Triangles typical of clergy work systems are the religious leader, the ruling body of lay people, and the rest of the congregation; a member of the clergy, the congregation, the budget deficit or a theological issue; a member of the clergy, the congregation, and any other professional religious leader in the same congregation (choir director, director of education, another minister, or the retired rabbi who has an emeritus position); a priest, the bishop, and the order (if not the entire hierarchy).

The two most pervasive triangles for all clergy are: (1) minister, rabbi, priest, or nun, each of his or her "charges," and that individual's own personal salvation (in this world or the next); (2) the triangle that is the basic thrust of this book: the clergy's own personal family, the congregational family itself, and any family within the congregation.

Emotional triangles have some very specific rules that they invariably obey. Awareness of these rules can help us to understand the emotional processes swirling around us, to remain more objective about intense situations, and to protect our position in counseling situations (where one spouse is bad-mouthing the other) or in congregational divisions: "Father, Mrs. Smith is out to get you, but I'm on your side." The emotional triangle concept focuses on process rather than content; it therefore provides a new way to hear people, as well as criteria for what information is important. It has been said, "What Peter says about Paul tells you more about Peter than it does about Paul." In the concept of an emotional triangle, "What Peter says to you about his relationship with Paul has to do with his relationship with you."

Here are seven laws of an emotional triangle. They are equally applicable to all families of the human species, of whatever religious persuasions, and in whatever variety of congregation of faith.

1. The relationship of any two members of an emotional triangle is kept in balance by the way a third party relates to each of them or to

their relationship. When a given relationship is stuck, therefore, there is probably a third person or issue that is part of the homeostasis.

2. If one is the third party in an emotional triangle it is generally not possible to bring change (for more than a week) to the relationship of the other two parts by trying to change their relationship directly. This includes anything from trying to make a child become more orderly, trying to make someone give up his or her "habit," or urging someone to come to church more frequently. It well may be that, in the history of our species, no family member upon trying to correct the perception of another family member about a third has ever received the response, "You're right honey. I don't know why I didn't see it that way myself."

3. Attempts to change the relationship of the other two sides of an emotional triangle not only are generally ineffective, but also, homeostatic forces often convert these efforts to their opposite intent. Trying harder to bring two people closer (brother and sister, child and parent) or another party and his or her symptom together (anyone and his or her sense of responsibility) will generally maintain or increase the distance between them. On the other hand, repeated efforts to separate a person and his or her symptom or any two parties (a spouse and his or her paramour, a child and his or her peer group, an engaged daughter and her "horrible" fiancé), or anyone and his or her cherished beliefs (a congregation and its conservatism) increases the possibility that they will fall "blindly in love" with one another.

For example, a mother became concerned when her 20-year-old son developed an imaginary girlfriend whom he used to bring home for dinner. She wanted him to see a therapist but he wouldn't go. She kept trying to "take her away" from him by forcing reality issues, but he only clung tighter. Then he said he was taking his "friend" with him on a vacation. Mother was encouraged not only to stop fighting his fantasy but to detriangle by buying Ms. Phantom a gift for the trip. He left his friend in the Caribbean. Had mother continued to try to straighten her son out, upon his return he and his friend might have moved in permanently.

4. To the extent a third party to an emotional triangle tries unsuccessfully to change the relationship of the other two, the more likely it is that the third party will wind up with the stress for the other two. This helps explain why the dysfunctional member in many families is often not the weakest person in the system, but on the contrary, often the one taking responsibility for the entire system. The concept of an emotional triangle thus creates an interrelational rather than a merely quantiative view of stress. (All diseases are communicable.) On the other hand, the concept of triangulation permits a style of leadership

that is healthier for both leader and follower, in both personal and congregational families. (See Section III.)

5. The various triangles in an emotional system interlock so that efforts to bring change to any one of them is often resisted by homeostatic forces in the others or in the system itself. In the opening case history, the efforts of the bride to detriangle from the groom and his former wife were resisted by the homeostasis in a second triangle between the groom, his former wife, and his inability to define himself in relation to women (his relationship with his mother). Another example of an interlocking triangle found in some clergy families is the one between a minister's responsibilities to his congregation, his responsibilities to his own family, and both interlocked with his wife's triangle between her mother and that woman's need for a highly achieving son-in-law.

A rather humorous example of this kind of interlocking triangle involved two ministers who were brothers-in-law. Mother frequently visited her son-the-minister and was close to his children but rarely came to visit her daughter and her children. It happens that son-in-law minister had been far more successful in his career. Suddenly grandmother started to visit her daughter's children more frequently. The shift coincided with her son-the-minister obtaining an equally prominent congregation.

Usually one triangle in an interlocking system is primary, so that change in that one is more likely to induce change in the others. The primary triangles tend to be those that involve family of origin, even when the other interlocking triangle is in the work system. In Section III we will see how this may be applied to the extended system of a religious hierarchy. In Section IV it will be shown that clerical dilemmas of faith are often connected to unresolved emotional triangles in family of origin, and can often be resolved by taking the issues back to the extended family. This is so in part because the choice of the clerical profession is often a way of dealing with such triangles in the first place.

6. One side of an emotional triangle tends to be more conflictual than the others. In healthier families, conflict will tend to swing round the compass, so to speak, showing up in different persons or different relationships at different times (even on the same day). In relationship systems that are not as healthy, the conflict tends to be located on one particular side of a triangle (the identified patient or relationship). It is often the distribution and fluidity of conflict in a family that is crucial to its health rather than the quantity or the kind of issues that arise. Systems in which the triangles are more fluid can tolerate more conflict (and therefore more creativity) because of that capacity for distribution. (This is also why other parts of a triangle, despite being upset by

conflict elsewhere, often resist change, since that would result in re-distribution.)

7. We can only change a relationship to which we belong. There-fore, the way to bring change to the relationship of two others (and no one said it is easy) is to try to maintain a well-defined relationship with each, and to avoid the responsibility for their relationship with one another. To the extent we can maintain a "nonanxious presence" in a triangle, such a stance has the potential to modify the anxiety in the others. The problem is to be both nonanxious and present. Anyone can keep his or her own anxiety down by distancing, but that usually preserves the triangle. Variations on this theme, as it applies to the counseling, administrative, and personal aspects of clergy life, will be discussed below. Sometimes it involves staying out of a triangle that is just forming when we first enter a new post. Sometimes it means getting out of one that is in existence, perhaps between our spouse and the head of an important committee. And sometimes, since triangles are by nature paradoxical, it requires reversing our input by being paradoxical ourselves, or playful, or even "irreverent." For example: Member of congregation, to minister (trying to avoid her own discon-tent—with spouse, parent, child, or life—by triangling minister into the middle as the *focus* of her discontent): "I wish you'd stop all this concern for the poor and stick to preaching the Gospel." Minister (trying to stay out of the triangling process by avoiding the content of her remark, which he would fail to do if he responded in a defensive or critical manner): "Madam, do you think the devil has got my soul?" or "I get all my ideas from *Playboy*, you know."

The most triangled position in any set of relationships is always the most vulnerable; when the laws of emotional triangles are under-stood, however, it tends to become the most powerful.

2

Understanding Family Process

This chapter will describe ten "laws" of family life derived from family theory. The purpose here, however, is not merely to offer more insight. It is rather to accustom the reader to think in terms of family process. This is not easy in a world used to the individual model, particularly where our own professional training, if not our own therapy, was conducted in that context. Thinking in terms of family process involves more than the application of new ideas. It represents a shift in paradigms, a change in the very manner of conceptualizing emotional phenomena. Thinking in terms of family systems rather than individual personalities is analogous to a shift between algebra and calculus, between Newtonian and quantum mechanics, or perhaps between seeing the crazy as bewitched or as emotionally troubled. As with all such paradigmatic shifts, there is a tendency to explain the new model in terms derived from the old.

In other words, family emotional process is not reducible to individual model psychodynamics any more than chemistry is reducible to physics. Molecules, for example, may contain atoms, but other forces are at play on the molecular level that cannot be explained in terms of elementary interactions. Worse, collecting data at an inappropriate level of inquiry tends to produce misleading information. This chapter, therefore, is an effort to demythologize several assumptions about family life that have resulted from the effort to conceptualize families as the interactions of individuals rather than individuals as the components of families.

BENEFITS FOR THE CLERGY

Familiarity with these laws of family process can also bring other benefits to members of the clergy. First, rather than having to keep in mind a catalog of all the symptoms known to the human species and their different remedies, these rules provide criteria for what information (in the encyclopedia that every family "publishes" about itself) is significant.

Second, these laws transcend culture. They are equally applicable to families from any background and are particularly useful when counseling cross-cultural couples who think their background differences make a difference.

Third, these rules are equally applicable to emotional processes in personal families and congregational families. They provide a map to the crossovers whereby problems in either of those relationship systems create symptoms in the other; conversely, they are also the keys to learning more about either family by observing emotional processes in the other.

Throughout this chapter, therefore, the word *family* always means church or synagogue as well as one's network of relations.

EMOTIONAL DISTANCE

When family members use physical distance to solve problems of emotional interdependency, the result is always temporary, or includes a transference of the problem to another relationship system.

Most family members think of distance as a physical category rather than as an emotional category. Accordingly, when they want more separation, they tend to resort to physical solutions. A husband who finds his wife's constant anxiety disturbing may spend more time on the golf course, in a bar, or at work; a wife who wants to get away from the constant surveillance of a perpetually critical husband may start taking half-hour showers; a child who finds her parents' constant focus oppressive may marry early or move far away.

While such efforts often bring relief, generally they require a great deal of energy to maintain the relief, and in many situations the same intensity just surfaces elsewhere. It is not really possible, in fact, to become totally independent from one's family except by fusing with another relationship system of equal intensity, for instance, a marriage where the spouses are poorly differentiated, or overinvolvement with one's child, a cult, or a volunteer organization.

Distancing comes about because there is not enough distance to begin with. Marriage partners may separate because they have grown distant, but most couples probably separate because they are not able to achieve any separation at all. Children may wind up undisciplined because their parents pay them no heed, but as many are problemed because they are the objects of too much investment. Emotional distance is perplexing. If there is too much, it is not possible to have a relationship; if there is not enough separation, it is also not possible to have a relationship.

The problem goes to the very essence of existence. It has been shown that if two microorganisms of the same species become close enough, often one or both will begin to disintegrate. But, the disintegration is not the result of aggression. It seems to come about as an adaptation to the relationship. It would appear that there are destructive processes at the very essence of protoplasm that can take over when loss of distance occurs with respect to other protoplasm.

For the human species, however, getting distance must go beyond obtaining physical space. As will be shown throughout this work, the capacity to define self in a relationship, and to control one's own reactive mechanisms, also creates space. The opposite is equally true: The quickest way to destroy distance is to *overfunction* anxiously in another's space. Emotional distance must be measured in terms of resiliency rather than in inches. The trick is to be able to have different distances at different times. It is the failure to understand this notion that makes ineffective most efforts to improve communication or show more feeling, by having people get closer.

It is also this confusion of physical distance and emotional distance that leads to the assumption that the family is breaking down. Actually, no matter how many miles apart people live, or how infrequently they communicate, it only takes a letter or call every now and then to trigger the programmed circuits. The family has only gone underground. Its emotional potential is always there. The family umbilical cord is infinitely elastic.

LOSS AND REPLACEMENT

To the extent a family rushes to replace loss, its pain will be lessened, but so will the potential for change that the loss made possible.

Nature also abhors a vacuum in emotional systems. When individual members leave a family, whether through death, marriage, relocation, or a cutoff, the system will generally be quick to replace the person who was lost. Whoever the replacement is, new child or new spouse, new in-law or new boarder, clergyman or clergywoman, in the same generation or the next, he or she will replace in all the family triangles the person who has left. They will have grafted onto them all the expectations associated with their predecessor, and un-worked-out problems that may have contributed to their predecessor's leaving (or becoming symptomatic) are likely to resurface in the new relationships. Replacement is a function of grief, and grief is always proportional to the un-worked-out residue of the relationship that was lost.

This is a homeostatic principle. It is the way the family maintains its balance. In work systems, it helps explain why the introduction of new blood often brings little change. In Section III, this principle will be applied to situations where a member of the clergy takes a new post, and it will provide some answers to how one may avoid the dangers associated with replacement.

As Table 2-1 illustrates, the replacement phenomenon also provides a reading on the degree of differentiation in any family around the time of nodal events. The table describes seven important life-cycle changes with respect to marriage, birth, marital dissolution, and remarriage. It shows that to the extent that family members make such transitions as a replacement or, to the contrary, are unable to separate at all from a loss, their decisions can be correlated to the time periods they allow for the new relationship to develop. Individuals who fall within the "benchmark period" are generally entering the new relationship with the least likelihood that they are using it as a replacement (everyone does to some extent). This benchmark period may be seen as an expanding slide rule that shifts along the continua, depending on the specific period or the cultural context. Its presence is there to highlight the extremes, and all these continua are more accurate as one moves toward the extremes. At either end, however, we will find family members who are most likely to have fallen into the replacement trap. This does not mean their decision was bad, or that those who fall within the benchmark period will be guaranteed success.

But to the extent that individuals make decisions within these extreme time frames, it is more likely that they are bringing important un-worked-out family residue with them. Thus, when problems surface in a new relationship, the problems of the old relationship are more likely to surface right along with them. Families and congregations that function near the extremes appear to ricochet down the alley of time, bouncing from loss to replacement to loss.

Skin Deep: A nurse who was dealing with various problems of loss, divorce from her husband, separating from her children, and changing her own family position as a replacement for her mother's mother, was helped through these dilemmas when she came across the following biological fact in a medical journal: "When a wound occurs, there are

TABLE 2-1. Life-Cycle Decisions

Decision	Extreme	Benchmark period	Extreme
1. Age when married	Teenage elopement	21–27	No marriage or marriage in mid-40s
2. Length of courtship	Love at first sight—10 days	6 months–1 year	5 years of going steady or living together
3. Length of engagement	Eloping right after decision to get married	3–6 months	Many years of putting it off
4. Time to birth of first child	Pregnancy before marriage	2–3 years	Childless for whatever reason
5. Time between separation and divorce	Attempt to hasten legal limits	1–2 years after legal limits	Never separated/divorced ('til death do us part), but withdrawal from mate and/or promiscuity with others
6. Time between separation from one mate and going steady with future mate	Affair with future mate	2–4 years	Same as example 5
7. Time between divorce and remarriage	Same as examples 5 and 6	2–5 years	Same as example 5

Note. Adapted with permission from E. H. Friedman, "Systems and Ceremonies: A Family View of Rites of Passage," in E. A. Carter and M. McGoldrick (Eds.), *The Family Life Cycle: A Framework for Family Therapy,* New York: Gardner Press, 1980.

two kinds of tissue that must heal, the connective tissue below the surface, and the protective tissue of the skin. If the protective tissue heals too quickly, healing of the connective tissue will not be sound, causing other problems to surface later, or worse, never to surface at all." She was able to make the analogy that in some families emotional wounds also close too quickly and, when they do, it is often very difficult to reopen them again, despite the promise of a more fundamental healing.

CHRONIC CONDITIONS

If a family problem is chronic (perpetual or recurrent), there must be reactive or adaptive feedback from somewhere in the system to sustain it.

This rule helps explain why it is often more effective to work with a family member who is not dysfunctional (and is unwittingly contributing feedback), rather than with the symptomatic family member.

Most traditional theories of behavior say that a person's problems in the present are influenced largely by his or her experiences in the past. More significant to the formation and perpetuation of a symptom, however, may be the past experiences of other family members who are important to the symptom-bearer (the identified patient).

There are major problems with the assumption that "past is prologue," it does not adequately explain why the pattern has remained chronic. (Clergy are in a position particularly suited for noticing this anomaly; we are almost unique in that our vocation allows us to become acquainted intimately with families who have no serious problems, but who have many of the same patterns that, when they appear in problemed families, are used to explain why they are troubled.) Second, this cause-and-effect reasoning only seems to work well backwards. If the past is so determinative, why can't it be used to make more definitive predictions? (Some would answer that no two situations are exactly alike. But with that logic, how is it possible to theorize about human behavior at all?) Third, linear, cause-and-effect reasoning is deceptive because, depending on other variables, any "cause" in emotional life can have exactly opposite effects, and any effect can result from exactly opposite causes. Over- and underaffectionate parents have the equal likelihood of producing either over- or underaffectionate children. (See "Symmetry," below.)

All human beings are programmed for far more pathology than could possibly become manifest in a lifetime. The major variable that selects out of anyone's past the behavior patterns or ways of thinking that are most likely to become symptomatic is the adaptive or reactive response of the most important people in our lives, our parents or our spouses. Furthermore, these selectively chosen patterns of behavior will be precisely those found in the "uptight" areas of other family members who are most important to the symptom-bearer. The chronic aspect of a symptom in a husband, wife, or child has primarily to do not with his or her own past, but with the spouse's or parent's past, not with his or her own childhood, but with the spouse's or parent's childhood. Otherwise the pattern would not have become chronic, nor perhaps even symptomatic to begin with.

A subtle proof for this comes from a frequent response nonsymptomatic family members offer when it is suggested that they change their response to the symptom. Frequently they will answer, "You are asking me to do something that is totally out of character." Were it not out of character, they probably would not have a problem. By definition, no one gets the problem he or she can handle. One family will tolerate and, indeed, not even notice what another family considers immediate cause for alarm. Family problems generally are not interchangeable.

Feedback and Change

The notion that chronic conditions require feedback also suggests strategies for change. (See Figure 2-1). The sine wave (A) represents the ups and downs of a chronic condition: depression, drinking, a school problem, a recurrent physical condition such as back pain or migraine, or the backsliding of a religious congregation. Generally, there is predictability about the highs and the lows of symptomatic behavior, and the frequency with which the symptom reappears, no matter what its nature. Chronic symptoms rarely go below or above certain thresholds, and they tend to reappear with a certain rhythm. (Anyone who doubts this should try to make a problem worse and keep it at that level.) This curve, therefore, is the curve of a relationship rather than a description

FIGURE 2-1. Sine wave of a chronic condition.

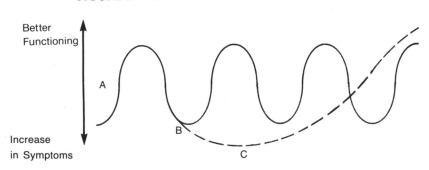

of only the symptom-bearer's functioning. For it is the feedback of an anxious other that gives any chronic condition its shape and continuity and, thus, provides its homeostasis. Where the person in the feedback position (family member or spiritual leader) can be helped to reduce his or her anxiety about the other's condition and to change his or her way of adapting or reacting to the symptom, the curve will often change to the dotted line (B). Paradoxically, the problem will appear to get worse at first, and it will take a longer period to go back to its previous best. Related here is the notion that it is not possible to eliminate any chronic condition without going through a phase that is acute. Acute stages are more painful, and most family members would prefer peace to progress. But if the nonsymptomatic member can sustain a nonreactive response, the condition will often get better than ever before. The problem in changing the curve comes at (C), when the *nonsymptomatic family member* (increasingly anxious when things seem to be getting worse) must avoid going back to merely adaptive or reactive feedback behavior. Where this can be done successfully, the change that occurs is more likely to be a fundamental (systemic) change rather than a recycling of the symptom.

Many family members or leaders can take the first step of trying not to respond with their usual adaptive or reactive patterns. Very few, however, can maintain their resolve to hold that position when the identified patient's symptoms become more intense. This increases their anxiety, sabotages their resolve, and begins to draw them back into the triangle again. Focusing on this feedback aspect of chronic conditions is basic in the "coaching" approach to counseling (to be described in Section II), and in the "nonanxious presence" view of leadership (to be discussed in Section III). It involves the concept of family responsibility: If we work on the areas of our own emotional inflexibility, those important to us will begin to function better, specifically in those same areas, generally in relationships, and eventually throughout their lives.

PAIN AND RESPONSIBILITY

If one family member can successfully *increase* his or her threshold for another's pain, the other's own threshold will also increase, thus expanding his or her range of functioning. All pain is, to some extent, "in the head," but this is not to say that it is psychosomatic, that is, imaginary. The degree of pain felt at any given moment is never simply proportional to somatic stimuli. Other variables always are the general attitude of the family member experiencing the pain, his or her attitude toward the pain itself, and also his or her attitude toward life. The more

47

that family members are motivated to achieve goals, the less their pain will bother them. A boy who has sprained a ligament playing basketball will tell his mother that he can't take out the garbage, yet he will run to meet his friends who are going to the movies. A husband on crutches will be unable to fix his own breakfast, yet he may stand in line for three hours to get into his favorite hobby show.

While recent research has shown that the brain can release its own analgesics called endorphins, which actually block pain signals, beyond such physiological phenomena, the degree of pain felt at any moment, as well as its debilitating effects, has something to do with threshold. Thresholds for both physical and emotional pain are lower when we are functioning dependently, and are higher when we are motivated to accomplish something. But there is also an interrelational aspect to this threshold dimension of pain. Where members of a family are too quick to spare another pain, the resulting dependency tends to make the other's threshold fall. In addition, he or she will become *addicted* to having pain relieved through someone else's functioning. Conversely, where family members can begin to increase their threshold for another's pain, the other person's threshold is likely to rise, even though he or she may at first go through "withdrawal" symptoms when the "addiction" is taken away. Those who focus only on comfort, on relieving pain, or filling another's need, tend to forget that another's need may be *not* to have their needs fulfilled.

Many symptoms first surface in children, for example, around the time mother has begun to think more about herself, and has inadvertently ceased to respond (positively or negatively) in ways that were comforting or familiar to her child. (Maternal anxiety may be the original addiction.) To some extent, the child's reaction will depend on the extent to which mother used the child as *her* own addiction, fusing with the child to ward off rejection or pain in her own life. The withdrawal phenomenon in a child is more severe to the extent that the child was originally mother's analgesic. Either way, the intensity of the symptom that surfaces will be proportional to the amount of pain the child was originally spared. This need for a "fix" can occur in any relationship, however, even between a shepherd and his flock.

A Low Threshold: An efficient, hard-working woman found it very difficult to function after a major automobile accident. Although able to move about, she was under heavy sedation to relieve her pain. Unaccustomed to an inactive life, she became more and more depressed. Her husband, a good-natured, helpful person, took over totally, doing all the shopping, the household chores, and the child-rearing, to make it as easy as possible on her. After her suicide, when the funeral was over, he turned and plaintively said, "I guess I should have kicked her in the ass."

But am I not my brother's keeper?

The Responsibility Triangle

The problem is that we cannot make another family member responsible by trying to make him or her responsible. The very act of trying to make others responsible preempts their own responsibility. This is equally true whether the issue is study habits, drinking, or failure to come to church. Harsh scolding generally should not be seen as inflicting pain. It often only succeeds in taking the sting out of their indolence, thus taking away the stimulus for motivation.

There is, however, a way to be our brother's keeper, to manifest responsibility for a fellow human being without getting stuck in a triangle between that person and his or her failure to be responsible. It is called "challenge," but it requires one to nonanxiously tolerate pain, and sometimes even to stimulate pain, thus forcing the other to increase his or her threshold.

A Stimulus for Motivation: A woman found her husband coming home from work ever more tipsy. Her anxiety increased. She tried everything she could to keep him sober, from constant warnings in the morning to harangues in the evening. As in all such emotional triangles, her own stress increased, and her husband seemed to feel more freedom to drink. Worried that she might be left a widow with two children, she was encouraged to get out of the triangle between her husband and his symptom, to shift the pain, by telling him (when he was not drunk) in as calm a manner as possible, "Honey, I've been thinking things over. I have decided that you have a right to drink all you want, to enjoy life to the hilt, and to risk it. After all, it's your life. I would like to stop nagging you, but I've got a problem. It's fairly clear to me that you probably won't make it for too much longer, and I don't want to be stuck with the mortgage and the car payment, so I'll make an agreement with you. If you will agree to triple your life insurance, I will agree never to mention your drinking again." Sticking someone with the pain of responsibility for his or her own destiny is far more "sobering" than giving the person black coffee afterwards.

A similar phenomenon occurs in work systems where leaders are always trying (usually unsuccessfully) to delegate responsibility. A far more effective form of leadership can be to delegate anxiety: "I just want you all to know that our collections have been so low to this point that we probably won't last to the end of the year. It would be my suggestion, therefore, that we establish a committee to see if we can still get a good price for our building, and merge with our rival across town."

Challenge is the basic context of health and survival, of a person, of the family, of a religious organization, or even (in the course of evolution) of an entire species. When it comes to life and growth, therefore, surely one of the most fundamental advances in modern healing is that it is no longer limited to treating symptoms after a disease has struck, or even to eradicating the causative agents in the environment. Today it is common practice to inject the germs and viruses directly into an organism so as to stimulate and help it develop its own system of defense.

THE PARADOX OF SERIOUSNESS AND
THE PLAYFULNESS OF PARADOX

The seriousness with which families approach their problems can be more the cause of their difficulties than the effect of the problems. Efforts directed at the seriousness itself often will eliminate the problem.

Seriousness presents a paradox. If family members are not serious about their responsibilities, the family may become unstable and chaotic. But seriousness can also be destructive. Seriousness is more than an attitude; it is a total orientation, a way of thinking embedded in constant, chronic anxiety. It is characterized by lack of flexibility in response, a narrow repertoire of approaches, persistent efforts to try harder, an inability to change direction, and a loss of perspective and concentrated focus.

Families that evidence such seriousness are as if surrounded by volatile fumes of anxiety, and any small incident can cause a flare-up. They will always assume that it was the incident that created the problem, but it is the way they relate and think that gives any incident its inflammatory power. The family, thus, tends to overlook the cause of its misery by focusing on the object of its discontent. On the other hand, if changes can be made in such a noxious atmosphere then the fumes of anxiety disperse, and the sparking incidents of life (that are necessary for creative existence) lose their explosive potential.

The antidote to seriousness is the capacity to be playful, which is not to be equated with making jokes. Some of the world's greatest humorists led personally tragic lives; and it is not unusual for the office wit to lose his timing in the presence of his wife. What gives to any playful response its remedial power is its relational affect and not its cleverness. This notion of playfulness has less to do with "one-liners" than with the concept of flexible distance; it has less to do with good "come-backs" than with the ability to distinguish process from content. Ultimately, it is more connected with responsibility for others than with being light-hearted. When playfulness is introduced into a "serious" relationship system, family or congregation, it can break the vicious feedback cycle that is keeping a problem chronic. In the family field, it is often called "paradoxical intervention." If we assume that any chronic condition that we are persistently trying to change will, perversely, be supported *not to change* by our serious efforts to bring about change, then it is logical to consider the possibility that one way out of this paradox is to be paradoxical.

Reversing Direction: A good husband and dedicated father found that his wife had chronically been having affairs. He took her once to a marriage counselor, but she refused to go again. He continued for two years, desperately trying to make her see the light. He showed anger. He threatened. He tried making her jealous. At his wit's end, ready to throw in the towel, he heard a discussion at church about how families never teach their members to push one another away. We are trained to hang onto others, or to withdraw (pull away). Pushing people we care about at others, or into activities we don't care about, is almost inconceivable. When a relationship is caught in a skid, we almost never think to turn the wheel the other way.

The next day, when the husband came home, he found his wife on the phone. Predictably she hung up quickly. Resisting the urge to berate her, he said, "Listen, honey, I know you want some privacy. I'll go for a walk around the block." Predictably, the wife's behavior escalated. At the end of the week, she informed him she was going to Miami to visit an old boyfriend. He went to a travel agency and got her brochures on places to have fun in southern Florida, adding some suggestions based on his own experience. She took them without comment and flew off, returned within three days, and announced that she had had a terrible time. The following week she joined him in counseling and continued long after he dropped out.

Some may hear this tale as gimmicky, manipulative, or game playing. But that would be a "serious" way of listening. Others may label this approach as simply reverse psychology. It is important to point out, therefore, that the major effect of playfulness and paradox is on the perpetrator. It takes him or her out of the feedback position. It detriangles and changes the balance of the emotional interdependency. It is the change in the structure of the triangle that gets the other person functioning or thinking differently. It is less the words than the emotional envelope in which they are delivered that determines whether any comment will be a put-down or a therapeutic challenge.

There is an important personal ramification here for members of the clergy. If it is generally true that it is not possible to be playful with those for whom we feel too responsible, it is especially true when we feel a responsibility for their salvation! Few religious traditions make much of playfulness, and even less of paradox or challenge. Or is that the way that we who are responsible for our traditions hear them?

SECRETS AND SYSTEMS

Family secrets act as the plaque in the arteries of communication; they cause stoppage in the general flow and not just at the point of their existence.

The communication system of many families is riddled with secrets. Favorite subjects are an affair, illegitimacy, elopement, terminal illness, abortion, adoption, institutionalization (crazy or criminal), previous marriage, black sheep in previous generation (skeleton in the closet), finances, and any minor matter where one family member says to another, "But don't tell Dad (Mom, etc.)."

Far more significant than the *content* of any family secret is the ramification of its *existence* for the emotional processes of the entire family. These effects are specific and predictable.

1. Secrets function to divide a family, as an avalanche would a community. Those "in" on the secret will become far better able to communicate with one another than with those in the outsider group, *about any issue*, not just about the secret. For example, a minister once complained how he was unable to help four sisters who were recuperating from an accident because they had yet to be told that their brother had died in the same crash. He spent so much time prethinking everything he said, for fear it would lead to questions about the brother, that he was totally unable to be the spontaneous self that was the basis of his pastoral effectiveness. When that same emotional phenomenon occurs in a family over a long period of time, very rigid triangles result.

2. Therefore, a second effect of secrets on a family system is that they create unnecessary estrangements as well as false companionship. For example, a father and daughter conspire not to tell mother about the abortion. Mother and daughter's relationship is likely to be affected well beyond the specific issue. An overall atmosphere of unnecessary

52

distance will develop between them. On the other hand, father and daughter will become closer, but it will be a shallow togetherness.

3. A third major effect of secrets on a family is that they distort perceptions. Family members will become confused or misled by information they obtain because they really are seeing only part of the picture. An ironic example of this is the husband who was considering leaving his wife because she had become "cold, selfish, and distant." She was having an affair, which she kept a closely guarded secret for fear that he would leave her if he found out. When she finally told him the truth at the urgings of the counselor, though he first expressed deep hurt and rage, breaking almost every glass in the house, he then began to feel better about things because he was now able to put together, in a comprehensive way, many messages and actions that had not made sense. Almost immediately, they found they were able to communicate better *on every subject*.

4. The most important effect of secrets on a family's emotional system is that they exacerbate other pathological processes unrelated to the content of the particular secret, because secrets generally function to keep anxiety at higher energy levels. When secrets are revealed, despite the fact that family members might at first be upset (either over the information or the fact that the secret is out), the anxiety level of the family generally decreases. This is particularly the case if the family continues to work at the issues that then surface, issues that often had precipitated the forming of a secret. The formation of a family secret is always symptomatic of other things going on in the family.

To some extent, secret formation feeds back to the previously mentioned issues concerning pain. Family members will say that they kept a secret "to spare" someone's feelings; the truth is more likely to be that they did so in order to spare their own feelings. Few of us are irreparably hurt by upset. Chronic anxiety, on the other hand, kills.

All of the above is equally true in the parish. The clergy are constantly triangled by various clandestine messages that parishioners report to them about one another, or about the other minister. That network of interlocking triangles is always in operation. But to the extent that messages about the minister are reported back and forth between "family members" *in secret*, then such secrets will promote pockets of pseudomutuality and unnecessary estrangements throughout the emotional system of the entire congregational family.

The ultimate proof of the function and the power of secrets within a family is that when they are revealed, more change usually takes place throughout the entire system than could have been attributed solely to the content of that secret. In short, secrets create and perpetuate triangles; they are always on the side of the existing homeostasis, the labeling process, and the chronicity of symptoms. They are never on the side of challenge and change. Secrets are very serious stuff.

SIBLING POSITION

The position we occupy within the sibling constellation of our nuclear family of origin foreshadows our expectations of the opposite as well as the same sex, our degree of comfort with our own various offspring, and our style of leadership in succeeding nuclear groupings.

Many studies have been published correlating sibling position to various social phenomena. The major pioneering work in the field is the very large cross-cultural investigation done by Walter Toman. He found, for example, that individuals are more likely to be satisfied if they marry someone of a compatible sibling position. An oldest would do better not to marry an oldest; a man who had an older sister should ideally marry a woman who had a younger brother. Toman has also suggested that parents tend to have the most sympathetic relationship with the child whose sibling position is closest to their own. A father who himself was the youngest would understand his youngest child best, even better if it were a boy; if he himself had an older sister, then it would be best if, before the youngest were born, he and his wife had a girl.

There are many exceptions to these feelings. Handled in too doctrinaire a manner, they can sound like astrology. Many individuals have rather complex sibling positions, and size of the family also makes a difference. Still, for all its exceptions, the general formulations about sibling constellation can be useful in counseling, helpful in understanding how people get along in work systems, and an aid in charting how emotional processes are transmitted from one generation to another, as well as from one emotional system to another. Sometimes it has such astonishing predictive power as to resemble an emotional genetic code. It probably has far more impact on a child's attitude toward relationships than whether he or she was "natural" or adopted. The following are some examples of its application in counseling situations:

1. In premarital counseling, if both consultees are "oldests," the potential for a king–queen conflict can be pointed out, as well as the dangers of always trying to resolve conflict by finding a middle ground that will satisfy neither. If he wants meat and she wants potatoes, they should not have hash.

2. An "oldest" mother disturbed by the "immaturity" of her youngest daughter (who is a delight to everyone else) can be shown that the extreme oppositeness of their sibling positions simply makes them function differently. She would do well not to graft the expectations of her own sibling position onto this child. Oldests are rarely as playful as youngests, and youngests rarely as superresponsible as oldests. Conversely, where both parents came near the bottom of the sibling line, their oldest is likely to be odd man (or woman) out. She, for example, will "naturally" want to go her own way, but she will find that her parents, used to tagging along, constantly thwart her desire. Neither child nor parent will really understand the other.

3. When assessing how to coach a family member not to be thrown off course by homeostatic resistance, oldests generally have the "go power" to push straight ahead. However, when an oldest is on the side of no-change, it is not likely that a youngest, married to this oldest, will be able to win a contest of wills. If, on the other hand, the youngest has some of the mischievous or playful qualities more natural to that position, she (or he) can often learn to skin the cat another way.

While other variables are always present, it can be generally said that the more reinforced the sibling position has been throughout successive generations, the more accurate the predictability of sibling theory. For example, if a man complains that his wife is spending him out of house and home, won't let him take responsibility for the children, won't come in for counseling, and won't stop nagging him about getting a better job, but he, his father, and his grandfather were each the youngest brother of three sisters, forget it!

Sibling constellations also function as semiautonomous systems in their own right. A trio of young adults, or even married siblings, can make seemingly independent decisions, about jobs, moving, college, or marriage, that really have been made relative to one another. The key is often the family's need to have at least one child close to home. A sibling system can also create herd-like panic, as when the marriage of one daughter triggers the marriage of all of her sisters within a year. This can look as if the houseboat is sinking, and it's every woman for herself. But it's more likely a game of hide-and-seek in which mother has just announced, "Anyone around my base is it!"

Sibling constellation theory can also be applied to work systems. It can help explain relationships, as well as be used to tone down conflicts between, for example, co-ministers, rabbis and cantors or educational directors, clergy and lay leaders, any two members of a religious hierarchy, "brothers" in a rectory, "sisters" in an order, or nuns in the way they respond to the mother superior and the way in which she responds to each of them.

DIAGNOSIS

The diagnosis of individual family members stabilizes family homeostasis and makes it more difficult for the diagnosed member to change.

Diagnosis in a family establishes who is to be the identified patient. It is inherently an anti-systems concept. It is linear thinking. It denies other variables that are present in the system. Existentially, it makes someone "other," and allows the remainder of the family to locate their troubles in the diagnosed member. It also disguises opinions and judgments; in an intense "congregational family" struggle, this hidden effect adds to the polarization.

Within the personal family, the labeling effects of diagnosis destroy the person. It decreases, in the diagnosed member, a sense of control over the situation, increases his or her dependency, and thus lowers their pain thresholds. The effect on nonsymptomatic members is that it fixes their perception of the diagnosed person's capabilities. Eventually a family member's label will become confused with his or her identity. Diagnosis also tends to concretize. It makes everything and everyone more serious.

Parents who are trying to make their young child concentrate in school, or their adult child clean up his or her act, will have an even harder time responding to that child's resistance if he or she has had psychological testing and the parents' perception of their child has been "corrected" by the lens of authority. This can be true even with the most disturbed children. In one instance, 80-year-old parents brought in their 45-year-old "schizophrenic" son who had never left home and could never hold a job, although he was obviously quite bright. The parents assumed that his failure to succeed was due to his "schizophrenia." It had to be pointed out that downtown (in Washington, D.C.) there were an enormous number of psychotics functioning quite effectively, and that their son's problem had less to do with his condition than with the overlay of immaturity (which is a family symptom). This can be true even where the condition upon which the immature functioning is blamed is physical, for example, mental retardation, cystic fibrosis, or cancer. With the elderly, the same identifying process fosters or reinforces senility when the family receives a diagnosis such as "chronic brain syndrome." (See Chapter 6.) To the extent that family members see the dysfunctional member as having a "condition," they will always stop short of those measures that are needed to bring about fundamental change.

Labeling also retards rehabilitation. For example, no one functions at peak capacity. Indeed, few people function at better than 50% of capacity on the average. Once a person has been diagnosed, however, there is a tendency to assume that he or she cannot do any better

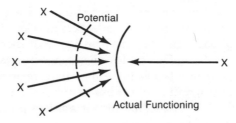

FIGURE 2-2. Actual versus potential functioning.

because of his or her condition. This is particularly true regarding the aged. To the extent the anxiety of others (family members or helpful professionals) causes them to rush in and be "supportive," their over-functioning will preempt the potential functioning of the diagnosed one and fix their "actual" as their "potential." (See Figure 2-2.) This can be true in any situation, but if someone has been diagnosed, there is more of a tendency to accept that he or she is not capable of function-ing closer to peak capacity.

When it comes to "psychological" conditions, there is an additional, more subtle reason why diagnosis inhibits change. Analyzing another person's being is a very slippery affair. It is not that the traditional interpretations are wrong; it is that, at any given moment, it is almost impossible to know if one has guessed right, because, in emotional life any cause can produce exactly opposite effects, and any effect can come from completely opposite causes. Worse, individuals are most likely to resort to diagnosis of others when their own anxiety has gone up. In fact, a good rule of thumb is that if you catch yourself diagnosing someone else, there is probably something in you that you are trying to hide. Recognizing these problems of objectivity, no psychiatrist would ever take his or her own spouse into therapy, yet every day husbands and wives are doing just that in the kitchen.

Diagnosis in a Congregational Family

The alienating and *ad hominem* qualities of diagnoses carry over to the congregational family philosophically and practically. Philosophically, religion has come a long way from the Inquisition. But the inquisitional potential in diagnosis is enormous. The word *sick* (and its various synonyms or euphemisms) has become one of the most pernicious words in the English language. It reeks of authoritarianism and allows labelers to think that they are being objective rather than judgmental. When we judge another person's form of existence in the disguise of diagnosis, it becomes too easy to consider what we do not like or cannot agree with as a symptom. Diagnosis thus used becomes a convenient tool in the armamentarium of a new "omni-science." However, when clergy employ diagnosis, they may be guilty of theological regression.

The practical ramification for congregational families is that anxious systems diagnose people instead of their relationships. Therefore, the amount of diagnosing of others going on in any religious institution is an indication of the amount of anxiety present in the system. And, since a major by-product of "chronic diagnosis" is polarization, the resulting alienation usually leads to two (or more) enemy camps.

SYMMETRY

In emotional life, every cause can produce exactly opposite effects and every effect could have come from exactly opposite causes, with the result that the more polarized things seem to be in a family, the more likely they are somehow connected.

This systems concept can be a powerful tool for explaining how parts of a family are related, for making predictions about other forces that may be operating unnoticed, and for noting what is being transmitted from generation to generation. Focus on symmetry rather than cause and effect also forestalls diagnosis. The most basic characteristic of a system is symmetry, the concept that all the emotional pushes and pulls in a family add up to zero. That is, they cancel one another out in a way that enables the overall family system to retain its homeostasis. In emotional space, paying attention to extremes can be more productive than focusing on specific emotions. In physics, where it is called "parity" or "complementarity," this homeostatic principle has enabled physicists to make accurate predictions about the existence of hitherto undiscovered particles by estimating what unseen forces must exist in order to keep what is observable in balance.

Here are some examples of symmetry, asymmetry, and crossover of causes and effects in family life. They will be followed by illustrations of how this concept can be used in charting family process.

Examples of how the same "cause" can lead to opposite effects in family life:

- Parental investment can promote overachievement or underachievement.
- An overly strict father can produce an overly strict son (when he is a father) or one who is too permissive.
- Alcoholic parents can produce alcoholic offspring or offspring who marry alcoholics.
- Dependency can lead to helpless or controlling attitudes.

- A "nice guy" clergyman may be beloved by his congregation or taken by them.
- Well defined stands can lead to admiration or revulsion.
- Surrendering and taking over are both ways of adapting.

Examples of how the same effect could have come from opposite causes:

- Someone who sleeps a great deal could be depressed or content.
- A family problem could surface after a business failure or a business success.
- An extremely rigid offspring can be produced by an extremely rigid parent or an overly flexible parent.
- Lack of change can be a by-product of polarization or of too much togetherness.
- Ineffective leadership can result from stands that are too authoritarian or too concerned with consensus.
- A crisis in faith can develop because of lack of self-examination, but the overexamined life isn't worth living either.
- Chronic means *always*; it also means *never*.

In the intensity of family life, we are prone to see only one of the possibilities in any chain of cause and effect, and the possibility we never think of is usually connected to our own emotional inflexibility in that particular category. In other words, we will tend to think of the explanation that makes us comfortable. Failure to keep this symmetry principle in mind leads to self-serving diagnosis or blaming of other family members, to the creation of a singled-out identified patient, to an artificial distinction between the unhealthy and the normal members of the family, and to a concentrated focus on the other family members' past and a blindness to our own.

Three tables of polarities (Tables 2-2, 2-3, and 2-4) show how the systems concept of symmetry can be used to understand the emotional forces in a given family. Table 2-2 shows how its application to any individual family member indicates an area of that person's inflexibility. When any family member's functioning can be placed at either extreme in this table, the category in the middle is an uptight area for them.

Table 2-2 can also be used in understanding chronic conditions. It suggests that to the extent that any family member tends to function at either extreme of an emotional category, other family members probably have difficulty functioning in the same category; otherwise the extreme behavior of the symptomatic member could not have become or remained chronic.

Tables 2-3 and 2-4 apply the symmetry principle to nuclear and extended families, respectively. And it is here that the predictive power

TABLE 2-2. Principle of Symmetry in Individual Family Members

Extreme	Emotional category	Opposite extreme
Rebellion	Authority	Blind acceptance
Just like parent	Identification	Totally dissimilar
Displace onto others	Pain	Hoard it for oneself
Can't leave home	Stuck in family of origin	Can't go home
Promiscuous	Libido	Low or asexual
Always avoid	Conflict	Must confront
Account to the penny	Budget	No planning
Hot-tempered	Anger	Soother
No mourning	Mourning	Extended mourning
Never give in to it	Handicap	Use as constant excuse

of this principle stands out most clearly. These tables suggest that, to the extent *both* of the opposite extremes of any emotional category are present in a family simultaneously, the following is predictable: (1) it is an uptight area in that family; (2) the extremes in some way add up to zero; that is, they are complementary and in some way maintain one another; (3) both extremes probably come from a similar source; (4) to the extent that any movement for change goes from one extreme to the other, it is transformation rather than change (in change something remains the same); and (5) if only one of the extremes listed in either end column is obviously present in the family, its opposite extreme must be around somewhere. (And in Table 2-4, to the extent

TABLE 2-3. Principle of Symmetry in the Nuclear Family

Extreme	Emotional category	Opposite extreme
(One spouse)		(Other partner)
Giver	Adaptability	Taker
Pursuer	Responsibility for relationship	Pursued
Spendthrift (loose)	Money (or any variable)	Tight
Optimist	Responsibility for hope	Pessimist
Anxious one	Anxiety	Reassurer
Along for the ride	Social life	Activities director
Symptomatic one	Soma (body)	Healthy one
Never remembers	Dates (family life history)	Historian/archivist
Permissive (good cop)	Discipline	Strict (bad cop)
Favorite	Any two siblings	Black sheep

TABLE 2-4. Principle of Symmetry in the Extended Family System

Extreme	Emotional category	Opposite extreme
One child takes all	Responsibility for parent(s)	One takes none
One child at home	Distance from parents	One child far away
Unable to conceive	Fertility	Pregnant before marriage
One sibling has affair	Infidelity (or obesity, or any variable)	Other sibling's spouse has affair
One child just like parent	Identification	Other child completely different from same parent
Exactly the same	Similarity between opposite-sex parent and spouse	Completely different
Diagnosed and isolated	Symptomatic family member	Allowed to tyrannize family with symptom
Surfaces in marriage	Severe problem in nuclear family	Surfaces in child
Exactly opposite to the last	Choice of new post or new clergyman	Exactly the same as the last

that any of these extremes is present in one generation, it or its opposite extreme is likely to surface in the next generation.) In both Tables 2-3 and 2-4, the parties also can be a congregation and its clergyman or clergywoman.

SURVIVAL IN FAMILIES

The major human factor that promotes survival in any environment is the same that has led to the evolution of our species since creation: an organism's response to challenge.

There is a general tendency to assume that the harmfulness of an environment is simply proportional to the strength of its noxious components. Such linear, cause-and-effect thinking is appropriate in certain cases (exposure to radiation, for example), but when it comes to family crises and many conditions of ill health, another and often more crucial variable also exists: the repertoire of one's responses to challenge. When that repertoire is narrow, either/or thinking develops, resulting in either an attitude of helpless victimization or all-out efforts to escape. When, however, the repertoire of responses to challenge is rich and varied, other alternatives can also be realized. One is a transformation of the organism, and a second is modification of the environment. Victim attitudes that measure the harmfulness of an environment only by the strength of its toxicity preclude these other two vital, evolutionary possibilities.

Responding flexibly to crisis, however, is not the same as merely being flexible (manipulable). It has more to do with resiliency (ability to maintain shape despite manipulation). After all, there are family members who are flexible because they do not know any other way to respond. Sooner or later the tendency to be automatically adapative will catch up with them, particularly when they are caught between interlocking triangles. The "rigidly" flexible family member is victimized by environments that require him or her to take stands.

Hostile Environments

To clarify, hostile environments can be divided into two categories: those where the human response is irrelevant, and those where it can make a difference. Category I hostile environments are absolutely hostile; the organism contains no resources that would enable it to adapt. Examples would be a land-based animal locked in an unbreakable tank of water, a "fish out of water," or a human organism near ground zero who could not withstand the heat, the aftershock, or the radiation.

The vast majority of survival crises that human beings experience with regard to relationships or their health belong in Category II, where the response of the organism is a variable in its own survival. Included in Category II are such hostile environments as plagues, epidemics, economic depressions, gas shortages, slavery, racial prejudice, ghettos, ship sinkings, miserable marriages, genetic defects, exposure to germs and viruses, many cancer and heart conditions, and a church or synagogue highly critical of its spiritual leader. In fact, much of what we label stress is the response of the organism rather than the impact of the environment. (See Chapter 5.) There is a marked tendency among human organisms to assume that whenever they are in an extremely hostile environment, *ipso facto* they are *in extremis*.

The Human Response

Even in Nazi concentration camps the human response to challenge could make a difference. Here was a hostile environment that came as close to Category I as could be found in human experience. Not only was it totally hostile by the nature of its harmful components, but also "dumb" chance, luck, fate seemed to rival the all-determining unintelligent *selection* forces that have shaped evolution. So often was this the case that it came to be called *"selectzia."* It was as if a "natural," that is, environmental, selection process was totally in charge. The truth is that even the natural selection processes in the evolution of our species were affected by the repertoire of an organism's responses. Concentration camp survival literature consistently shows that even in that environment the response of an organism could optimize the possibility of survival. It did not guarantee survival. What can, anywhere? But it could make a difference where a difference was possible. As small as the crack in the door of fate was, some saw it and some did not. Indeed, some apparently looked for it and some did not.

One way to preserve the importance of the human response variable, yet also allow for the variables of luck or other determinative factors in an environment, is to think of all these forces as dials on an amplifier that can vary the mix. This avoids the opposite alternatives of linear cause-and-effect thinking, on the one hand, or simplistic mind-over-matter solutions, on the other hand. In some circumstances the dial marked "chance" is low, and in some situations it is all the way up; the same is true for the dial marked "physical environmental determinants." But there is still the dial for the "human response to challenge." It also can be tuned low or high, and most often the final "mix" is dependent on its fine tuning. In fact, this is the real difference between Category I and II; in Category I the tuning of this dial does not matter.

Today the contemporary phenomenon that perhaps most emphasizes the survival ratio between challenge and response is recombinant
DNA. Many have expressed concern that in recombining DNA from
different organisms a new toxic substance will be created for which
there is no remedy. But, as several less anxious scientists have pointed
out, the fact that something is inherently toxic to the human organism
is not enough to destroy it. The toxic substance must also have the
capacity to bind itself to the cell wall and defeat the immunological
response. Toxicity, therefore, may be viewed as a relational category,
not merely as a matter of a Category I, noxious threat.

In family relationships, as long as individuals focus primarily on
the toxicity of their relatives' behavior instead of what makes them
vulnerable, they will fail to realize that it is a far healthier response to
work on their own "cells," as a way of immunizing themselves against
"insult." Actually, such responses accomplish more than self-protec-
tion; they also tend to modify the insulting behavior.

A couple asked to have in their wedding vows "I vow not to
abandon (the other)." They had seen a family counselor for 6 months
during courtship and learned that this is what they had been doing to
one another. The minister replied, "That is an unworkable basis for
marriage." He suggested: "I vow not to be abandoned, when (the other)
abandons me!"

These ten rules of family process are not the only ones that could
be formulated, and to some extent they could be reformulated differently. As a group, however, they touch on most of the major elements
in family process; they help create a way of thinking that is not moored
to symptoms or enmeshed in content; and they provide a matrix for
deciding which information is important. They are equally applicable to
all families irrespective of cultural background. And they are equally
applicable to the three families of the clergy: those we counsel, those
we lead, and those which consist of our relations.

THE FAMILIES WITHIN
THE CONGREGATION

3

The Marital Bond

The purpose of this chapter is to describe family emotional process in the context of marriage, and to illustrate how members of the clergy can employ this perspective to enrich their counseling at various stages of the marriage cycle (courtship, marriage, and divorce). It will also lay the basis for a family systems understanding of clergy–congregational partnerships (to be described in Section III). In fact, all the chapters in this section have a two-fold purpose: first, to describe emotional process in an area of family life that we encounter in our parishioners, and second, to establish a framework for understanding those same dynamics when they appear in the interlocking emotional systems of our congregational "families" and in our own

THE MYTH OF INCOMPATIBILITY

There is an ancient story in which a Roman woman comes up to a rabbi and asks: "What does your God do now that he has created the world and set it in order?"

She is answered: "He tries to match up couples."

"Is that all?" she says. "Why, I could do that myself."

"Maybe so," she is told, "but for Him it is as difficult as splitting the Red Sea."

In another version the rabbi tells her, "Go try it!" She tries, but returns after total failure; in her "matchmaking," the partners had afflicted one another in various ways.

The antiquity of this story suggests that it may be misleading to assume that marriage failure is more a modern phenomenon. Mating, whether it is between man and woman or between a religious leader and his or her flock, is, and always has been, a very difficult experience for our species. If this 2000-year-old story seems to refute one myth about the marital bond, it perpetuates another. The framing of this parable supports the widespread assumption that the key to successful marriage is finding the "right match." Emphasis on compatibility confuses cause and effect. When partners do not make it together, this kind of thinking leads to the notion of "incompatibility." Then, when strikingly different personalities, or partners from different backgrounds, do make it, thinking in terms of compatibility reverses its explanation to say that "opposites attract." A more accurate perspective is that it is not the ingredients of the mixture but the emotional crucible into which they are poured.

Incompatibility in marriage has less to do with the differences than with what is causing them to stand out at any given time. All differences, cultural or personal, tend to stand out more at times of stress, but in any relationship, the same difference is not necessarily "differed over" every time it appears. In addition, while partners when they are "differing" can remember every issue between them back to day one of their relationship, if they can achieve a more comfortable level of interdependency, they will forget all those "sore points" as if they had never existed, even though they are still there.

Emphasizing compatibility is also misleading because it tends to isolate the marriage relationship from the two emotional fields in which it is always situated, the nuclear family and the extended families of origin of both partners. It is precisely these two emotional systems that are most likely to influence or change the balance of a marriage.

A SYSTEMIC VIEW OF MARRIAGE

THE NUCLEAR FAMILY

With respect to the nuclear family, it is not possible to judge the health of any marriage without also taking into account the health of the children and the health of the partners. It is only too easy for unworked-out parts of a marriage relationship to surface as symptoms in the children or as a symptom in one of the spouses that is then seen as "his" or "her" problem. A systems way of rating marital success must take into account the entire nuclear family. If there are important unworked-out aspects of the marriage, then, depending on the nature of the triangles, a symptom can surface in any of three locations in that nuclear system: (1) in the marriage relationship itself, as conflict, distance, or divorce; (2) in the physical or emotional health of one of the partners; or (3) in the emotional or physical health of one of the children, or in a relational problem with one of the parents or with a sibling.

In family systems terms marriage relationships are not simply divided into categories of "successful" and "unsuccessful." Instead, a continuum is established that says all marriages are successful *to the extent* that the entire nuclear family is symptom-free. In reality, no human marriage gets a rating of more than 70%.

Approaches to marriage counseling that focus on the marriage relationship alone, especially on personal differences, can create deceptive results. If a couple comes in troubled by constant bickering, or because one spouse has had an affair, and after months of counseling they seem to be "compatible" again, but a year or so later he has a heart attack, or she sinks into a severe depression, or their child has a psychotic break, the question has to be asked: Did the marriage really change? By focusing on differences, it is too easy to splint a marital relationship so that one spouse becomes the only self-destructive "Wild Duck," or the other invests all his or her feeling in a child (who then may dysfunction several years later).

As we shall see in Section III, which examines clergy–congregational partnerships, the same failure to distinguish congregational emotional *process* from the *issues* that tend to surface in those kinds of families is a major reason why clergy find that, despite brave efforts and best intentions, problems refuse to go away permanently.

THE EXTENDED FAMILY

It is also misleading to regard the marriage, or the entire nuclear family, in isolation from the extended families of the marriage partners. Many nuclear family problems, no matter between (or in) whom they are located, surface within 6 months of a major change in one of the broader, extended systems. And many marriages are contracted within 6 months of problems or change in the extended families. It is forces emanating from those emotional fields that often set the marital centrifuge spinning. Sometimes the opposite can happen when too much distance from families of origin takes away the modulating effects of extended family connections and a suddenly jolted marital top spins increasingly out of control.

It may well be that the sociological phenomenon that makes modern marriage most different from the marriages of Roman times is not the wide variety of life-styles, liberated women, or the complexity of society, but, rather, the attenuation of extended family connections. Even 2000 years ago the human institution of marriage would not have been able to carry the load of emotional satisfaction it is *expected* to bear today. In a similar manner, many of the issues that plague contemporary synagogues and churches are the result of intensified relationships in the nuclear systems of member families (or clergy) when individuals try to substitute their religious organizations for their extended families.

A SYSTEMS APPROACH TO COUNSELING

The focus of this chapter, however, will not be the specific symptoms of marital stress, for example, conflict over children, money, in-laws, sex, lack of communication (whatever that phrase is supposed to communicate), etc. Rather, an approach to marital and premarital counseling will be illustrated that emphasizes the *position* of the clergy counselor, and how his or her special entrée into families can induce fundamental change by focusing on systemic factors within the relationship itself, between the partners, between them and their children, and between the nuclear family and important extended family members.

The fact that family emotional process and the entrée of the clergy are the same at every stage of the marital cycle, and regardless of the specific symptom, means that a unified approach can be taken to marriage, separation, remarriage, and premarriage counseling. This brings several important practical benefits to the clergy. First, it provides a file system for storing information. Since we often come into contact with the same person or family at different nodal points in their life, such continuity of perspective also enhances our capacity to make predictions. Second, because the emphasis is on emotional process and the healing power inherent in the *position* of the counselor, it is less dependent on his or her expertise in dealing with any type of premarital, marital, and separation problems. From a systems perspective, every marriage is also to some extent a divorce. Third, counseling approaches that emphasize emotional process are far more protective of positions that are susceptible to triangles, a major concern when doing marriage counseling within the parish or congregation. Fourth, as will be seen in Section III, because the emphasis is on emotional process rather than specific symptoms, these marital counseling approaches can be just as effective in understanding and resolving similar problems of bonding and separating in the congregational family. This creates a bridge for reciprocal insight into both kinds of partnerships, not to mention the clergy's own marriages.

Before beginning, however, a comment is in order about my use of case material in this work. While the case histories that appear are intended as illustrations of the potential effectiveness of the family systems approach, they also serve as metaphors. The overriding purpose of this book is not to turn clergy into "experts" but, rather, to teach a way of thinking that integrates the varied dimensions of our lives. It is important to keep in mind, therefore, that case illustrations telescope time. They always appear "miraculous," and convey an illusion of rapid change. It can take years to alter the emotional processes of a family. (The cases are all composites, of course, and the names are fictitious.)

The framework for this exposition will be as follows: Six case histories will be used to illustrate three different angles of entry into a family system. Some are designed for working with both partners together, some for those situations where only one of the partners is motivated. They will be applied to married couples, separated couples, and courting couples and include remarriage and blended or reconstituted families.

1. The couple seen together
   A. The counselor as a catalyst for self-definition
   B. The systemic effects of the counselor "detriangling"
2. Coaching one partner with the focus on the relationship
   A. The wife alone
   B. A divorced husband alone
3. Coaching either partner with focus on the extended family
   A. A separated woman alone
   B. During the premarital phase

1. THE COUPLE SEEN TOGETHER

A. THE COUNSELOR AS A CATALYST FOR SELF-DEFINITION

Couples usually come in with specific issues. One partner is angry about how the other keeps house, dresses, acts at parties, disciplines the children, drives the car, spends money, etc. Some have a list that goes back for years. If they are caught up enough in one another, they constantly interrupt to correct the record. Their perceptions of the nature of the problem often differ. If the counseling focuses on "the issue," it is dealing with a symptom and not the underlying emotional process. Effective healing occurs when the counselor is less anxious to relieve the symptom and instead uses it as a pathway into the emotional system. Then, if changes can be made on that level, the symptom is likely to atrophy.

In both the following examples the counselor "pretends" to buy the issue but uses his *position* in the triangle that reforms around him to disrupt the homeostasis of the predictable response pattern. In the first example, "John and Mary," the basic approach is to ask questions designed to stimulate each partner to differentiate his or her self better. The purpose is not to get them to agree (their own emotional process won't permit that) but to define their positions. The more differentiation of self there is, the less stuck-togetherness, and the less stuck-togetherness, the more they can get together. There is also no effort to bring about confrontation directly between them. Partners will often listen far more attentively when they *overhear* their partner's answer directed to the counselor than when the answer is spoken directly to (at?) them.

An approach that primarily asks questions, sometimes consciously naive, also keeps the counselor out of the dependency-encouraging, expert position that fosters giving wise advice. Furthermore, it is hard to give answers if you are the one asking the questions. Some of the questions are designed to bring out the symmetry in the relationship, others are playfully designed to tone down the emotionality so that the partners can hear, and so that the counselor can retain his own objectivity; some have a paradoxical intent, designed to challenge the thoughts of one of the partners by taking his or her thinking to its ultimate extreme. Indeed, sometimes questions are deliberately directed to the wrong person. Such "three-cornered shots" often fake out the demons of resistance. In no way, however, should this approach of asking questions be confused with being nondirective. It is *very* directive and tries to make the most of the experience of the session itself for bringing about change. Actually, it is probably very effective to conduct entire sessions where all we do is ask questions, and never point out things, that is, if our anxiety will permit it.

The last rule of triangles (see Chapter 1), and the key one, is that the way to bring change to the relationship of two others is to try to stay in touch with both sides while not getting caught in the middle of their unresolved issues. Success in such an effort will usually modulate the intensity in the relationship of the other two. This is why the term *catalyst* has been used. A catalyst is by definition something that causes change in the relationship of two other substances without losing its own integrity in that relationship. There is probably no better way of explaining the effectiveness of a nonanxious presence in counseling, in our administrative functioning, or sometimes at home. Asking questions is a great way to remain both nonanxious *and* present.

John and Mary: John and Mary came to their clergyman 5 years after their marriage. They had just had their second child. John was successful but unhappy in his work. He was distant from his family, who lived across the country. Mary had lost her mother when she was 18 and hated her father's second wife. Both of them felt that their marriage had been going downhill steadily because of "increasing conflict" and "inability to communicate."

MARY: Things are terrible; John won't stop hounding me. "Take off weight, buy new clothes, keep the house in better order, show more enthusiasm."

COUNSELOR: What would you say to that, John?

JOHN: It's not like she has to go out in the fields and start harvesting. She's in good shape physically. It's for her benefit too, you know.

MARY: He just doesn't realize that it takes time. I'll get to it, but it takes a little time, that's all.

COUNSELOR: John, your wife says you're rushing her. How much time will you give her? I mean, do we have a deadline we're working with here?

JOHN: No. I don't have a deadline, but she's been saying that for months. I mean, some of this was going on long before the baby was born.

COUNSELOR: John, what would you say has been your success in getting your wife to change?

JOHN: Sometimes if I get on her enough, but she rarely keeps it up for more than a week.

COUNSELOR: Maybe you're not trying hard enough.

JOHN: What? Are you kidding? Hardly a day goes by that I don't have to remind her about one of these things.

COUNSELOR: Maybe if you reminded her more often.

JOHN: Nah, that won't work. I remind her every day as it is. What would you suggest?

COUNSELOR: You could try thinking more about the problem.

JOHN: More? I think too much about it already. I guess it's not doing any good at all.

COUNSELOR: How would you explain your lack of effectiveness in trying to improve your wife?

MARY: Improve me! He wants to make me into his image.

COUNSELOR: John, Mary says you are playing God.

JOHN: It's not my image. Why shouldn't a woman want to look beautiful? She doesn't seem to care.

COUNSELOR: Well, everyone knows when a woman doesn't care for her appearance, she really doesn't love her husband.

JOHN: Sometimes I think that.

COUNSELOR: Mary, when did you stop loving him?

MARY: That's not true, and he knows it. That's the problem; I really want to please him so much. But I just can't.

COUNSELOR: John, can you make Mary defensive any time you want?

JOHN: Absolutely.

COUNSELOR: What's your batting average?

JOHN: One hundred percent.

COUNSELOR: One hundred percent! What works best? I'm not saying you do this on purpose, mind you, but let's say you wanted her to justify herself, what would you do?

JOHN: Oh, I don't know. I never really thought about it. I guess telling her to take off weight.

COUNSELOR: Mary, what would you say to that?

MARY: You're right, I am too defensive. But weight isn't the big one. I know I'll get that down. It's the cleaning. I just feel I'm a pretty good housekeeper.

JOHN: You used to be.

COUNSELOR: John, what got you to say that then?

JOHN: When she talks that way it really makes me angry.

COUNSELOR: Talks what way?

JOHN: Uses that tone of voice.

COUNSELOR: What is it about her tone? Is it the quality? The amplitude? The timbre?

JOHN: I guess it's a combination.

COUNSELOR: You mean all she's got to do is strike the note and you sing? Mary, if you got that tone down you could get him going every time.

JOHN: I don't like to think of it as if I'm being controlled.

COUNSELOR: It doesn't sound like an exercise in free will.

JOHN: Maybe I am too sensitive to her.

COUNSELOR: What is your response to that?

MARY: If he's so sensitive, why can't he see how he upsets me?

COUNSELOR: John?

JOHN: I hear an awful lot from her too, especially how I'm supposed to spend more time with our son.

MARY: Well, you're not around much on weekends, you know.

COUNSELOR: Why don't you two make a trade? He'll stay around on weekends and you can agree to take off weight.

MARY: That's ridiculous. I used to think that way. One has nothing to do with the other. I want him to share responsibility; he wants to change me.

COUNSELOR: John, what would you say to that?

JOHN: The changes I want for her are for her own good.

COUNSELOR: Mary, when John starts pushing you harder to lose weight or to keep up the house, what's the effect of his efforts?

MARY: Turns me right off. He has a way of beginning all his demands. "Honey, we gotta sit down and talk," or, "Honey, listen." Everytime I hear the word *Honey*, I don't hear anything after that. I'm not perfect, but I can't stand all those put-downs.

COUNSELOR: Mary, why does your husband have so much power to determine your view of yourself?

MARY: That's a good question. I just love him too much.

COUNSELOR: If you two keep loving each other you'll absolutely destroy one another. How would you both see the difference between love and dependency?

MARY: I guess I always thought they were the same.

JOHN: I would have to agree with Mary. I always thought that if you loved someone, dependency didn't matter; it was just part of the package.

COUNSELOR: Mary, how do you deal with that double message? Be close and loving, but don't be needy.

MARY: Not very well.

Eventually changes came about in John and Mary's marriage, not because either one finally convinced the other of the correctness of his or her own position, but because Mary became less defensive as a result of reworking her relationship with her guilt-inducing father. This type of refocusing will be explored later. However, it required several sessions like the one described here, where the counselor used his entrée to be a nonanxious presence within the marital triangle (rather than trying to offer sagacious advice), before Mary became motivated to examine her own emotional "baggage."

B. DETRIANGLING

The second use of position to affect process is detriangling. Throughout the previous dialogue, the counselor was trying to stay out of, but in touch with, both sides of the marital triangle. Detriangling occurs where the counselor, having been put in the middle when one partner reports information about the other (creating the pseudoalliance common to secret-sharers), responds by sharing the information with the other partner. This often happens where one partner misses a session or comes in late. Under such circumstances, simply by taking notes of what the first partner is saying (and might not have said so clearly had the other partner been present), and then later asking the other partner his or her perceptions of the same issues, preferably while the first partner is present, can fundamentally change the marital system. In fact, more positive change can occur in the marriage as a result of such a detriangling opportunity than if the triangle had never formed in the first place.

Jack and Jill: Jack and Jill had been married for 20 years. They had two daughters in college. While the relationship had been peaceful, there had been a great deal of distance. Each had had an affair. They clearly cared for one another, yet seemed almost incapable of being open with one another. It was almost as though they didn't know how. Generally he tended to distance and she to manipulate.

Just before their fifth appointment, his secretary called to announce that he would be late. During the early part of the session, the wife talked about her divorce anxieties, punctuating all of this with details about her husband's personality; for instance, he relied heavily on his older sister, he thought the counselor didn't like him. She insinuated that he might be homosexual because he had a kind of scarf "that gay people carry around." Moreover, he had once asked her if it would surprise her if he were.

JACK: Sorry I'm late. I couldn't get out of an important meeting. Did my secretary reach you?

COUNSELOR: Come on in. Your wife and I were just discussing the possibilities of your being gay.

JACK: (*hearty laughter*) That's one problem I don't have.

COUNSELOR: (*to Jill*) I guess you had it wrong.

JILL: Then why did you ask the other night, "What would you say if you found out I was gay?"

JACK: I was just teasing. Boy, you are serious!

COUNSELOR: She was worried about your scarf also.

JACK: I told her it was my sister's. You really have a nose for evidence, don't you?

COUNSELOR: Speaking of your family, one of the things that Jill and I got into was your heavy reliance on your sister. I wonder how that came about.

JACK: Is she on to that again? She has blamed my sister for everything from my affair to my job. Lady, you better start worrying about your relatives, not mine! (*to counselor*) You know, since our last session I decided that you were right about the way I let this woman take charge.

COUNSELOR: I'm surprised to hear that. Your wife mentioned that you thought I didn't like you.

JACK: Wow! That was taken totally out of context. (*to Jill*) You really hear things the way you want to, don't you? (*to counselor*) I was referring to your remark that I ought to give her a report card every week so she can shape me up. You really got me with that one. I've been thinking all week how, if I really want her to become less dependent, I also have to be less dependent on her. (*to wife*) You've been painting some picture of me.

COUNSELOR: You mean it's not accurate?

JACK: Not accurate? She's never seen me as I am, only as she thinks I am.

COUNSELOR: What is the effect on you of trying to explain someone you aren't?

JACK: It confuses me. I get frustrated and I just say the hell with it.

COUNSELOR: I would like to get into something you both might be reluctant to talk about, but which I think is important for partners who have engaged in extramarital sex. Jill, Jack discussed your recent affair. I understand that the young buck was only half your age. What was it like with him?

JILL: O.K.

COUNSELOR: Just O.K.? How would you compare it?

JILL: Oh, Jack's really better.

COUNSELOR: You mean this old guy here isn't bad.

JILL: Well, there's more to sex than strength or beauty.

COUNSELOR: Who'd you think about?

JILL: What do you mean?

COUNSELOR: You know what I mean. Who'd you think about, Jack or the guy you were with?

JILL: I never could achieve much of an orgasm with Ted.

COUNSELOR: Maybe you stopped the affair too soon. It takes time. Maybe if you had continued, something really beautiful would have come out of it.

JILL: Sometimes I wonder about that. But I really don't think so. Sex for me really has to include love.

COUNSELOR: Jack, how about with your extramarital sex? Who'd you used to think about?

JACK: I always thought about Jill. I used to compare a lot. I don't mean technique. But even when I really got stimulated by another woman, I used to think — no, I used to wish it were Jill.

COUNSELOR: Maybe you could both pretend you were having an affair with one another.

JACK: We really have a problem with intimacy, don't we?

After this session, Jill called for a separate appointment, and in that session she switched her focus to her own need to develop a sense of self that was less dependent on a man. Jack become visibly stronger throughout the remaining sessions, and continued in that much more self-assertive direction.

By using the opportunity of having been triangled and purposefully unhooking himself, the counselor was able to help the couple to unhook from the triangle they were each caught in with each other. Such a process approach, when it becomes available, can accomplish more change in one session than hours of discussing the content of the relationship.

The counselor also admitted that he himself felt freer and more objective about the couple once he had detriangled. This can be particularly the case where the minister had performed the wedding. In those instances, the clergyman or clergywoman often feels an increased sense of responsibility that can make it very difficult to be effective. The other side of this problem is that when a couple goes for marriage counseling to the person who had originally "hitched them up," they probably have greater expectations of what that counselor can do for them. The detriangling process is especially effective with such couples.

Some might be concerned that the counselor was betraying confidences here. A far deeper issue for the health of a family is why one member is telling a counselor something he or she should be telling the other member. When the counselor can convey that "the entire family is my concern," and when the "revealing" can be done in the presence of the informer, in a nonanxious manner, and the underlying process issues can be worked on immediately, then the teller of the tale is generally grateful. The key is to keep the focus on the relationship, not the issue. That is what detriangling is all about.

Catalyzing definition of self in the partners' relationship will work equally well with courting and separating couples. In the former relationship, the self-definition enables them to come together and, in the latter, to separate more cleanly. Members of a religious hierarchy will also find it effective in their triangular position between congregations and their clergy partners. (See Chapter 10.)

2. COACHING ONE PARTNER WITH THE FOCUS ON THE RELATIONSHIP

In the foregoing examples, husband and wife were equally motivated to seek help. Often, however, only one partner comes in, or one partner drops out after the counseling has begun. Were marital counseling always dependent on both partners attending, as many troubled spouses unfortunately believe, the less motivated partner could consistently sabotage progress by merely refusing to work on the relationship. It is often possible, however, to bring change to a relationship by "coaching" the motivated partner alone on how to get out of the "feedback" position and how to gain more self-differentiation. Indeed, progress can often be made faster this way. The more motivated and therefore more coachable family member is generally the one who calls, generally is the one who articulates the problem and always is the partner who is more capable of defining his or her positions in a nonblaming way. He or she also tends to be an overfunctioner rather than an underfunctioner, which works both ways. It is usually their overfunctioning which has put them in the more stressful position, thus supplying their greater need to upset the status quo. But it is also their quickness to initiate and willingness to function without waiting for the other which makes them the better candidate for coaching.

Such an approach, does run the risk that the counselor will become triangled, or be seen by either partner as having joined in an alliance against or with him or her. But to the extent that the counselor's main goal is to pursue differentiation throughout the relationship ("listening" for the dependency issues that always show through the "facts"), he or she will be able to stay fairly objective about the underlying process even when the partner being coached is lying, and even though the minister might appear at times to be on the side of one or the other. Actually, the partner who is not coming in often cannot change until the one who is coming in can. Therefore, while it might appear at times that the advice given to the partner seeking coaching is an effort to manipulate the other, its true aim is to free the other, and often that other comes to appreciate this even while he or she cannot articulate what is happening or, from time to time, appears to be angry about it.

More fundamentally, the coaching approach is an effort to stimulate strength in a family, rather than shore up its weaknesses. This is a prospective approach that is concerned with the future health and development of all the family members. It is also a focus on leadership, with regard to parenting (see Chapter 4), and in relation to the congregational family (see Chapter 9).

There are several components to the coaching model. First, the marriage partner being coached is encouraged to gain an understanding of the emotional system that surrounds him or her, and how his or her own feedback into the system might be retarding change. The counselor tries to convey that mistakes are as profitable for learning about the system as is success. Thus, when suggestions are made for new initiatives, it is not just to bring about change but also to learn how the family black box functions. Some of the more dependent trainees must be constantly reminded that a coach can only teach rules (the proper forms) and the probable results of various actions based on his or her experience and understanding. The trainee ultimately must carry the ball. A blackboard or other demonstration device can be used to diagram the family and to help family members and consultant to remain more objective.

After some initial focus on the nonattending partner in order to enable the differentiating partner to change course, ultimately we want the partner being coached to focus on his or her own course. As will be shown later, a major way of supporting that shift in focus is to have the differentiating partner work at unresolved issues in his or her own family of origin rather than on issues in the marriage.

Indeed it is with this approach that the most change occurs in the marriage relationship. When the differentiating partner becomes thoroughly interested in his or her own goals, destiny, or salvation (which is not the same as being selfish), he or she automatically reduces his or her own dependency to a minimum, and can decrease feedback to the partner's systemic responses. At that point, the differentiating partner makes changes in his or her own response pattern that could never have been brought about by continuing to focus on the problem, and the whole system shifts. The differentiating partner becomes the more attractive one, and the recalcitrant one becomes the pursuer. This is equally true in marriage, parenting, and spiritual leadership.

A. THE WIFE ALONE

The coaching approach begins with helping the partner who comes in to accept that he or she is the more motivated one to seek help, and not the one who is problemed. We want to avoid making the motivated partner into the *identified patient* (which the spouse would often prefer). The partner who comes in is probably feeling the pain because he or she has taken the responsibility for the relationship; but, if that partner can learn how the pain may be shifted, the other will then become more motivated to change, whether or not he or she ever participates in the counseling process. Of course, with the coaching model, whether the context is marriage, parenting, or leadership, the nonattending partner is always participating, like it or not.

Ms. Green: Ms. Green, a woman of 28, came in to her minister when she was on the verge of leaving her husband because she was distraught over her continued ineffectiveness in changing her marriage. She and her husband had been to a counselor several years previously, but he had dropped out. She had continued to see the clinician alone to work on what she described as "my own problems" of loneliness and isolation. Recently she noticed that she was again becoming phobic about being alone. She had asked her husband to come to the counselor, but he said she was the one who was bothered and, therefore, she should be the one to seek help.

Regarding Ms. Green's desire to leave her husband, the counselor said if she had reached that point, then presumably she could feel freer from her partner's responses. Would she be willing to try to leave without leaving? (Often change can be brought to a marriage only when one partner is fed up, or no longer cares.) Would she be willing to imagine how she would live her life if she really were alone, and, other men aside, start living that kind of life while she was still married? Ms. Green would, in effect, have to make her own functioning and goals as nondependent on her husband's functioning as possible and, at the same time, try to hold herself back from compensating for his failures. If she wanted to do something for herself and he somehow benefitted from it, that would be fine; but she should get her head out of his, and chart her own course without constantly checking the marital radar scope to see how he was functioning. Ms. Green said she would try, but she thought it would be very difficult. (If she really were unaffected by his responses, there would have been no problem.) The counselor agreed that it was always easier to leave, but there would be little chance for change if she stayed and continued to function as she had.

A Foreign Service husband in a similar situation, upon hearing this idea, said that in the diplomatic corps, it was generally known that "defecting in place" was far more effective than going over to the other side.

Ms. Green took the suggestion. She stopped worrying about the checkbook; she was not the spendthrift. She no longer rushed to clean up her "mess" if she was working on a project for school, and she started going to events that she liked but that her husband said bored him, but she continued to invite him.

Most people immediately recognize, after a suggestion that they "defect in place," the intensity of their own emotional dependency, their difficulty in sustaining an independent course of action, and the fact that, despite the loud bark of their partners, if they really were to function more independently, the partners probably would never bite. Along with this realization is an awareness of their own power in the relationship if they can learn how to use it in the right way. This process (described in Chapter 9) is also a way of helping clergy to stay in and bring change to henpecking congregations with whom they are fed up.

It is, however, not easy to continue to live more independently in a situation previously conditioned by interdependency. When any partner in a relationship begins to try to differentiate (and this includes parents, children, or clergy and their congregations), it is absolutely predictable that the other partner will respond with efforts to triangle the differentiating partner back into the previous stuck-togetherness. This response is almost always either seduction or sabotage, which are different forms of the same thing. It is to be emphasized, however, that this is a mindless, automatic response designed to maintain the homeostasis of the system, and that it originates in an emotional level so deep that it makes the concept of the unconscious appear shallow.

Fundamental change in a relationship does not begin when the partner being coached starts to change his or her own functioning. It comes about when, after initiating changes and after the other partner reacts, the differentiating partner is able to avoid getting triangled in the other's automatic reactivity. It is important, early in the coaching, to ask the partner being coached, "If your spouse were to do something to get your anxiety up, what would it be?" Most marriage partners know this clearly and will respond with comments like: get drunk, have an affair, become depressed, start complaining about a physical symptom, pick on the kids, complain about the budget, become critical of my cooking, my housework, or my appearance, etc. In more anxious systems, they will respond: have an accident or a heart attack, commit suicide, etc. It is, therefore, helpful to suggest to partners being coached that they be prepared in advance for the symptom, and not to let it throw them off course. In fact, it can even be suggested that if they become anxious about the possibility of such a symptom-for-togetherness, they would do well to tell their spouse their anxious fantasy and, thus, make their partner responsible for it. It can be done straightforwardly, such as, "I must tell you that I expect you will probably get sick (become depressed, be critical), but I will not cater to you this time," or more playfully, "Well, if you are so upset, why don't you have an affair (get drunk, pick on the kids). That usually makes you feel better." Of course, the straightforward approach may run more risk of being a dare, while the mischievous response usually challenges the other to keep self-control.

For Ms. Green, a major problem was her husband's know-it-all criticisms. She never won an argument because he was so articulate. Every argument left her feeling stupid. Since Ms. Green was a younger sister of brothers, it was suggested that it would be far more natural for her to be playful than to try to take charge, especially since her husband was an oldest (brother of brothers who tended to treat all women like men). Thus, she was armed with verbal shields to ward off his verbal onslaughts. "Honey, what I can't understand is why you married someone as stupid as me." "You know, honey, what confuses me is why someone as bright as you was so stupid as to marry someone as stupid as me."

A second area of vulnerability for Ms. Green was her husband's sulks into which he invariably withdrew when his "squaw" forgot her place. Ms. Green had a very low threshold for her husband's emotional pain and always felt she had to make things better. She was unwilling to put her "brave" in more pain. But she did understand that it was important not to reward his sulks. She was coached, therefore, to be oversympathetic—for example, "Honey, you look terrible. I think you'd better go to bed." What she said was less important than the emotional envelope; it was not her words that communicated, but the position they allowed her to take.

The coaching process also includes straightforward defining of a position, taking what some have called an "I" stand. An "I" position is one that defines self; it is saying, "I like," "I don't like," "I believe," "I don't agree," "I am going to do this," "I am not going to do that," etc. It is mutually exclusive of "you," "us," and "we" positions such as, "You always —," or "We should —," which are cohortative, or coercive, blaming.

When one partner in any relationship can concentrate on an "I" position, defining in a nonreactive marriage where he or she stands, many other things also seem to happen—conflict diminishes because it takes two to fight, the passive partner usually becomes more active, and the "I" position-taker generally appears more attractive. (The ramifications of this type of self-definition for leadership will be elaborated in both Chapter 4 on raising children and in Chapter 9 on "raising" congregations.)

At one point Ms. Green said she hated faking to her husband about their sex life. His generally passive and controlling nature just turned her off. "Why not tell him that?" asked the counselor. "Well, I don't like to use sex to get my way." She was assured that being openly honest about her feelings in this matter would have a greater chance of disturbing the locked-in homeostasis than her apparent adaptation to his needs. It was also an opportunity for her to increase her threshold for his pain, and to challenge him to take more initiative.

The next time her husband approached her sexually, she told him in as nonattacking and well-defined an "I" stand as possible, that she simply did not enjoy sex with him and did not want to fake it any longer. His response was a monument to passivity: "How long is this going to last?" From that time on, there was no stopping Ms. Green in her efforts to get out of the position of being her man's "pacemaker."

No longer feeling any responsibility for her husband's functioning, or his failure to function, and free of his guilt-inducing dependency, Ms. Green found herself able to channel most of her energy into her own personal goals. She was soon spending more time pursuing her interests; solitude turned from a feared state into one she eagerly sought. Shortly thereafter her husband "lowered his standards," and joined her in counseling.

B. A DIVORCED HUSBAND ALONE

The coaching model can also be used with one motivated partner even after divorce, as well as in premarital consultations. Even *after* a couple is no longer married, if they have children, and even *before* a couple has "tied the knot," the rules of emotional process operate to the exact same extent.

Divorced but Not Separated: Mr. Carpenter came in to see his minister several years after his divorce because he was still caught up in some of the same issues that had plagued him during his marriage. Neither he nor his former wife had remarried, and most of the conflict still revolved around the children. They were, in other words, divorced but not separated. His wife, despite a legal agreement, always found excuses to frustrate his visitation plans. She insisted that he pick the children up and drop them off at specific times, would not let him see the children if he took them to places she disapproved of, and claimed she had extra rights because she was the "custodial parent," a phrase that left him with no answer.

He loved his children and did not want them to become pawns in a power struggle, so he hesitated to take her back to court. His lawyer agreed, and suggested that maybe the minister who married them, and still knew both of them, could help conciliate things. The minister, however, also knew how recalcitrant the wife could be and how timid the husband was. He had tried unsuccessfully when they were married to urge the husband to take firm stands with her, but he seemed to have been "fileted of his back bone," and went wishy-washy whenever the moment of truth arrived.

Remembering this, the minister, instead of plunging in to help this "poor guy" deal with his "bitchy" former wife (all "poor guys" are married to "bitches," of course, and vice versa), first challenged him by saying that while he had some ideas that might help, he wasn't sure Mr. Carpenter could hack it. After all, Mr. Carpenter had never been able to deal with his wife before and, therefore, rather than get involved in all that strain, maybe he should just take what he could get and not rock the boat. Mr. Carpenter responded that the situation had made him lose all dignity. His son was now a teenager, and he felt embarrassed that he could not be more of a man himself.

The following program was outlined. First, Mr. Carpenter was not to make legal threats, but simply to define his own positions, whether it was to disagree or to "disobey," and he should keep a record of any of his wife's responses that broke with the separation agreement. This would build a case if he ultimately needed to go to court; but under no circumstances should he mention "court" and "case." The real purpose of the notetaking was to keep him cool in the face of her diatribes, and to let her react with all the hysteria she could mobilize. Without defensive or aggressive feedback to sustain her behavior, a systemic change should follow.

He never needed the evidence, although at times he was glad he had it. The first thing Mr. Carpenter was coached to do was to tell his wife straight out that he intended to take the children places that she disapproved of. (In the past, when he had done so, he would ask the kids not to tell their mother—a conspiracy that was probably far more harmful to the children than going to court.)

She responded predictably, by telling him that he never cared for the kids and that she was the "custodial parent." In the past, that phrase had always stopped him short; he would usually respond by calling her a name and, in the escalating argument, one would walk out on the other. This time, however, he had been coached in advance for his vulnerability. Armed with a response, his own anxiety was low, and he was able to say, "I've been thinking of that. You always say you are the 'custodial parent,' and I guess I never realized what a burden you bear. So I want to offer you the opportunity to get out from under it. I am prepared to take them totally off your hands and . . ."

He was never able to complete his sentence. His wife went from astounded, to speechless, to amazed, to a verbal barrage. Prepared for this reaction, he did not respond anxiously with the usual counterattack. Instead, he took out a piece of paper and started making notes. (He improvised further: The pencil tip broke and he had the "audacity" to ask her for another.) "What are you doing?" she asked. "I'm taking notes," he responded. She retorted, "Oh, gonna take me to court? Well let me tell you something, I've got a note or two myself." He replied very quietly, "No, no. It's just that when you start telling me my faults, you speak so rapidly, I don't remember everything. I thought if I took notes, I could look them over later . . ." Again, he never got to finish. "Get out!" she yelled. "From now on, you get the kids on the front porch!"

He walked out, pleased as punch, calm, yet excited. He also, for the first time, told the children what had happened, not in a complaining, conspiratorial way that might force them to choose sides, but rather with straight reporting, and even added an excuse for their mother that put him on her side of the triangle—"I guess she's a little tired today."

He later reported that he had the best time of his life with the kids that day and that his daughter, far from being sullen as usual, became friendly almost to the point of being seductive. Indeed, so did his wife! After several more visits in which he managed to become bolder yet still parry all her verbal thrusts, and after two more direct reports to his children about how they wouldn't be able to get together as planned because mother had changed her mind (often making excuses for her; "guess she's not feeling well today"), on the fourth week his former wife met him at the door, looking sexy, smelling great, with his favorite drink mixed for him on the table and an invitation to stay a while because the kids were still at a neighbor's.

Things did not always go smoothly from then on, but they never regressed to where they had been. And, probably as a result, within a year, both Mr. and Mrs. Carpenter had separated enough from one another so that each was able to establish a lasting relationship with someone else.

One can only speculate about what would have happened to their marriage had Mr. Carpenter been able to function within it as he had outside of it. But maybe he never could have done this while they were still "hitched."

A self is more attractive than a no-self. This simple, rather obvious idea is crucial to coaching a member of a family in a direction toward his or her own differentiation, rather than on a path of adaptation to the other. The other may say by word or deed that adaptation is what he or she wants, but each is also more likely to be bored by it. This is just as true concerning clergy and their congregational partners. In the next chapter it will be demonstrated how this same concept can be applied to relationships with children who are so sullen, contrary, and totally expectant that the parent will take all the initiative for the relationship. Actually, coaching one marriage partner is sometimes strikingly similar to coaching the parent of a child. Everyone evidently marries the irresponsibility of their in-laws. Whatever immaturity our partner's parents failed to correct when they had the opportunity now becomes the problem, but also the opportunity, of the spouse.

3. COACHING EITHER PARTNER WITH THE FOCUS ON THE EXTENDED FAMILY

A third angle of entry into the problems of troubled marriages is coaching one or both partners to focus on relationships in their own families of origin. As described in Chapter 1, the influence and impact of the extended family emotional field, either by its presence or its absence, continues long after someone has left home. It is the degree of emotional distance, not the length of time or of geographical physical distance, that is important. In addition, our position in extended family triangles is likely to remain unchanging over the years, whether that position has been "positive" (the family caretaker) or "negative" (the family ne'er-do-well).

It can be stated generally that the first partner in any marriage who begins to work at unresolved issues in family of origin becomes better able to define positions in any context, more objective about feedback contributions to a chronic situation, more capable of appreciating where he or she ends and where his or her partner begins. For the most part, the changes do not have an obvious one-to-one correspondence. They seem to be far deeper, that is, more systemic. When a change comes about in a marriage after changes have been made in the partners' families of origin, these changes always are far less likely to recycle.

Coaching family members to work at issues in their extended families is best done by seeing them separately because one partner can be made anxious by changes the other partner wishes to make and can, by reactions, wear down the other's will. More importantly, working on our own extended family is coming to grips with that which is most exclusively our own. It is the source of all differentiation. It is an experience that is not really shareable, however tellable the tale may be. Since the major purpose of encouraging husband and wife to work at unresolved issues in their own respective families of origin is to create more selfness in each of the partners, it can defeat the purpose if they work on it together.

Sometimes one partner has become very involved in the other's extended family, either to make up for the other partner's distance or as a replacement for his or her own extended system. While it is nice to get along with one's in-laws, that type of overinvolvement will diffuse the lines of self in the marriage, and short-circuit the entire emotional system. Such network crossovers can reduce the therapeutic power in contacts with one's family of origin. The partners' parents are not always available, of course, but that is not crucial. Just reentering the emotional system of a family of origin can help, whether it involves grandparents, other relatives, visits to the original family homestead or, sometimes, to a gravesite. It must be added, however, that for some people this can be such an anxiety-provoking experience that they will avoid it; given a choice they might even prefer chemotherapy.

For most family counselors, a focus on the extended family cannot be introduced when people first come in for help. Often the couple has first to reach the point of feeling totally fed up with, or helpless to change, their marriage. For the clergy, however, because we ourselves often know some of the extended family members, the refocus upon the family of origin can often be a much more natural part of the counseling process.

A. A SEPARATED WOMAN ALONE

Interlocking Triangles: Marie Murphy had been separated for 2 years. Her daughter was living with a man, and Marie did not approve. One son, upon completing school, had returned home; he kept promising to find a job, but refused to help around the house. A second son, who was soon to graduate from high school, looked as if he might not graduate.

Her husband was living with another woman and showed no interest in the children or their problems. If she made efforts to involve him, he fobbed her off with assurances, but never kept his promises, and he always left her with the feeling that she was just a worry-wart. In her family of origin she also had wound up the overresponsible one, unlike her younger sister. She was constantly in the position of giving her mother advice on how to deal with the irresponsible younger sister. It was suggested to Mrs. Murphy that if she were willing to work on that triangle, it might help get her out of similar ones in her nuclear family. She could not imagine how this would help because they lived several hundred miles away, but she agreed to try it.

The conversations with her own mother were predictable. Marie regularly called once a week and asked her mother how she was; mother would respond with worries about her sister. Marie would then tell her mother to make "sis" grow up, but mother would only worry even more about the younger daughter and her children. Next, Marie would offer "reasonable" advice. Mother would either protest or agree, but never followed up the advice. At other times, Marie would call her sister and give her strong advice, acting either as mother's agent or out of frustration with her mother. Marie and her sister would then end up in a fight.

Marie's father had died several years previously, after years of occupying the very stressful position of trying to keep the entire family together. Marie seemed to have inherited that position. It was suggested to Marie, therefore, that she begin operating less predictably and more paradoxically in the triangle: not call her mother as regularly, or call her at odd times, or call her sister first. Familiar patterns, therefore, would not be as apt to recur so automatically. Second, when she did call her mother, it was suggested that Marie be the depressed one who wanted to talk about her own problems. Third, it was suggested that under no circumstances should she ask her mother how she "feels." This otherwise normal expression of concern had, over the years, become a trigger for chronic patterns of triangulating complaints. Fourth, if mother did begin to complain about sis, Marie was to be supportive of sis, thus pushing mother toward her sister rather than trying to separate them further.

To illustrate how the telephone conversations changed, the following is a typical conversation of the past:

MARIE: Hi, Mom, how are you?
MOM: It's your sister, again.
MARIE: What's the matter this time?
MOM: She's left the kids alone again, and that little one absolutely needs to be better fed. He's so skinny.
MARIE: Mom, leave well enough alone. She's got to work this out herself.
MOM: I can't.
MARIE: But it isn't doing any good.
MOM: I know you're right, but when I think about those little ones . . .
MARIE: But Mom, she's over thirty!
MOM: I know, but if I could just get her to settle down a little.
MARIE: But Mom, it hasn't worked, anything you've done. Get yourself interested elsewhere. Go away for a month. As long as you infantilize her, she is going to infantilize her own kids.
MOM: You mean just try to ignore her? What if she calls?
MARIE: Tell her you're busy.
MOM: I guess — I could try.

But try as she would, mother had no staying power beyond a week.

The new conversational approach with mother went something like this:

MARIE: Mom? (*pause*) is that you?
MOM: Marie? (*silence*) What's the matter?
MARIE: I don't know. It's nothing, just a little down.
MOM: Well, you've got no reason to be down. You've got fine kids, a good job. I'm the one who should be depressed, your sister has started to . . .
MARIE: (*interrupting*) No, Mom, I don't think you understand. It's different this time. I don't know what's going to happen. I just don't seem to be able to make it any longer. I've lost all my joy and verve.
MOM: What can I do?
MARIE: I'm afraid you can't do anything. Maybe I'll write you about it.

MOM: Well, I don't understand. You were never the one I had to worry about. Your sister started some of her old shenanigans again. Maybe you could call her and tell her to straighten out.

MARIE: Mom, sis's problem is that you don't help her enough

MOM: What? Why do you say that? I try all I can.

MARIE: Well, let's face it, Mom, sis wouldn't have these problems if you had raised her right.

MOM: I used to think that way, but I'm beginning to think she's just a spoiled brat.

MARIE: Whatever you do, don't tell her that.

MOM: You know, I'd like to.

MARIE: She might not be able to take it.

MOM: She's tougher than you think.

MARIE: I don't know, Mom, she doesn't have our strength. She needs a lot of help.

MOM: When she needs me, you mean. Don't think I'm going to be so quick to run to help her every time she needs it. I'm getting older, you know, and it's getting hard on me. Besides, there are things I want to do with my own time.

MARIE: But, Mom, if you died and sis still needed you, you would never rest in peace.

MOM: I'll worry about that when I come to it. Tell me more about your life. Maybe you're the one who I should be thinking about.

Marie called her sister after this phone conversation and, in a similar way, got herself out of the responsible older sister position by complaining about her own lot, and asking for advice instead of being set up as the one to give it. She also began pushing her sister at her mother by continually reminding sis how lucky she was to still have a mother available to take care of her.

As she continued to detriangle with her mother and sister, she found herself better able to hear similar suggestions regarding her behavior with her own children and her husband. For example: The school called to say that her youngest son was not completing his assignments and probably would not graduate. Instead of talking to her son or pushing her husband to get involved, she gave her husband's private number to the school and told them the boy was his responsibility. When her husband called, irate, she delegated the anxiety rather than the responsibility. "Well, you don't have to do anything about it, but you might want to get some good connections at court in case we are sued for what he does next."

Regarding her daughter who was living with a man against Marie's wishes, Marie defined her own position better. Rather than trying to change her daughter, she told her that she could do what she wanted outside her home, but that she could not sleep with this man anymore when they came for a visit. To her lazy oldest son who had recently moved back, she gave a deadline: either start paying rent or get out. She also made a list of specific responsibilities that he would have to take charge of if he were going to be the "man of the house." When she told all three kids that she was going to sell the house at the end of the school year and move into an apartment, everyone reacted and told her she was selfish, and, naturally, everyone made their own efforts at sabotage. Husband lost the support check that month. Younger son got two speeding tickets. Daughter came home sick and needed to be cared for. Oldest son spilled out the punch "by mistake" before a dinner party she was giving for friends. She persisted, however, saying, "It's them or me. I don't want to end up like my mother." And she didn't. After the initial sabotage, everyone began to show more respect. She found herself quite able to follow through on the divorce, began a lasting relationship with another man, and then went down to the docks to see off her mother, who had decided to take a trip to Europe.

B. A SYSTEMS APPROACH TO PREMARITAL COUNSELING

It may well be that it is in the premarital phase that coaching with respect to families of origin has its greatest value. What makes the family approach particularly applicable at this juncture in the life of a couple is that the emotional phenomena of engagement and disengagement (from previous relationships) are the opposite sides of the same coin. These processes of entering and leaving are always found in the development of any new bond. And these reciprocal processes do not end with the wedding. This is another example of how concern with compatibility, and focus on a marriage relationship, in isolation from consideration of the extended family fields, can be misleading. We will come back to this theme in Chapter 10 where it will be seen that the course of any new relationship between clergy members and their congregations is greatly affected by the nature of their respective separations from their previous "partners," and the way in which they continue to relate to those former partners after they have separated. This is also why premarital counseling is discussed here after marital counseling, and not before. Ideally, it should be discussed after the issues in the next chapter, which is concerned with the difficulties of leaving home.

The Failure of Premarital Counseling

The failure of premarital counseling to affect the divorce rate today may be due primarily to the fact that the approach is often directed toward the couple's *relationship*. The focus on personality, psychody-namics, and transactions has deprived couples of a more enriching perspective from which to evaluate their problems and their future. Here, especially, the individual model has diluted the healing power inherent in the position of the clergy, whose entrée into families during courtship is almost an exclusive bailiwick. By switching the focus to the bride and groom's families of origin, not only can premarital counseling be made more effective in its own right, as was shown in the first example of Chapter 1, but the very experience also becomes an oppor-tunity to affect more than one couple and for more than one genera-tion.

As will become more explicit in Chapter 7, all life-cycle events, nodal happenings in the life of a family, are moments of great relational flux and are, therefore, propitious opportunities for derailing patholog-ical processes as well as heading healing processes in the right direction. The extended family emphasis can be employed in premarital counsel-ing either as a general prophylactic measure or as a means of dealing with specific problems that arise during courtship.

Family History

In using the family approach as a preventative measure, if each partner would be willing to work up a genogram of his or her family of origin, and then be allowed to respond to what each has learned about the other's extended family field, it often becomes possible to make accu-rate predictions about where they are likely to have some "rough sledding." For example (as illustrated in Chapter 1), a pattern might show marriages breaking up (by death or divorce) after the birth of a child. Or a pattern might emerge that, in one branch of the family tree, the nuclear groupings tend to show symptomatic problems in individu-als, and in another that problems in the marriage are projected onto the children. Both of these patterns can sometimes be correlated to the gender of the people involved. Also, the sibling positions of the respec-tive bride and groom, and the general position and expectations they have inherited from their families of origin, can be discussed by noting how the marriages of those whose positions they may have taken turned out.

Such specifics often are important indications of the future, and the opportunity to discuss them often enables couples to talk about things they might not otherwise have mentioned, or even realized were important. The counselor also may glean information that he or she would never have thought to ask for. In addition, the contact with extended families that is often necessary to obtain information for the genogram sometimes catalyzes discussions (about sex, death, or affairs) that might not otherwise have been discussed. And in the latter case, talking with parents about their parents will always help the couple getting married to separate more easily, because that type of focus helps their parents to let go with less of a struggle.

Genogram information can make the difference in the life and death of a marriage, for, like any malignant process, many marital problems would never have had such influence had they been recognized and treated at an earlier stage in their development. It must be admitted, though, that with engaged as with married couples, those who most need to become involved in such research will be those most reluctant to engage in it.

Communicating with Courting Couples

Beyond its specific informational value, the extended family approach also comes to grips with several major aspects of the courting process that generally prevent couples from hearing or taking any counsel at that time. First of all, people generally can only hear you when they are coming toward you. When couples are courting, they are moving toward one another and, relatively speaking, away from everyone else at the speed of light. Messages just do not catch up, no matter how they are broadcast. In fact, the faster the couple is coming together (which at its highest speed is always an indication of unresolved issues elsewhere), the more likely it is that well-meaning advice will be perceived as an effort to slow them down or pull them apart, and the more likely that those efforts will increase the partners' acceleration toward one another and away from everyone else.

Because the extended family approach is less specifically pointed toward a couple's relationship, the same distancing, reactive phenomenon is not as likely to occur. In fact, the couple is more likely to see such premarital counseling as fun. Individuals always enjoy learning about their partners' backgrounds, and they often reply, "Now things (in my own background) are coming together." In addition, couples are far more likely to remember information and suggestions given by clergy in the context of the extended family investigations than in the context of a symptom orientation that concentrates on their own relationship. The atmosphere also establishes a camaraderie with the clergy member.

A second reason that most couples cannot hear most premarital advice is that before marriage they have yet to experience the kind of fusion that will develop in their relationship after the vows. It is almost impossible for couples before marriage to appreciate the loss of self that marital fusion will promote, even if they have already experienced it in other relationships. The emotional interdependency characteristic of this kind of fusion only seems to emerge after the final commitment,

often appearing like some printout, programmed in a previous generation. It even occurs with couples who have lived together for some
time, and provides a reason why trial marriage will not solve the
contemporary problems of mating. Actually, many couples live together, unmarried, in a quite harmonious state for years, only to start
experiencing severe difficulties once they decide to "get serious." There
seem to be two nodal points in life, marriage and becoming a parent,
after which individuals, who have sworn they will never function like
their parents, suddenly find themselves "spooked."

Little of this is predictable from looking at a couple's relationship
alone. The degree of fusion any couple can expect to experience after
marriage is only predictable from a family systems approach that
explores the evidence for fusion in the partners' extended families,
their own respective positions within those systems, and the way they
have functioned in previous states of relational commitment.

Ironically, clergy have an experience in their own professional lives
that approximates this inability to hear before experiencing the real
world of commitment. This is when advice is given to them in their
"prenuptial" seminary training about how they should function when
they become committed to the relationship systems of church and
synagogue. Clergy in the field constantly lament that what they learn
in workshops after ordination should have been taught when they
were still in school. It was. Couples during courtship are no more
capable of hearing advice about how to fight, budget, communicate,
and have sex, than are clergy capable of learning about how to deal
with unjust criticism, triangles among congregation members, or
separation anxiety when their charges can't find them in the office; at
least this is true until after they have taken their "vows" and after they
have spent some time in the committed responsibility of their own
post.

A third deception promoted by the compatibility model of courtship (and not found in the extended family approach) is that individuals getting married tend to judge one another primarily on the basis
of personality. (This one also has its analogue in our seminary experience.) A major key to "knowing" another is to know how he or she
will operate in a crisis. If the courtship has been relatively calm, the
couple will assume that the absence of crisis is proof they are well
matched. The absence of crisis actually deprives couples of the opportunity to test and understand one another. Couples who experience
problems in courtship are often luckier, if the crisis has motivated them
to work on the relationship. Either way, a family history that can show
the links between dysfunction and change from a multigenerational
perspective can penetrate deeply into the capacity of family members to
deal with crisis. The parallel to our own training is that, in the effort to

be modern, seminaries often choose their candidates with the aid of personality tests designed to ferret out potentially inappropriate traits. Aside from avoiding the aforementioned inquisitorial dangers in such diagnosis, an extended family history might go much further in predicting how individuals will function after ordination (commitment).

As a general approach to all couples "tying the knot," therefore, the extended family focus in premarital counseling can enable future marriage partners to gain a depth perception of their partner not available when the focus is only on the fit of their personalities, and whether or not their relationship has been calm.

Here now is an illustration of a family systems approach to premarital counseling when the couple is experiencing problems. The following extended case history is presented as a way of summarizing all that has been said earlier about the marriage jewel in the extended family setting. Each partner was formerly married, and both had troubled relationships with their parents and their children. I will describe how the issue between these two individuals was defocused and how it eventually atrophied when their attention was directed to their extended family fields. As will be seen, in the course of the counseling systemic change occurred. Not only did the relationship with one another change, but also their relationships with their parents, their children, their siblings, their respective former spouses, and even the relationships of their parents with one another, as well as their sibling relationships with their parents.

This approach unifies premarital counseling and separation counseling from divorced spouses, and foreshadows an important part of Chapters 4 and 6, the stimulating of growth in both children and aged parents. It, thus, illustrates the aforementioned relationship between engagement and disengagement. Here, the disengagement is not only from triangles in the families of origin but also from triangles with children and former spouses. Almost all these opportunities are present for every couple, but few have the motivation to work at things long enough for all the vital issues to surface.

Putting It All Together: Mike Chin, 49, and Pam Harris, 46, came in to see their minister after their relationship of 2 years had not gone anywhere. They seemed to be foundering over differences in religion. Pam was from a Quaker background and Mike from a Catholic home, although his father was of Chinese ancestry. Both had been married before and both had custody of their children. Relationships with their former mates, both remarried and living in the community, were polite but distant. Both sets of parents were alive. Pam's lived in town, Mike's a thousand miles away.

Mike had said he would not marry Pam if she did not convert. Pam, having been very adaptive to her previous spouse, was afraid that if she converted she would be setting the same course again. Both were serious about their desire to work things out, came regularly, and taped each meeting so that they could review what had been said. However, no matter how much Mike and Pam rehashed their religious differences, no new ideas or positions came forth. It was suggested, therefore, that whatever was really hindering their relationship might be related to other things going on in their extended families. They were encouraged to stop discussing their relationship at all, and to focus instead on unresolved issues with their parents and children.

As a means of shifting the field of focus it was suggested that at first they discuss their problem with their parents. They did. Mike's mother was adamant; their kind (Catholic) didn't marry her kind (Quaker). Mike's father went along with mother. Mike also had a brother, aged 40, who had never left home, had been diagnosed manic-depressive, and had never held a job. It never occurred to Mike to ask him.

Pam, on the contrary, found her parents unwilling to take a stand. They were more interested in the problems of Pam's daughter who was majoring in urban studies and totally immersed in the problems of the black community. Pam was upset about this, too, but more concerned about her son, who had become a model and who Pam was afraid would become homosexual. Her former husband had little to do with either child, and Pam felt the burden of raising both, as well as the responsibility for her aging parents since her own brother had moved out of town.

Mike, likewise, carried the whole burden of his two children as well as his parents. His first wife had left him for another man and was totally cut off from her own parents. It also became clear that one of Mike's sons was somehow triangled between Mike and his former wife, and had recently begun to show preulcerative symptoms.

Pam and Mike's relationship may be viewed three ways: by itself (Figure 3-1); in the context of their previous marriages and offspring (Figure 3-2); and in the context of the extended family force fields (Figure 3-3).

Over the next year, Pam, with biweekly coaching, got out of the following triangles: (1) She involved her former husband in her children's lives by reporting their anxiety-provoking behavior to him in nonanxious tones. When he would respond with his usual laconic, "What do you expect me to do about it?" she answered, "I'm not asking you to do anything about it, just thought you'd like to know." (2) She got herself out of the middle between her brother and her parents by doing something similar, by reporting to him regularly how badly their parents were doing, but not suggesting that he do anything about it.

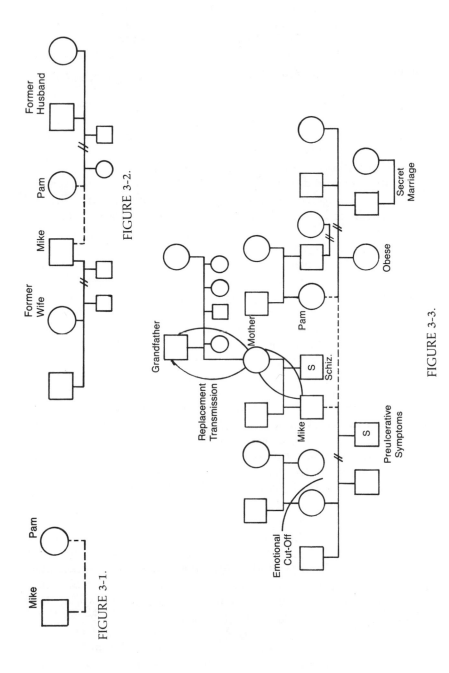

FIGURE 3-1.

FIGURE 3-2.

FIGURE 3-3.

(3) With regard to her parents themselves, she began to tell her father all the complaints mother dumped on her about him. When mother gave her a hard time about how Pam was raising her own daughter, instead of defending herself, she asked mother to adopt her.

The new self-emergent Pam also got out of the middle between daughter and daughter's destiny. Instead of continuing to give her wise advice or letting her take advantage of mother's financial resources, Pam began to make firm rules regarding the conditions under which she could live in her house. Daughter predictably threw a tantrum, screamed that mother never loved her, and moved in with her grandparents. This gave Pam a double opportunity because she could now tell her mother how to raise her granddaughter.

As she began to detriangle everywhere, Pam became stronger in her resolve not to convert in order to make the marriage work. She said that she could see herself joining Mike in family celebrations, but that she was just not a very "religious" person. She would not submit to the indignity of a false confession. As she became stronger in her resolve, Mike (the head of a government agency) also began to throw tantrums and started blaming her for putting him in the middle between her and his mother. But she was no longer willing to get herself into the middle in order to help him get out of the middle. Mike now became motivated to work on his relationship with his parents.

Fearful that he might lose a woman he really loved, Mike began to look at his position in his own very large family, many of whom had intermarried. With the aid of a genogram he began to understand his mother's special position in her family and why she was the most religious member, saw how he had replaced his grandfather (her father) in her affections, and consequently saw more clearly how he carried away from his nuclear family of origin the burden of the patriarch's expectations of his children. Then he began to get out of the position of expert to his parents and counselor to his nonfunctional brother. First, he asked his brother's advice on what to do about Pam. To his utter shock, his brother assumed the helpful sibling position almost naturally. Regarding his parents, he made sure that they not favor him over his brother when he went home for a visit. In addition, instead of telling his parents, as he had for years, that they were getting on and should start thinking about themselves rather than about their younger son, he began to praise their martyrdom, telling them that while they would never have any joy in this world, there could be little doubt it would come in the next. When he began to tell members of his extended family how his mother and father were reacting to his possible marriage, all of them were extremely supportive. He also made direct contact with his former in-laws. He had maintained distance from them in an unthinking conspiracy with his former wife. He talked to them frankly about their distance from their daughter, and how their grandson's "nervous stomach" might get better if they would cease distancing from her. He was surprised at how much better that made *him* feel.

About this time Pam, totally fed up with the absence of a commitment, told Mike she would not go on this way indefinitely. She loved him, but she didn't want to wait beyond her attractive years. She was going to start dating other men. When, and if, he ever got ready, she would see where she was then. Mike became terribly depressed and called his psychotic brother who said, "Love is more important than duty." An able lawyer, Mike soon came up with a brilliant legal fiction, based on different kinds of corporate mergers, and decided that his marriage did not have to be based on an association in which there was total merging (fusion?) but, rather, on one in which the association was more "participatory." They were married within a month.

Around this time, Mike's mother traveled back to her "homeland" for the first time in decades, and his "kid brother" went out and found a job. Pam decided to sell her house right out from under her daughter so that she could begin to bear her own "weight." At the wedding, Pam's son introduced Pam and Mike to the woman he had been secretly married to for a year.

There can be no clearer picture of the systemic quality of marital bonding. The logical conclusion, which leads naturally to the subject of the next chapter, is that the most effective form of premarital counseling would be working with the parents of the bride and groom when they are about age 6.

4

Child-Focused Families

Ruth and Joe Harris came frantically to their clergyman, anxious about their daughter's involvement in the drug scene at college. Her parents were chagrined because they had tried to maintain a very close family. As it happened, Mrs. Harris was expecting a visit from her mother that week, and she said that her mother seemed to have a better relationship with her troubled granddaughter than she (Ruth) had. The minister, therefore, suggested a family session that would include Ruth's mother as well as her child. In that session, he succeeded in defocusing the daughter, and managed to keep most of the family's attention on mother's relationship with her own parent. Soon after, her own daughter decided to move back home and finish her education at a local school.

THE CHILD-FOCUSING PROCESS

If the world of counseling generally tends to focus on individual symptoms rather than on family emotional process, this is particularly the case when the symptom is located in a child. This is most unfortunate because children tend to occupy the least influential position in the family hierarchy. At the bottom of the totem pole, they are usually the most helpless to affect a process that has made them into the family symptom-bearer. It is also unfortunate because it allows the other family members to avoid their own contributions to the problem. The fact that models of individual therapies tend to organize their thinking and their clinics around children's symptoms often reinforces such family process, even when the parents are seen "in addition" in order to "help" the child.

100

It is possible today to find therapeutic institutions, books, or work-shops devoted to: enuresis, school phobias, drug and alcohol abuse, delinquency, poor school habits, nightmares, teenage pregnancy, an-orexia, cults, teenage suicide, juvenile arson, adolescent obesity, etc. But the key to lasting change in symptomatic children, whatever the symptom, is changing the focusing process so that it does not recycle again, either on the same child or on another member of the family. This focusing process always appears to be a result of parental concern that has been *caused* by the child's problem. But almost always the concern *predated* the symptom and was part of the emotional process that made the child's symptom chronic. (See "Chronic Conditions," Chapter 2.)

Focus on a child's symptom, therefore, is not only part and parcel of the family's "disease," it is that symptom's natural manure. (It must be added, however, that the focusing process can also produce an overachiever and even a "genius.") Either way, a child in the path of multigenerational focusing processes will have more difficulty dealing with his or her problems. Family anxiety will always be more height-ened when the symptom is in the focused member, and the child who occupies such a position will have less flexibility to adapt to the condi-tion in a way that optimizes survival. This may be equally true for recuperation from physical illness (see Chapter 5).

This chapter will apply family process thinking to families focused on a symptomatic child. It will continue to develop the coaching model introduced previously and show how it may be used when one or both parents are motivated to seek counseling. Similarly, it will be applied to both the nuclear and extended family systems.

ADVANTAGES FOR THE CLERGY

As with marriage counseling, the family approach carries several par-ticular advantages for the clergy as counselors. Some advantages have to do with their pastoral efforts, others with their own position in the congregational family. First, there is the "expertise" problem again. It is just not possible for any professional counselor today, much less members of the clergy who have other areas of concern as well, to be adequately knowledgeable in the content of more than one or two areas of child symptomatology. Second, since the parents that a minis-ter, priest, or rabbi counsels are also his bosses, there are multiple triangular pitfalls when we come between a child and our "elders." However, because of the long-term association that members of the clergy often have had with a parishioner family, the appearance of a symptom in a child can be an unusual opportunity to gain entrée into the entire family system. This advantage has many other positive spinoffs. For example, time and again, clergy who have been trained in the family approach have reported that where they have avoided the temptation to become the advocate for the child *against* the family, and instead worked from the direction of coaching the parents to differentiate themselves from the child (and in the process from one another), the latter have consistently shown gratitude within the congregational family, generally siding with the cleric on important issues. In addition, the family has been quicker to return to their minister as other problems surface throughout the years. Also, the child is less likely to dismiss the minister as a "fink" for the "establishment" even when the minister is supporting the parents to be firm. Since any problem in a child is the result of multigenerational processes, one can expect its source to be energized again and again in the change and stress of life-cycle events. Over the long run, therefore, a family approach to problems in children ultimately unifies the minister's priestly and shepherding roles (see Chapter 7).

FAMILY LEADERSHIP

There is also another type of integration that works to the advantage of the clergy when they adopt a family approach to symptoms in children. This one has to do with leadership. It is worth highlighting immediately because it establishes a bridge for reciprocal insight between parenting "charges" (responsibilities) in a personal family or in a congregational family. In fact, everything to be said here about the importance of leadership in families with problem children will be just as relevant for leadership in congregational families.

In our society today, much is made of treating children as persons, human beings who have a right to be heard. But many family leaders today bend so far in the direction of consensus, in order to avoid the stigma of being authoritarian, that clarity of values and the positive, often crucial benefits of the leader's self-differentiation are almost totally missing from the system. One of the most prevalent characteristics of families with disturbed children is the absence or the involution of the relational hierarchy. While schools of family therapy have different ways of conceptualizing this condition, which may also be viewed as a political phenomenon regarding congregations, it is so diffuse among families troubled by their troubled children that its importance cannot be underestimated.

What happens in any type of family system regarding leadership is paradoxical. The same interdependency that creates a need for leadership makes the followers anxious and reactive precisely when the leader is functioning best. This is as true in personal families as we saw in the previous chapter, as it is in congregation families. Family systems thinking suggests an approach to leadership that diminishes the stress of sabotaging resistance. It will be called leadership through self-differentiation and is designed to put to use the very interdependency that usually obstructs a leader's efforts. It is a systematic approach because it depends less on personality and more on position. A full elaboration of this leadership model appears below (see Chapter 9).

Its analogue is the following, not uncommon situation in the Jewish community today. A father calls his rabbi for the name of a nontraditional colleague who would be willing to officiate at an inter-marriage, maybe also on the Sabbath. Both of these acts are contrary to traditional Jewish values. Often the very parent who is making the request is not in favor of it himself, but he has been reluctant to take a stand because at this point it is "too late," or he doesn't want to lose his son. The same situation could arise in Catholic families around issues of abortion, in Methodist families around issues of divorce, or in any family even when the issue is not a religious one.

If that father could have been coached to define himself, to take an "I" position, as described in the previous chapter, it would not have been "too late," and instead of losing his child with such a stand, he is more likely to find his son drawing closer. "Son, I've been thinking things over. I said I would try to find the kind of rabbi you want, but I really do not agree with the way you are going about this. You have a right to marry whom you want and in whatever type of ceremony you wish. I, however, also have a right to be true to myself. Therefore, if this is the way you want to go about it, you will have to take the responsibility for putting it together. I will probably come to the wedding because you are my son, although I will not be happy about it. Perhaps that is my problem. In all events, some other time, if you want, we can discuss the issues more calmly." A position like this does not guarantee that the son will do a sudden "I now see the light" turnabout, but there is probably even more guarantee that "leadership" by threatening to cut him off financially or emotionally, no less than by other "guilting" or wise parental advice, will fail to change his mind.

What the self-definition approach is guaranteed to do is lay the groundwork for an entirely different type of relationship between leader and follower (here father and son), one that maximizes the possibility that eventually the son's ears will open to his leader's values. Difficult as it is to formulate and take such positions during intense family struggles, parental, marital, or congregational, the effects on a follower can be extraordinary. Involved here is a different use of language, a different concept of communication. The leader does not use language to force ideas into the follower's head. Rather, a leader uses language to define his or her own being. It is the resulting effect of the *leader's well-differentiated presence* that will communicate with the follower. Because of the intrinsic connection between the head and the body, in any organism, family leaders who can take such stands will influence the entire system far more than had they simply tried to change the heads of others. Indeed, had this father understood how to function that way over the years, the odds are that the problem would not be there now. Children have a right to be heard, but parents have an obligation to be clear.

In Section III we will see how the leadership issues discussed in the context of the congregational family double back to become a therapeutic modality in parishioners' families. The most effective form of parental counseling that we can give the members of our congregations may not be how we counsel them in their moment of crisis but, rather, the style of leadership we ourselves exhibit daily regarding our own "charges" in the congregation, particularly our capacity to define ourselves. At the very least, if we are not aware of this connection, we may undercut our "sage" pastoral efforts, well-meaning though they may be.

The subtle but very powerful connection between congregational family process and the family process that is characteristic of child-focused families also works the other way. Parents are as likely to displace unresolved family issues onto their priest, minister, or rabbi as they are onto their own children. Therefore, when clergy unwittingly collude in child focus, they reinforce the same displacement processes that then ultimately come to focus on themselves and make them into symptom bearers for their own congregations. Similarly, where they are too quick to respond anxiously to that displacement they support the habit of parental displacement at home.

Once again, however, the emotional interlock between the clergy's families can also work to our advantage. To the extent that we can teach families not to focus on their problemed children, we discourage the process that leads to displacement on ourselves. And to the extent that we can learn not to buy into the displacement process in our congregation members, we become their children's advocates in the deepest sense.

THREE EMOTIONAL COORDINATES

Family therapy began as an effort to help children. It is worth noting, therefore, how one of the primary models developed before illustrating its application. This model formulated three emotional coordinates necessary to map the course of a family's focusing process, and they still are valid today. The specific counseling pathways to be described later all are derived from that map.

When Murray Bowen conducted his pioneering research at the National Institutes of Health, about 25 years ago, hospitalizing entire families, a pattern began to emerge in the relationship between child and mother. Universally, their emotional functioning was almost the reciprocal of one another. While mother's anxiety appeared to be concern over her child's poor functioning, if the child began to function better mother's anxiety often rose. Similarly, it was noticed that if efforts to help mother gain some measure of control over her anxiety were successful, the child seemed to get worse! It is now generally realized that this type of reciprocity can be found to some extent with almost any mother and her children. But it will always be descriptive of mother's relationship with her most impaired child.

While many a child's symptoms begin after increased focus, for example, after a mother (in the replacement phenomenon) rushes to fill a void created by the loss of one of her own parents. Many symptoms also surface in children when mother begins to think *less* about a child and more about herself, perhaps because the mother has lost a parent she has been parenting. This kind of "wound" in the child, however, has great capacity to heal itself if the parental anxiety (the inflammation) can be reduced. The important thing for the counselor to do in such instances is to coach the mother to preserve her new-found self.

A second consistent pattern that emerged in those early studies concerned the functioning of the father. The fathers tended to be of almost no account, and by their emotional absence contributed mightily to the problem. To what extent a mother's intense involvement in her children is due to father's distance, and to what extent father's distance is an adaptation to his wife's involvement in their children, is not always ascertainable. What can be stated as a very specific rule of family life, however, is this: *An emotionally distant male is a necessary precondition for the perpetuation of an intense mother–child relationship.* However, as the principle of symmetry suggests, a father who is too reactive to the mother–child axis will also perpetuate stuckness in that relationship.

Father's input into the impairment of a child is as important as mother's, but generally the direction is somewhat different. (See Figure 4-1.) His main contribution to the problem often has more to do with how he relates to mother (1) and to mother's relationship with the child (2) than with how he himself relates directly to his child (3). It is his response to mother's anxiety that tightens the loop. Even where father is a child abuser, the source of that family symptom is often to be found in his relationship with his wife. This can be just as true where mothers work or where fathers share more of the child raising. Mothers who work are not necessarily less intense about their off-

105

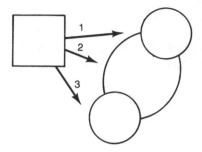

FIGURE 4-1. Father's contribution to symptom in child.

spring. Fathers who share more of the mothering are not necessarily less reactive. Contemporary life styles do not necessarily change family emotional processes.

The third pattern that showed up consistently is the least obvious, and yet it may be the most influential. It was found that mothers who were uncomfortable in their relationships with their children rarely were comfortable in their relationships with their own mothers. In fact, to the extent the mother–child relationship was stuck, a similar degree of inflexibility almost always appeared in mother's relationship with her own mother (who usually also had married a "distancer"). Eventually the theory developed that it took several generations to create severely impaired children, several generations of a mother "selecting" out of her brood one particular child with whom to complete herself, and successive generations of a narrowing of focus. Some readers may perceive such a theory as chauvinistic. Mother is not being blamed. That would be an individual therapy model. The systems model is saying that mother tends to be the quarterback. She is not to be exclusively blamed for any failure of the team. It is her position that tends to lay the failure at her feet. On the other hand, as we shall see, this same position generally gives her more power to engineer success.

The multigenerational hypothesis provides a very important third emotional coordinate for creating strategies to help problemed children. When grandparents are involved in the counseling process (either directly in the office or through contacts with them by the parents), it can often stem an otherwise pernicious tide. Here are two case examples; one failed to involve the three generations, the second succeeded.

A Family Projection: A highly energetic, willful mother of three sons went into an agitated depression after leaving her extremely dependent husband and began to act so "irrationally" that she got herself committed. Both she and her husband had been seeing separate therapists. Her parents accepted the institutionalization as proof of their daughter's illness. The minister tried to get the family not to identify her as the problemed one. First he called the husband to see if he would stay more in touch with his estranged wife, also hoping to get him to work on his relationship with his own extremely possessive mother, whom the minister knew. But the husband, as always, nicely begged out. The minister tried to show the wife's parents how the institutionalization kept everyone in a posture of seeing their daughter as sick. He said that if they would instead view her as a brat who was willful and demanding and who needed someone to stand up to her, they might be of significant, long-term help to their "child." The parents listened politely, but theirs was a relationship in which the wife was totally dependent on her husband, and he wanted no disruption in his marriage, such as the growth of his mate.

Their daughter eventually reentered society, and she and her husband both continued to see their respective counselors for several years after the divorce. For the next few years there was no severe crisis, and so no one was motivated to seek additional change in the family. Then, 6 years after the separation, mother's oldest son, the one with whom she had had the least amount of trouble, just before his graduation and in the midst of applying to graduate school, blew his brains out one night.

But even where a symptom shows up early, relieving that symptom only is about 25% of the problem. It is only a one-base hit. A parent changing his or her relationship with a parent is a "home run." Here is an example of a successful team coached in a family systems approach.

Clearing the Bases: The Meyers came in concerned about a child who was preanorexic. She had lost 10 pounds in a month. Within several weeks, however, mother's anxiety had been considerably reduced and she was able to see her daughter as petulant rather than sick. Then, through paradoxical techniques, she was able to stay loose about her anxiety, able, for example, to serve her daughter absurdly small portions and warning her about calories when she was hungry. The child began to eat regularly again. We now have the family on first base. The wife then began to focus on her marriage, and many hidden conflicts came to the surface. In the course of the counseling, father was seen alone and encouraged to work on a relationship with his widowed mother whom he treated in a distant but protective manner. He succeeded in changing that relationship. The family now was on second base. The automatic, predictable effect of this change was that his wife started to become anxious again. Without her husband's efforts to dampen her anxiety this time, she was forced to take responsibility for her own anxiety and, as a result, blamed him less for her discontent.

107

The family was now on third. At this point, the wife became motivated to understand her own chronic anxiety and, in working on her relationship with her mother, was able to differentiate her own basically happy view of life from her mother's constant pessimism. Home run! There is little likelihood now that her daughter will become anorexic even though she may refuse to eat from time to time. The focus that equates mere disappearance of a symptom in a child with a fundamental change in the system leaves a lot of families on base.

THE SYSTEMS APPROACH

The systems approach to child-focused families will now be illustrated in four clinical settings. As in the previous chapter, each one will emphasize the position of the clergy–counselor, the position of the family member(s) being coached, and *not* the content of the child's specific symptom.

1. Family and child together.
2. Mother alone with focus on nuclear family.
3. Mother alone with focus on her family of origin.
4. Father alone with focus on his family of origin.

These different angles of entry all are derived from the aforementioned three emotional coordinates: relationship of parent and child, relationship of parent and other parent, relationship of parent with own parents. As will be seen later in Section III, the relationship that the clergy maintain with those above them in their hierarchy strongly influences their capacity to parent their charges in the congregation.

1. PARENTS WITH CHILD

When mother and father come in with a child, they are anxious to eliminate the symptom and the child is defensive, wishing he or she could change but also wishing to be anywhere but there, sometimes cooperative, sometimes sullen. Often, to the counselor, the kid is just a kid. Without the emotional investment of the parents, if the counselor can avoid trying to force change and just use his or her own nonanxious presence as a catalyst, through the use of questions, it is sometimes possible in just one meeting to reduce family anxiety significantly, and to shift the problem from the "kid's" to the "family's."

Here are two short examples, one with a shy young'un, and one with a chip-on-the-shoulder teenager.

Billy: The Gray family called their minister early one morning in a dither about their son Billy's angry behavior. He had sassed his mother, beat up his kid brother, was sent home with notes the first two days of school, and was brought home by a neighbor who said he was playing with matches near their house.

MRS. GRAY: Billy has been impossible. He has come home from camp like a wild animal. Nothing seems to keep him still.

MINISTER: Mr. Gray, what's your perception of this problem?

MR. GRAY: Billy sure has been impossible.

MINISTER: Billy, how'd you get to be impossible?

BILLY: I don't know.

MRS. GRAY: That's his typical response, (*mimicking*) "I don't know." Well, I don't know what we are going to do with you. (*to minister*) Can you recommend someone who can find out what's wrong with him, or at least teach him some sense?

MINISTER: Mrs. Gray, what makes you so helpless?

MRS. GRAY: Helpless? I'm not helpless! Why do you say that? I don't want to see him grow up to be one of those addicts.

MINISTER: Is there something else you haven't told me? I mean, where does that "addict" stuff come from?

MR. GRAY: My wife tends to get nervous about things. Actually, I don't have that much trouble with the boys.

MINISTER: Billy, how come you don't give your father as much trouble as your mother?

BILLY: He won't let me.

MINISTER: Won't let you? Your mother is giving you permission?

MRS. GRAY: He's never listened to me like he listens to his father.

MINISTER: Billy, is that true?

BILLY: A little. It's just that I know that if he says something, he means it.

MINISTER: Mrs. Gray, how would you explain your failure to get respect from your child?

MRS. GRAY: I don't know. He just won't listen to reason.

MINISTER: Billy, how come you don't listen to reason?

BILLY: My mother talks a lot.

MINISTER: And your father?

BILLY: He doesn't talk as much as my mother.

MINISTER: What would you say to that, Mrs. Gray?

MRS. GRAY: My husband hits the boys. I can't do that.

MINISTER: Spare the rod and spoil the child.

MRS. GRAY: My mother never spared the rod. She abused us. I vowed I would never hit a child of mine.

MR. GRAY: I don't think they obey me because I hit them. They just know I won't stand for nonsense.

MRS. GRAY: Well, then, tell me what to do.

MR. GRAY: That's what gets me furious. A day doesn't go by that she's not upset about something the boys have done. And then she comes around and complains that I shouldn't hit them.

MINISTER: No one ever taught you how to catch a "sidewinder"?

MR. GRAY: I think we spoil them too much. I didn't like it when my father hit me. I'd think of running away. But I shaped up.

MRS. GRAY: Well, I just can't hit them.

MINISTER: Mr. Gray, you seem to have a pretty well-worked-out idea for how to raise your children. I mean the hitting isn't the issue. You have some convictions that you think are workable. Why do you need your wife's permission to raise your children the way you think they should be raised?

MR. GRAY: I don't like to upset her.

MINISTER: Well, which is worse? Her being upset because she doesn't like the way you keep the kids in line or her being upset because the kids are out of line? Billy, I don't think you've got a problem. I think it's your parents who've got the problem. And I'd like to see them again without you. Would that be O.K.?

BILLY: Sure.

When the parents were seen without Billy to focus on, father turned out to be an extraordinary overfunctioner who insisted on an immaculate home. Busy all day with a responsible job, he vacuumed every room every night, and woe to Billy and his brother if they did not keep things in order. The minister managed to bring out the absurdity, got the parents to be more outrageous than outraged, and father eventually loosened up. Within a week of father being able to get "down on the floor" with his kids, instead of watching over them in an effort to keep it clean, Billy ceased his "delinquent" behavior, and the parents began to work at their marriage.

Murray: In the second example, the child, Murray, is an openly belligerent teenager. Mother once again is the protagonist, but this time father fades into the walls, letting his wife take over totally. The reactivity in the family is so automatic that no one hears anyone else. As in all argumentative families, they can't see the process for the content. They consult their parish priest.

MOTHER: Father, we want you to talk some sense into him.
PRIEST: What's the problem?

MOTHER: He stays out at night. He's failing all his courses. He sneaks the car, he steals . . .

MURRAY: I did not steal that money, I told you . . .

MOTHER: We both know you did. His stealing isn't the worst of it. He lies, and . . .

MURRAY: You never believe me anyway.

MOTHER: How do you expect us to believe you when you lie all the time?

MURRAY: You ask Jack's mother. She was there. She'll tell you.

MOTHER: I don't have to ask someone else. Besides, this isn't the first time I caught you.

PRIEST: How long has this been going on?

MOTHER: What would you say, honey? Three or four years now?

FATHER: Yes.

MOTHER: And it keeps getting worse.

MURRAY: My marks are the same now as they have always been.

MOTHER: You brought home two "Ds."

MURRAY: It was one. The other didn't count because . . .

MOTHER: That's what you think. The counselor told me . . .

MURRAY: He doesn't know. Go ask Mr. Wilson.

MOTHER: I asked him too, and he said . . .

PRIEST: (*interrupting to modulate the emotional tone*) Murray, just what's your view of what's going on?

MURRAY: They just don't leave me alone. "Do this." "Do that." "You should be doing more of . . ."

PRIEST: If you would just do everything they want, they wouldn't have to be on you all the time.

MURRAY: That sounds good. But even when I do something right, they're always looking for what I did wrong.

MOTHER: That's just not true. When you came in first in the model competition, we . . .

PRIEST: Mrs. White, you said this has been going on three or four years now. He just suddenly turned bad, like an apple?

MOTHER: He was always good. Then after his sister left . . .

PRIEST: I didn't know you had a daughter.

MOTHER: We don't hear from her much.

FATHER: Actually, we didn't hear from her for about ten years, until last December. We have three children.

PRIEST: Another son?

FATHER: Yes. Wait till you hear about him! One of those artists. Work is beneath him.

PRIEST: What I don't understand is that there's no drinking in this family, no wife beating, no drugs. You live comfortably, come to

111

church regularly. How would you explain why a family like this has had so much difficulty?

MOTHER: (*emphatically*) I don't know! Some parents don't seem to care half as much as we do, and yet their kids are all doing fine. We've tried so hard and where did it get us?

FATHER: The kids are not that bad. My wife is always concerned about a whole bunch of things that don't mean diddly.

MOTHER: That's easy for you to say. You don't have to take care of them all day. You just come home for dinner and watch TV, or go out with your friends.

FATHER: She's always like that. Gets upset easily, but she simmers down.

PRIEST: Mrs. White, what's the effect on you, when you're upset and your husband does not take you seriously?

MOTHER: I could kill him.

PRIEST: How come you can't remain cool like your husband, Mrs. White?

MOTHER: He isn't cool, he just isn't there.

PRIEST: What would you say to that?

FATHER: Well, you wouldn't stay around either if you had to live with all that screaming.

PRIEST: What goes through your head when you come home at night and she and Murray are really at it?

FATHER: I just say, "Why can't we have any peace around here?" And then I either go into the bedroom and try to read, or I get a quick dinner and get the hell out.

The priest has successfully defocused the child at this point. Murray can be left out of future sessions. Change will come faster if he were not there to keep mother intense. What we have now is marriage counseling, though if a counselor ever called it that, this couple might quit on the spot. Some parents are quick to recognize that it is their own relationship they have to look at. Often, however, the counselor has to maintain the pretense that the child is the problem, and permit the couple to continue to focus on the child. But he can use the content of the discussion about the child's problems as a way to help the parents disengage from one another.

Quite often, a child will be resistant to being helped. From a family systems point of view this is not always the complication it seems. As it was shown in the previous chapter, it is possible to bring change to a marriage when only one partner is motivated; it is also possible to bring about change when the symptom surfaces in the child but only the parents are motivated to seek help. In fact, it often is more possible. The case of the Hermans is a good example.

112

Seen but Not Heard: The Hermans' daughter had dropped out of high school in her senior year and had withdrawn completely into her bedroom. She would sleep till 3:00 P.M. every day, never get dressed, and refuse to do the most basic household chores, including changing the litter for her cat. She had recently taken to copying a novel, longhand. The parents had put her in a psychiatric day care center and went regularly for therapy sessions with her, but little change came about.

An extremely serious couple, the Hermans had never thought to ask whether their own efforts were counterproductive rather than simply ineffective. They were coached to cease pulling their daughter out of her reclusiveness and instead to push her into it; to stop trying to treat her crazy behavior with reasonable attitudes but to "out crazy" her; to stop putting up with the stench from the cat box because she was too lazy to change it; to make her suffer the consequences of her own irresponsibility; and, instead of trying to push "sense" into her life, to encourage her to be more senseless.

They stopped asking their daughter to come out of her room. Mrs. Herman managed to avoid looking into the room periodically to see if she were still breathing. When she did come out to use the bathroom, Mrs. Herman was coached to tell her that she looked tired and ought to get more rest. She also took to bringing daughter's meals in so that she "wouldn't have to use up more energy." Mr. Herman got a cheap typewriter and gave it to their daughter so she could copy the novel "with less effort," and they put the cat litter box in her room so she could be "closer to her cat."

Within a week, the daughter started coming to the dining table; the Hermans were coached to push her back into her room. Within two weeks the daughter started calling friends. The parents stayed on course. Within a month, she went out and got a job, and the following month came, looking "ravishing," to her cousin's wedding. More was required, of course, to cement such changes. But the Hermans are a good illustration of the fact that the process of change can be initiated, even where the family problem involves an apparently severely impaired child, through a coaching approach that leaves that child out of the counseling altogether.

Similarly, coaching ministers, rabbis, and priests away from their charges can be far more effective than meeting with the whole brood as a way of reducing symptoms in a congregational family.

One of the added benefits provided by the systemic approach to problems in children is that it will work even after they have left home. Letters, after all, are a much cooler, far less reactive medium of exchange than phone contact. Familiar voices are experienced by some as physical touching. The person writing a letter has a chance to employ second thoughts and the receiver of the letter a chance for a second perception before any escalation of response. Parents can be coached to use letters to define self or to take a playful initiative, and sometimes it is more effective than person-to-person communication. Some parents may not think they can influence their children after they have left home, in which case it is only necessary to ask them when they stopped being affected by their own parents' calls.

2. COACHING ONE PARENT WITH EMPHASIS ON THE NUCLEAR FAMILY

As with marriage problems, often only one parent is motivated to seek change. Father, for example, may see mother's anxiety as so disproportionate that he will not support her wish to seek counseling or, as previously described, when he senses that the change mother has to make will affect his marriage (e.g., she will cease being as adaptive), he might quit the counseling abruptly or even try to stop her from continuing. In other situations, father is the key, and sessions with him alone, in order to teach him how to be a "nonanxious presence," can be the starting point for real change within the family network.

Here is an example where mother alone is motivated.

Breaking the Resistance Barrier: Harriet Fisher had raised her children mostly by herself. Her husband, a military pilot, was often away for several months. As in many military marriages (or those of hard-driving professional men), the balance was provided by husband's intense relationship with his "mistress," that is, his work system, and wife's counterbalancing "affair" with her children. In addition, Captain Fisher was as frugal as they come, insisting on detailed expense records of every penny his wife spent. As Harriet's children became teenagers, symptoms began to surface in the youngest son, who was failing in school, had only "flunky" friends, and never stopped eating. Mother occupied a position that could be called "central," the old term for a telephone operator. All messages seemed to go through her. She was totally ineffective, however, in trying to communicate to her children that they should be nicer to one another, or to her husband that he should spend more time with the children.

She was coached to begin by "defecting in place": to let the dishes pile up, the laundry go unwashed, and the living room be messy, and to focus on something she had always wanted to do, perhaps a "secret ambition." Most women cannot do this until they are thoroughly fed up. Luckily, Harriet had had it before the problems got worse. She had an untutored, beautiful singing voice, and decided to take lessons.

Almost immediately, her husband worried about the cost, and her kids found more ways to involve her in their lives.

Whereas in the past most of Mrs. Fisher's free-floating think-time went into her household responsibilities, now she was thinking scales. She also imagined herself in recital. Her "solo-ing" became "dis-con-cert-ing" to everyone. One day, for example, her youngest daughter came home from school and found, incredibly, mother's stockings still soaking in the bathroom sink. She immediately called father to see if anything was wrong.

Within a few weeks, ambushes came from every direction. Son got caught driving a car without a license. She managed to keep her anxiety down and not bail him out. She simply reported the event to her husband. He jumped into the breach, hired a lawyer, and soon the triangle with this child shifted. In the past, it had been Harriet and her son constantly fighting, with her husband remaining calm. Now it was the husband and son fighting, with Harriet maintaining her distance. It seemed, however, that her husband had infinite capacity to endure sloppiness, and she was still worried that her kids would soon fall apart. One idea kept her going, however. She had found a book at the military base about breaking the sound barrier. It described how pilots had always fallen short of the objective because the closer they came the more the plane vibrated, until Yeager said to himself, "Maybe once you get through, everything calms down," and sped up at the point where everyone else had slowed down.

One Saturday after a week filled with criticism from her family, Harriet "revved up." She usually reserved this day for the family. This time there was an all-day workshop being conducted by an artist she admired. With little more than a short explanation Mrs. Fisher left early in the morning and returned late at night. Her kids were furious: "How can you be so selfish?" "Where do you come off leaving without warning?" But she also noticed that her husband had cleaned the house. What sped her up enough to get totally through the barrier, however, was an appointment she still had to keep with her son's school counselor.

A very conventional and doctrinaire man, the counselor told mother that her son's problems had to do with the fact that she was separating herself out of the family at a critical moment in her son's sexual development. She should give up some of her career ambitions for a while. Harriet came out of the session depressed and confused. It was her husband's complete lack of responsibility that created the pressure at home. It was he who was stingy with economic resources. Why, she asked her minister, should she be penalized to compensate for his problems and failures? Sensitive to contemporary women's issues, the minister jokingly told her that the problem with the women's movement is that it got females thinking they were equals. She laughed, picked up the challenge, and began to turn things around overnight.

First, Mrs. Fisher sat her son down and took a strong, well-defined position. "I have decided that I am no longer going to take any crap from you. If you think I have not paid much attention to you recently, I can only say it's going to get worse. I'm fed up with your irresponsibility and I am not going to give you the convenient excuse of a psychological problem." (Mach .7.)

Next, she called her husband and said they had to talk about the money problem. She presented him with a request for more money than ever before. When he got upset, as she had expected, she managed not to get defensive. When he calmed down, she said, "This is only the beginning. As I figure it, given inflation and the needs of teenagers, the total you will need to come up with in the next six years is. . . ." At this point their daughter happened to come in. Instead of shielding her from her father's parsimony, Mrs. Fisher turned to her daughter and said, "Honey, Dad just decided that your teeth don't need straightening out." He retreated to the "rec" room, quiet and depressed, but the following week he agreed to start giving more. (Mach .8.)

Next, husband began to drink a little. Harriet, despite an alcoholic father, managed not to play Carrie Nation. Then her husband began ruminating about a transfer that would take him away from the family for another 6 months. That did it! Harriet told him flat out that all he had to do was have his orders cut, and she'd be out before him. (Mach .9.) She never heard another word about the transfer. As she continued to pursue her own artistic and commercial interests, husband began to find fewer extracurricular activities around the post. And the following spring, the youngest son began to talk about how one day he would like to go to the "Point." (Mach 1!)

The exact same type of coaching is also applicable to the separated woman who is "stuck" with all the responsibility for raising her children, whether or not her husband lives in the community, when she is in the position of trying to "squeeze" more money out of him for "her" children's clothes, teeth, or tuition. It rarely occurs to her that it is still possible to involve him through her defaulting, that even after separation his underfunctioning is as much an adaptation to her overfunctioning as her overadequacy is an adaptation to his distance. She will be far more effective if she will allow the children to confront him, rather than triangling herself as their advocate against him. She can be coached for example, to say: "I'm sorry, I would like you to stay in college, but your father and I had an agreement to split the tuition and I have paid the first two years." That does not put the child in the middle—provided these statements are made without efforts to create an alliance. On the contrary, the child who is protected from potential conflict with the other parent winds up more in the middle. Making children responsible for their own relationship with the other parent gets both the child and the overfunctioning parent out of the middle. And the detriangling process can make a symptom in that child— whether it is poor school work, antisocial behavior, or even psychotic fantasies—disappear overnight.

3. COACHING MOTHER ALONE
WITH EMPHASIS ON THE EXTENDED FAMILY

The following example of the role extended family contact can play in the elimination of child-focused symptoms also touches on one of the most eerie aspects of family process, the uncanny way in which the anxiety demons in one generation become transmitted to the next. This multigeneration transmission operates to some extent in all families, personal or congregational, but it is not always so blatant. What often disguises the transmission is the fact that, according to the principle of symmetry, it may switch from one extreme to the other, particularly where a child *vows* to be a different kind of parent. (Actually every time any family member "vows" to do it differently, we will have transmission.)

Staying in Touch: A middle-aged divorcée had a younger daughter who seemed to be bothered by any efforts on mother's part to improve communication. She never wrote or phoned, except when she needed something. She was also given to long periods of depression that frightened mother. When asked from where came this need to be in constant touch, mother answered that her own mother, living in a retirement community in Florida, had always urged her to remain friends with her children because she, the grandmother, saw so many women whose children no longer spoke with them. It was pointed out to mother that her family genogram showed a great deal of "always staying in touch"; her own sister spoke to all her children every week, and her brother, a builder, had built homes for his sons so they could remain near him. Mother was urged to explore her own mother's family history for the origins of the pattern.

She uncovered the following story. When her mother was a teenager, an older sister had been bitten by a dog. Father took her too late to a doctor who said she would die in a few days from rabies. Rather than let his wife feel guilty her whole life, it was arranged for the ill child to "run away from home" and "die in an accident." Great-grandmother was never told the truth, but grandmother, mother's mother, vowed she would always know what was going on with her children, and the anxiety about staying in touch was passed down to the next generation.

Supported by this knowledge, mother found it much easier not to pursue her own daughter, who finally did initiate contact several months later, whereupon the relationship shifted considerably, since mother was no longer the pursuer.

4. COACHING FATHER ALONE WITH EMPHASIS ON THE EXTENDED FAMILY

A Father's Self-Differentiation: Phil and Kitty Fogarty's two sons had done well, but their daughter was a total dropout from life. A study in contrariness, the criteria for all her life's choices seemed to be the opposite of what mother did or stood for. Mother was concerned about good grooming; daughter tended to go barefooted and had gotten a tattoo on her left shoulder. Mother was pleasing and considerate; daughter was sullen and self-centered. Mother was efficient and responsible; daughter was sloppy, made silly mistakes, and could never be counted on to keep her promises.

Father and two older brothers were in a business that had been started by their father. He basically was its mainstay, the partner with the creative ideas and the persistence to make the business expand. He was also extremely kind, very sensitive to his wife's feelings, and quick to help anyone in trouble.

They had sent their daughter to a psychologist when she was a teenager, but she had made little progress. They had also tried counseling on their own, but nothing seemed to work. Even when they first went for systems approach counseling, progress was slow. And then a regression took place. After Mother learned not to pursue her daughter, daughter went on drugs. Mother began to work on her relationship with her own mother. Daughter married her "pusher." All of mother's efforts to differentiate herself in the relationship with her daughter seemed to result only in daughter becoming more stubborn. Daughter had all the intelligence and "stick-to-it-iveness" of her father and brothers, but it had become totally perverted to a contrary service of the dark side of life.

One avenue that had not been tried was to work with father alone, to see if he could differentiate himself more in his own family of origin. There was no apparent relationship between father's position in his extended family and the lack of change in his nuclear family, but where there is a family business, the financial interdependencies often reinforce the emotional interdependencies. It is generally harder to disturb the homeostasis of business families.

Father was seen alone and coached to change the way he usually operated with his own mother and brothers. Traditionally, he had been the prime mover in his family, the one who kept things together. (In recent years his blood pressure had begun to rise significantly.) He was asked if he had ever thought of "striking out on his own," and responded that he would love to, but his own father had told him "keep the business in the family."

It was then suggested to Mr. Fogarty that he go to his aged, very dependent mother, and ask her advice about how to deal with her other two sons. He did and also told her about father's message to keep the business in the family. Mother was astounded; she never knew her husband had said anything like that, and added that he had once confided in her that this particular son "probably should not be held back by the family business" because he "had too much promise." Released, he offered to buy both his brothers out although he wasn't sure where he would get the money. They responded, predictably, by "guilting" him about his "selfishness," and reminding him that this was a "family" business. He answered only that he had been thinking about the family since he was born (maybe before), and now he would start thinking about his own. Both brothers came to realize that they really needed him, and neither seemed to have the motivation to replace him. Eventually an agreement was struck, giving Mr. Fogarty several years to pay them off.

Sometime during this period, daughter called mother for lunch, perhaps for the first time since she was in high school, and the two women began to go shopping together (she was still on heroin). Then, suddenly, the daughter's husband overdosed, and the young widow came back to live in the family apartment.

Several weeks later, after a crisis-filled night of attempted withdrawal, during which father stayed painfully awake, fearing her suicide but refusing to let her sustain the kind of habit that he said would turn her into a whore, father offered her a position in the business if she would work seriously to detox. Daughter agreed. She entered a methadone program, eventually licked her habit, went to her own counselor, and as the basic strength natural to her oldest position came out, entered the family business.

There is no way to show in simple cause-and-effect ways how father's differentiation from the triangles of his own family of origin unlocked this nuclear system, although family theory predicts that it should happen that way. In addition, the personal qualities of this father made a difference. Mr. Fogarty had an uncommon capacity for persistence, mixed with a rare ability to step back and look again.

119

But the finest character traits can always be countered by the triangular forces in a system. Father's blood pressure was doing him in despite his strength of character. In all events, when Mr. Fogarty went for his next annual check-up, his blood pressure had gone down. Once again the cause-and-effect chain may be impossible to verify here, but, as we shall see in the next chapter, there are many reasons to assume that this man's health and his family position were inextricably connected.

5

Body and Soul in Family Process

A widower with five children married a divorcée, and his teenage son came into conflict with his stepmother. Father was pained over the situation, but whenever he tried to temper his wife's demands for the son's punishment, she had a physical reaction. She suffered from lupus, an autoimmune disease in which the body's systems of defense attack the body in various ways. In her case, one effect was a reduction of her blood platelets, causing her to bruise. Finally, fed up with the tyranny of his wife's symptoms, he told her that he would not continue to support her strict punishments. The boy needed more flexible handling. She could let her white count go to zero if she wanted, but he was through responding to her anxiety. She began to show more bruises and told him that she had to go to the hospital. He told her to "go ahead" without offering to take her. She went to bed instead. Within a week her count had gone back up, higher than it had been in years, and the lupus stabilized after that.

Everything said thus far about the concepts of the identified patient, the homeostatic aspects of illness in a family, and the pernicious effects of triangles applies when the family symptom is physical. Physical health and mental health, their loss and their recuperation, are both influenced by the same family emotional forces. This view suggests an interrelatedness of body and soul that is far more essential than the concept of the psychosomatic, and has important consequences for traditional approaches to pastoral visitation. In fact, it revolutionizes them. Not only does it shift the pastoral aim from comfort to healing, in the most fundamental sense, but, also, viewing physical dysfunction as a family symptom means that *visiting the relatives often can be more salutary than visiting the sick*. This is the same healing

121

approach suggested in previous chapters that has emphasized family strength rather than weakness.

In no other area of a minister's ministry is the distinction between "family counseling" and "family therapy" so crucial. The thinking traditionally associated with "counseling" families to "deal or live with" the illness and its symptomatic member, may offer comfort, but it also allows the disease process to dominate the family's thinking and serve as the organizing principle of its existence. Consequently, it tends to make the diseased member "other." Indeed, it may be that such "alienation" is what disease is all about.

The theoretical premises of family therapy, however, view the entire family as one organism, and urge no such accommodation or surrender, and no such "excommunication." On the contrary, it sees opportunity in the crises crystallized by the manifestation of disease: an opportunity to modify those aspects of the family's emotional system that may have helped to initiate, or may be still helping to sustain, the pathology in the symptomatic member.

Far more is at stake here, however, than pastoral technique. This chapter is really about thinking. The capacity to conceptualize physical illness in a unified body/soul context underpins the broader conceptualization of this entire work, that human relationship systems, personal or congregational, function as organisms and that, therefore, it is natural for these various forms of "organ-ization" to interconnect. This chapter therefore also lays the basis for the organic model of leadership (between a "head" and its "body") to be explored in Chapter 9 that similarly conceptualizes the relationship between a congregation and its spiritual leader. Such an integrated perspective hints at an uncanny similarity between cellular functioning in the human organism and the functioning of humans in a family or work organism; the likeness may not be analogous, but rather homologous, a similarity that is connected through parallel, evolutionary pathways. Nor is this intended as a mechanistic concept of behavior. It is rather a homogeneous view of Creation. A biological bridge to the spirit does not materalize it; rather, a recognition of the link opens new paths for connecting up with it!

Not only can the clergy's unique entrée into families enable us at times to foster physical healing processes but, also, a use of a systems approach to physical healing can foster a reciprocal spiritual healing as well. When members of the clergy use their entrée into families to help modify the emotional processes that might be contributing to the physical illness of one of their members, the beneficial effects of coaching family members to achieve differentiation are never limited to physical healing processes alone. (This obviously is relevant to our own health as well; see Chapter 12.)

In many ways, therefore, this chapter, which is devoted to "material" symptoms, carries more theological import than those devoted to the "mind." This should not be surprising. For millenia, theology and medicine were quite intimate. Such a relationship should not be dismissed as medieval: All contemplations about the "image of God" lend themselves to one another. It is the contemporary concern with expertise that maintains the "cut-off" between these "queens of science."

A great error may have been made when healing "advanced" to the point where some "medicine men" decided to concentrate on the body and others to focus on the spirit. The resulting specialization served to limit the healing range of both. Today, family systems thinking supports a reversal of that specialization. Such a reversal is also going on within medicine itself. For example, staff members at biofeedback clinics, as well as those more traditionally devoted to relief of pain, are finding themselves inexorably drawn toward philosophical speculation about the human condition, as well as about the condition of the human body. The future of healing may well see a shift to a different, more potent kind of healer.

A NEW MEDICAL MODEL

An organic view of body and soul is not a mind-over-matter approach to medicine, an advertisement for holistic treatment, a deprecation of the vital importance of physicians and their skills, or a rationale for faith healing. On the contrary, it is new discoveries in medicine itself that have laid the groundwork for understanding the emotional and, therefore, the interrelational aspects of physical illness, and have thus diminished the notion that individuals are simply "victims" of disease.

These new findings have made it possible to reconstruct our traditional beliefs about the relationship between *psyche* (the Greek word for *mind* or *soul*) and *soma* (Greek for *body*). The relatively modern and often loosely used term *psychosomatic* conveys a false dichotomy. Rather than saying that a mental state can *cause* a physical problem, new theoretical models and research findings suggest an organic relationship between them. "Psychosomatic" is not a systems concept because it conveys a linear relationship between "A" (a thought or feeling") and "B" (a physical symptom). By applying the systems model of Chapter 1 to physical illness, both "A" and "B" are seen as constituent parts of a larger emotional process and, along with other elements in that process, only function as they do because of the presence of one another.

Figure 5–1 illustrates the linear model, where "A" is the promoting agent, and "B" through "F" represent the major physiological systems of the body: autonomic, endocrine, immunological, genetic, cortex, etc.

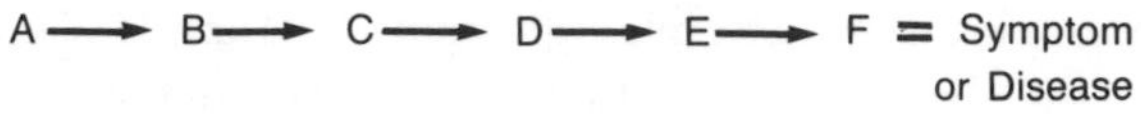

A ⟶ B ⟶ C ⟶ D ⟶ E ⟶ F = Symptom
or Disease

FIGURE 5-1. Linear model of disease.

Figure 5-2 illustrates a systems model of disease wherein all the physiological subsystems relate to one another and, together, operate as one larger system within an emotional field.

One way of formulating this organic context is to say that, for any physical symptom to become manifest, more than one condition, some physical and some mental, must be satisfied. In other words, a family member could have all the physical prerequisites for a disease, including the promoting agent (bacterium, virus, carcinogen), but the disease that those agents can "cause" might still not become manifest until some of the emotional conditions (prerequisites) in that family were also satisfied. Conversely, a person who already occupies certain family positions (to be described later), upon being subjected to certain triggering emotional, contextual, or physical factors would then be particularly at risk for "picking up" a disease, "catching it," or "getting" sick. All this does not mean that if only a person "thinks right," or "thinks positively," he or she can avoid getting sick. But it strongly suggests that the way we think about ourselves and our relationships may minimize the dangers of getting sick and, when illness strikes, may maximize the hope of recovery. It is because of this organic body/soul interconnection that the word "psychological" has been avoided throughout this book and the term *emotional* employed instead. The

FIGURE 5-2. Systems model of disease.

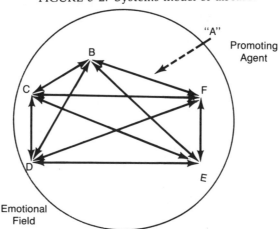

124

consistent use of the word "emotional" also supports the organic, that is, systemic connection among the chapters, namely, that anything said earlier about family process and "psychological" symptoms has equal validity for anything said here about family process and "physical" symptoms, and vice versa!

This chapter will be divided into three sections. The first will discuss some of the recent medical findings that point to new ways of understanding the relationship between body and soul, that is, between physical illness and our emotional being. The second section will combine these findings with basic formulations of family theory to show how emotional process in a family can create an identified physical patient, and how understanding of that process creates guidelines for survival and strategies for rehabilitation. The chapter will conclude with specific examples of how clergy can sometimes contribute to physical as well as spiritual healing processes in a family by shifting their efforts from comforting the sick to coaching their relatives.

NEW MEDICAL THINKING ON THE RELATIONSHIP OF BODY AND SOUL

Within medicine today, the effort to understand physical illness in an emotional matrix is producing radically new social approaches to the treatment of disease. Fifteen years ago a physician might have said, "I can see where heart problems may be influenced by psychological considerations, but cancer?" Yet today some cancer specialists have begun to ask how the thinking of the patient, his or her doctors, and his or her family might affect the course of the malignancy, and how family reunions might affect the recuperation. The factors that are contributing to this change in perspective are a broad range of new findings about the impact of emotions on the body's major physiological systems, as well as how those systems are interrelated.

Since an individual's thought patterns and feelings can often be seen as symptomatic of his or her position in the stress fields of the family, it is but a short step to the next conclusion that physical dysfunction can be viewed as a family symptom that sometimes can be healed by healing the family, or at least by helping the patient gain differentiation within his or her emotional field. Here are some examples of new evidence for the interconnection between emotions and the major physiological systems of the body, as well as evidence for the essential relatedness of body and soul. Each will be followed by some *metaphorical* analogues or practical ramifications for a family approach during ministerial visitation of the sick.

125

AUTONOMIC NERVOUS SYSTEM

The autonomic nervous system includes the brain and the neuron network. Today, biofeedback clinics hook patients up to various measuring devices, which enable them to monitor some of these physiological systems, in the effort to give individuals more control over what is controlling them. This method is used with more than 100 autonomic nervous system ailments, among them hypertension, asthma, migraine headaches, circulatory problems, colitis and other gastrointestinal diseases, dysfunctions in blood chemistry, lack of sphincter control, and some sleep disorders.

One analogue of biofeedback is the coaching technique used to achieve differentiation in families. Essential to the biofeedback technique is information. When individuals are given the opportunity to observe aspects of their physiological functioning, they often can, while still connected to their source of information, change that functioning. Similarly, when family members can learn about and, thus, learn to be more objective about what is happening in the family organism, the information feedback loop can enable them to bring about changes in it not, as has been shown, by trying to change others, but by changing their own responses to the emotional environment.

ENDOCRINE SYSTEM

Endocrines are hormones secreted by organs such as the pancreas, the thyroid, the pituitary, the adrenal gland, the ovaries, and the testes. Some of the better known endocrine secretions are insulin, estrogen, testosterone, cortisol, and epinephrine. The general function of these substances is to trigger and turn off various parts of our metabolic processes needed for normal or emergency functioning. Their flow is regulated through a complicated system of feedback loops so that homeostasis is maintained within certain thresholds.

Once a danger is past, the system of glands needed for flight or fight stops secreting so as to allow other substances to be released for repair or for resumption of ordinary functioning. But if an acute state becomes *chronic*, then the longer the fight/flight hormones preempt the replenishment and repair hormones, the more vicious the enervating cycle and the more difficult it becomes to rebalance the homeostasis.

Analogously, to return to the functioning within a family system, the major emotional force that will keep an endocrine level abnormal for an extended period of time, thus throwing it permanently out of balance, is chronic stress; and many of the most stressful situations likely to remain chronic are those found in the context of the family. Most individuals chronically stressed by their family positions really do not want to leave (flight). They are often more likely to work harder (fight) to change those aspects of their environment that elicit a stressful response. To the extent they are unsuccessful, the original stress is compounded. In addition, the capacity (or need) to adapt, essential to human survival, often makes family members unaware of how much stress they are experiencing. Therefore, their love (or need) for a family and their family's need for them can simultaneously disguise and increase their stress. That is the paradox of the "family endocrine system."

IMMUNOLOGICAL SYSTEM

Today it is known that the human body has a very sophisticated set of defenses equipped with early warning systems, embarkation centers, and "Pentagons," all capable of recognizing various foreign agents and dispatching exactly the right counteragent (antibody) against a specific enemy (antigen). A given illness can be the fallout of that ongoing war, the failure of its defense system, or its overreaction.

There is increasing evidence that the immunological system is also influenced by emotions, both directly and because it is interconnected with the endocrine system. Indeed, we have long heard the phrase, calculated to explain illness in a stressed individual, "His resistance was low." More significant, however, for a family approach (analogue) to physical illness is the possible intricate relationship between immunology and self. It is one that may have deep roots in the very structure and evolution of our species, and it puts together biological and existential survival. It has three dimensions.

First, it may only have been with the evolution of an immune system that the existential category of self even became possible. Otherwise, all protoplasm would have remained one fused, "undifferentiated" mass. The intricacy and integrity of higher organisms was only made possible by the development of an immune system. This could well mean that on a biological level it is only with some significant degree of self-differentiation that the immune system functions well.

Second, if the immune system is essential to warding off a foe, it may be equally crucial to the expression of love! With extremely undifferentiated forms of life that have yet to develop an immune system, when they touch (lose space between them), they disintegrate, literally lose their integrity. But this suggests that intimacy (touching and family closeness), and therefore *FAMILY*, are only possible because of the same immune system that protects against an enemy. It also suggests that the forces for preserving physical health in a family line up with the forces for preserving differentiation.

Third, under certain conditions, however, as in this chapter's opening example, an organism's immune system will lose the capacity to distinguish self from non-self and, in the face of challenge, attack its own being. This has been dubbed the autoimmune response. Such biological (or emotional) phenomena seem to resemble anxiety at a glandular level. This behavior is not to be confused with self-fulfilling prophecy, however, where fear of something in the environment promotes behavior that brings the very fear into realization. The autoimmune response is an inner phenomenon in which the response of the organism causes it to lose its own integrity.

One ramification for clergy visitation is that self-differentiation and the immunological system appear to be so much part of one another that, when it comes to recuperation, there is good chance that whatever works to stimulate self often works to stimulate the immunological system. And if that is so then, conversely, whatever works to suppress self, such as encouragement of dependency or shielding from challenge, could also work to suppress systems of defense.

GENETICS

In recent years the term "genetic programming" has become a popular way of describing the set of genes we inherit from our ancestors. It is becoming increasingly possible to know some of the configurations that "code" for different parts of the human organism. But a genetic program is not like a computer program. It is a far more dynamic state than miles of wires and specific leads that rest comfortably in place, doing only what they know how to do. Not all the genes we inherit necessarily express themselves during a lifetime. Some can be switched on and off by viruses set loose by a depressed immunological response. A person's gene "pool" is just that, a reservoir of potentialities, some of which only are activated or deactivated depending on other influences within the body's chemistry. As mentioned earlier, there is even some evidence that the same gene will produce different results depending on its relationship to another gene, and that genes can rearrange themselves on the same chromosome or reverse their roles in the body's chemistry. Genetic predisposition can make a person more susceptible to an illness, it can transmit form and malformation from one generation to another, but it does not always guarantee that an illness will become manifest. The Genius of Creation did not say "the sons must always be punished for the genes of their fathers."

Understanding of this dynamic quality of the gene pool is crucial to fostering responsible attitudes rather than victim attitudes for physical disease; it is as vital for survival in the context of physical illness as it is in the context of any other hostile challenge. The analogue to family systems thinking is that what counts is not thinking about our symptoms but thinking about our thinking, in particular, the extent to which such thinking falls into category 1 (victimization) or category 2 (responsibility). It is obviously not possible to will a gene on or off, any more than it is possible, at this point, to regulate by thought the body's level of high density lipids. And yet, the major thrust of all the above findings is that the physiological systems to which these basic substances belong are affected in their own interrelatedness by the total emotional state of an individual.

This is the notion that is important: Not that we can regulate specific glands or genes by concentrated thought but, rather, that on some level the organs of the body are susceptible to nonphysical influences while, at another level, they are subject to physical regulation. It is no metaphysical leap to say that care of our soul can affect the overall health of our body, even though all the processes of body and soul are yet to be (and may never be) understood. But all the ways of conceptualizing biological responsiveness may be extended to a family's response to a physical problem in one of its members. As we shall see, with physical as well as with emotional symptoms, a major impediment to the recuperation of any part of an organism is the anxiety (inflammation?) in the rest of the system.

THE IDENTIFIED PHYSICAL PATIENT

In this section, the previously discussed medical findings will be combined with basic family theory to show how family emotional process can create and perpetuate an identified *physical* patient, how such understanding of physical disease creates strategies for survival, and how these approaches can be tailored to clergy visitation.

EMOTIONAL STRESS AND PHYSIOLOGY

Recent studies on physical stress provide an important link to understanding body and soul in family process. While they tend to be framed in terms of the individual, they are basically systemic in conception and can easily be extended to the organism of the family.

1. *Physiological stress* is not the outside pressure of the impacting force upon a person but the body's own response to that pressure. This

distinction is vital for taking personal responsibility for soma and symptoms and, as we shall see later, in a systems view of clergy burnout.

2. *Stress* itself is a nonspecific response of the body. A person might somatize through lower back pain or a heart attack. The particular form of physical dysfunction, however, is not a direct linear cause-and-effect result of the outside pressure but, rather, the way that body's own set of systems has characteristically responded to its stress.

3. Individuals and perhaps families tend to express their stress in ways that are idiosyncratic. Some will tend to somatize in their respiratory system (asthma), some in their gastrointestinal tract (colitis, ulcers), some in the cardiovascular system (varicose veins, angina). But, since that part of the body has acted for the whole organism (has become the identified organ, so to speak), efforts to relieve stress in the total person have the potential to systematically affect whatever type of dysfunction has become manifest. Extended to the organism of the family, this means that efforts to reduce stress in that system have the potential to affect the identified patient's illness, no matter what the specific symptoms.

4. As previously mentioned, *it is chronic stress rather than acute stress that tends to promote the most serious symptoms.* This emphasis on chronic stress links the homeostasis of the family organism with the homeostasis of the individual cellular organism.

HOMEOSTASIS

The concept of family homeostasis takes on enriched meaning when it is realized that it is isomorphic, that is, family emotional systems mirror the same kind of balancing act that goes on within our bodies. Sometimes family functioning seems to mirror the most elementary metabolic processes. Whatever the true nature of the connection, family interactions are extraordinarily complex and deep, and whether expressed orally, emotionally, or physically, thought processes often seem to have been totally bypassed, not sublimated, not suppressed and relegated to the unconscious, but communicated directly from "heart to heart," even as different organs of the body that sometimes communicate through brain-mediated broadcasts often have their own private line.

This unified concept of homeostasis helps explain the creation and the perpetuation of an identified physical patient. As with behavioral symptoms, physical illness also can serve to stabilize a family and thus impede rehabilitation of the sick member. The following example illustrates how the response of a family to a member's illness, as well meaning as it was, can lock the ill member into illness every bit as much as similarly adaptive responses can trap a person within an emotional or behavioral problem.

Killing with Kindness: A football coach, known for his toughness and persistence, developed cancer. After surgery, his wife and grown children responded by making life as easy for him as they could. He appreciated their efforts but, as he became stronger, he found that they did not lessen their helpfulness. At first he thought they just didn't realize he was better; then he found he was fighting with them over issues relating to how he should sit, eat, take a bath, etc. He decided he had better fight harder for his independence, but reported that "trying to overcome the resistance of their 'niceness' to my regaining strength and autonomy seemed to take more energy than going up the middle on 4th and one."

This resistance phenomenon can be conceptualized through a diagram of the "vicious circle" (see Figure 5-3). At the top is an arrow (1) labeled chronic family anxiety. This leads to a physical or emotional symptom (2). The eruption of the symptom, however, creates a specific anxiety (3) in response to the symptom. Focus on the illness now deflects the original chronic anxiety (4). When the identified physical patient begins to recuperate (5), the specific anxiety that had been focused on the illness goes down, but the original chronic anxiety, if there is no change in the system, will begin to rise again (6).

The family at this point will often, inadvertently, function in ways to keep the focus on the recently developed illness. It is natural to want

FIGURE 5-3. The vicious circle.

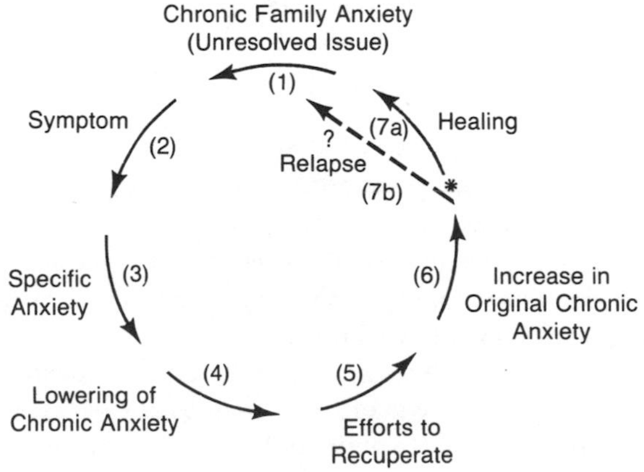

131

to avoid the alternative of the more painful, chronic anxiety, no less than the possibility that its return could create dysfunction elsewhere. Here now is the moment of truth, the critical turning point. If the patient is motivated enough, he or she will be able to push through the family's "resistance," in which case there is an opportunity for fundamental healing (7a), provided that the chronic anxiety is also treated, or the patient learns to function differently within the family. If the patient cannot push through, there is likely to be a relapse (7b) and a recycling of the whole process.

We are not talking here about willful efforts to do another in, but rather the frailties of being human, our great need for others, and the kinds of homeostatic relationship systems that naturally form around those qualities. Figure 5-2 only illustrates how a family system might rebalance itself around an illness. The logic of the concept also suggests that illness can be symptomatic of shifting balances within the family. The following case example of the Miller family points up some of the homeostatic aspects of physical symptom formation in a family.

'Round in Circles: The Millers' teenage daughter was described by her pediatrician as "a preulcerative personality." Her stomach was constantly out of whack. She drank Maalox as other kids gulped Coke. Then her father had a sudden heart attack from which it took him several months to recover. After he had gone back to work, and everyone had returned to their normal patterns, it was suddenly realized that the daughter had not needed any Maalox since that fateful event. Several months later, however, her stomach began to act up again. This time the parents, recognizing that there was a nonphysical component in their daughter's physical symptom, went to their minister for suggestions about a child counselor. He managed to defocus the child, and get the parents to work instead on unresolved issues in their own relationship, as well as problems each had with his or her aging parents. Shortly after this, the daughter's stomach returned to normal, and without recycling into a different family health problem.

THE MALIGNANT FAMILY POSITION

There have been many efforts in recent years to identify specific personality traits for particular illnesses. Most notable is the correlation of the Type A personality with heart problems. Many researchers have also suggested sets of attitudes common to cancer patients: inability to express anger, show feeling, or take charge (particularly after a loss). All such studies, however, are inadequate because they ignore other emotional variables. It is not that they are wrong; they simply do not have all the answers. A systems model, instead of diagnosing a cardiac or cancer "personality," looks for the cardiac or carcinogenic position in the family—positions, in fact, not so different.

Such a model is not incompatible with personality theories of disease. It complements them by saying that personal attributes may be related to *how* a given individual will dysfunction when he or she gets "sick," but, additionally, that whether or not that person is going to "break down" physically will have much to do with his or her position in the family and its confluence of stressful forces, as well as how he or she tends to function within that position.

It is in fact possible to list, in order of decreasing frequency, some of those positions and some of that functioning. Many, if not the vast majority of, physical problems tend to show up in a family member who occupies one of the following three positions (see below for case examples):

1. An intense, locked-in triangle, either within the nuclear family or the extended family or, most noxiously, a triangle between both.
2. A deeply dependent relationship with another family member that has been disturbed, often unwittingly, by the other member's efforts to differentiate his or her own self.
3. (Almost the opposite of 2.) Self-sabotage whereby the symptom or illness emerges almost immediately after the individual succeeds in taking more self-responsibility.

Example 1: A woman is caught in the conflict of her parents' marriage. (See Figure 5-4.) Her husband then goes to work for her father. As the triangled child while growing up, she was the most sensitive among her siblings to disturbances in her parents' relationship. In her own marriage, she was extremely adaptive to her stern husband because she felt she desperately needed him as a buffer against her parents. A huge crisis suddenly develops in her parents' marriage which results in her mother seeking more support than ever from this daughter. The marital crisis is related to father's desire,

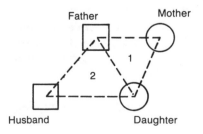

Father Mother

1

2

Husband Daughter

FIGURE 5-4. Triangling of a nuclear and extended family.

supported by this woman's husband, to merge with another partnership. Six months later, daughter finds that a lump she has had in her breast for years has become malignant.

Example 2: In this marriage, the husband was extremely passive about all family matters. He provided well but took almost no initiative in the home. He was also a complainer. His wife, given to hearing others' problems, always had time to listen, making sure also that he never felt alone. His company transferred them to another town, one effect of which was to take his wife away from her dependent mother. Within a year the wife had changed exceedingly. She returned to her own profession and, in ways not quantifiable, simply reduced the amount of thinking she did about the family. Within a year, he began to experience severe "angina" pains, although medical tests showed no pathology.

Example 3: A woman with endometriosis was so plagued with pain during her menstrual cycle that a hysterectomy was advised. A pleasant person of quiet dignity, she had been raised to be adaptive to her mother's needs. She had been working on a marital problem in which she was being encouraged not to give in to her husband's whims. The counselor suggested that her physical problems might be tied up with the denial of her true self. Spurred on by the hope that she could kill two birds with one stone, she "screwed her courage to the sticking point," and began to stand up to her man and say "no" more frequently. She was beginning to feel better than ever about the possibilities life had in store for her when her next menstrual period arrived and brought with it cramps so severe that she had to be hospitalized.

The frequency with which physical breakdowns occur in the context of these types of relational situations warrants a family approach to physical illness. At stake here is not only recuperation, but also the possibility of relapse.

A FAMILY SYSTEMS VIEW OF PHYSICAL HEALTH

Family systems theory also provides a relational perspective on which family member is most likely to get or stay well, and, indeed, on which family is most likely to remain healthy. It is a far more complex matter than merely avoiding the pitfalls of triangles. We cannot simply reverse the *personality model* for heart problems or cancer and say that those who do *not* fit the cardiac or carcinogenic personality models are more likely to survive. The reverse of the model also leaves too many exceptions.

Salutary family positions and ways of functioning that promote health are to be found at the opposite extremes of the continuum of self: dependency and differentiation. It is the differentiation end of this continuum that is to be emphasized because dependency only buys health at the cost of illness elsewhere. But the relationship between dependency and survival is worth notice because it explains many exceptions to the general thesis about to be developed, that there is a powerful relationship between good physical health and recuperative potential, on the one hand, and differentiation of self, on the other hand.

It has been emphasized that extremely dependent attitudes do not optimize recovery, and are conducive to making that family member more likely to become ill in the first place. In certain types of family homeostasis, however, it is precisely those dependent attitudes that can keep someone from becoming ill—provided that he or she can find some other family member to take over the symptoms for the relationship: "She was never sick a day in her life till her husband died." Dependency can take away symptoms. Indeed, over time it can kill.

Symbiosis: One very nice but extremely passive widower described how, while undertaking psychoanalysis four times a week, his allergies went away and a small benign growth under his arm disappeared. Three years after termination of analysis both symptoms returned. Several years after marriage they disappeared again. A year after his wife died of a stroke, they returned once more. (Luckily for his analyst, he never made this patient too important to him!) The virus, after all, even though it often has less resources for independent existence than the host it infects, can outlast its "partner," simply by drifting on to another symbiotic relationship after the latter's demise.

Physical survival in families is always a more complicated process than simply biological strength or weakness; in families, the naturally weaker often winds up as the survivor. But, having paid homage to this exception, there is a perspective that is salutary for the entire family. It takes into consideration the interconnectedness of body and soul; it deemphasizes specific symptoms; it does not get ensnared in a false dichotomy between physical and emotional (i.e., mental) illness; and it allows for the random permutations of environmental and genetic fate.

The less well-differentiated a family relationship system, the more probability exists that stress in any family member can produce dysfunction in any other family member. Which member is most likely to become the ill one may seem almost random, but it actually depends primarily on a number of variables beyond that person's control over

135

his or her own functioning, such as the impact of external forces: general health at that particular moment, the number of noxious physical (or emotional) pathenogens in the environment, etc. In less differentiated relationship systems also, the survival of the family member who becomes physically ill will depend primarily on the functioning of other family members.

On the other hand, the better differentiated the relationship system of a family, the less probable it is that one will somatize the stress for others, and the more likely it will be that the health of each family member will depend primarily on his or her own functioning, rather than on illness-causing variables in the environment. In addition, in the event of physical illness, recuperation will depend primarily on the ill person's own functioning, rather than on the functioning of others. Sometimes recovery will be *despite* the functioning of others.

This perspective formulates the following rule: To the extent that family members pursue a style of life aimed primarily at togetherness and interdependency, they set a course that actually risks the survival of their loved ones. Depending on other variables in the environment, they either luck-in and everyone enjoys the fruits of good feelings, or they eventually luck-out when the times and conditions are ripe for dysfunction. On the other hand, to the extent that family members pursue a course for differentiation, they maximize the possibility that every member will remain in good health despite other variables in the environment (whose pathogenic potential they may reduce), and they foster a family emotional atmosphere in which the health and survival of each member is more under his or her own control. This formula is equally applicable to situations in which failure to survive means biological death, existential death, or institutionalization.

The bottom line for clergy visitation, therefore, is that wherever members of the clergy can support or stimulate differentiation in a family emotional system, they stand on the side of systemically affecting the recuperative processes within that family, *no matter what the illness*, and no matter where the "patient" is located—home, hospital, or hospice. As with other problem areas of family life, sometimes that stimulation is best accomplished by working directly with the ill family member, but sometimes it is best facilitated by coaching his or her relatives.

A FAMILY SYSTEMS APPROACH TO VISITATION

Following are four cases subdivided into two pairs. This division reflects the two major ways in which members of the clergy learn about physical problems in the lives of their congregation members—thus the two different types of entrée available for promoting healing: (1) those where members of a parishioner's family seek help regarding a relational problem, but where a physical symptom or disease is also part of the package, and (2) those where the family seeks help directly for the physical problem itself. (See Table 5-1.)

In the first type of entrée clergy can potentially foster physical healing without ever focusing on the specific illness at all, that is, by trying to promote differentiation in the family around the *relational* issue that has been presented. Where successful, the physical problem may go quietly away. In such circumstances the clergyman or clergywoman will probably do better not to focus on the illness at all, although exactly where in the family the "dis-ease" is located can be important evidence for how that system is functioning and also provide specific clues to the creation of strategies for change.

In the second type of entrée, where the family is directly focused on a physical problem, by refocusing the family on their relationship system and using the physical dysfunction as a *context for relational change*, a curative process can be promoted.

Note that the "remedy" is never correlated with the *type* of physical symptom involved. The "right medicine" is dictated by the particular entrée that the family offers the healer, and not some prescribed formula for that particular physical affliction. It also seems appropriate at this point to remind the reader that case histories always seem to offer more promise than any approach to healing can truly deliver. But, as already stated, their primary purpose here is to loosen up conventional ways of thinking about physical and emotional problems.

Case 1: The Winslows had been married 14 years. They had two children, ages 10 and 5. Some time after the younger was born, they began to experience severe marital discord precipitated by Mrs. Wins-

TABLE 5-1. Two Types of Clergy Entrée and Case Examples

Nature of family request	Location in family	Entrée through
For relational problems (physical problems also present)		
Case 1. Diabetes, insulin shock (Winslow)	Child	Mother
Case 2. Infertility (Wallace)	Wife	The couple and their families of origin
For physical problems		
Case 3. Sundry aches and pains (Edwards)	Wife	Husband
Case 4. Cancer—mastectomy (Miller)	Wife	Herself

low's desire to obtain more emotional support from her husband. She also perceived him to be too involved with his parents, whom he called twice a week. While distant from her own family of origin, she thought there was probably some happy medium.

Mrs. Winslow had been in therapy on and off, trying to learn how to make her husband take more initiative or, failing that, to leave him. Whenever she made the effort to leave, however, he seemed to move just enough to make her think things were getting better, and she would lose her resolve.

She tried to make the best of it. But his passivity regarding sex, his parsimonious attitudes toward money, and his demands that she be present whenever possible (but not make trouble) all combined to make her realize that this could not go on indefinitely. In a last desperate effort she threatened to leave if he would not come in for counseling, and he agreed to go with her to their minister. But during the sessions he let her do all the work, and had no complaints himself, except the fact that she had complaints.

Several months went by in which each tried to accommodate a little, then he had to miss an appointment and did not return again. She continued alone saying, "Things are somewhat better, but the situation is still stuck." Then their little son became sick. A medical workup revealed that he had juvenile diabetes. He would need daily injections of insulin, regulated according to his sugar level for that day. Because he was only 5, the parents would have to give the injections. This too became an issue between them. Again the relationship became stuck around a seemingly simple issue.

During this period, on several occasions, the little boy went into insulin shock in the middle of the night. At this point, it was suggested to the couple that their son's diabetes, cause and course, could be related to the chronic stress and unresolved conflict in the family. Both parents agreed, but neither seemed to be able to do anything about it. Each kept pulling from his or her own direction, the wife trying to leave and the husband doing nothing to aid or abet any resolution.

In desperation, Mrs. Winslow finally agreed to the suggestion that she try to get closer to her own family. She was reluctant because her parents always had put her in the middle. Her mother had been alcoholic and her father was a roué, and each would complain to her about the other. In addition, being far better educated than her younger siblings, she thought she had little in common with them. The minister was able to get her to see, however, that the real issues in the family were emotional, and that differences in lifestyle did not mean that siblings could not be important to one another.

Mrs. Winslow then made a series of trips home during which she tried to detriangle more from her parents' marriage. Instead of quietly absorbing each parent's complaints, she began to tell each what the other had said. She made similar detriangling moves regarding her mother and an important aunt, and between her mother and a kid brother.

As she became an integral part of her extended family again, she found herself less triangled in her husband's passivity and argumentativeness. Several months later she told him in no uncertain terms that she was leaving. When he refused to cooperate regarding a separation, she continued on, unilaterally, and eventually left with both children.

Around the time Mrs. Winslow left, she realized that from the moment of her resolve not to get caught overtly or covertly in her husband's obstructiveness, her younger son had ceased having nocturnal insulin crises. In addition, the quantity he needed for his daily injections also had gone down, and remained low for years after the separation.

Case 2: The Wallaces came to see their minister for marriage counseling. But it was hard for them to pinpoint what had gone wrong. As Mrs. Wallace described it, she would get the feeling that her husband was not paying too much attention and she would withdraw. When he sensed her withdrawal, he would precipitate a fight to bring her closer, and the cycle would start again.

During the course of some questions about their respective family backgrounds, the minister noticed that all their siblings had children, but after 5 years of marriage they were still childless. The comment produced a flood of tears on Mrs. Wallace's part, and alternating defensive–aggressive responses by her husband. The Wallaces had indeed been trying to have children, but with no success. They had seen a fertility expert, were having sex only during the right time of the month, and were tracking her ovulation cycle with the usual temperature charts.

MINISTER: Have you ever related the infertility to the marriage?

MRS. W: You mean we might be angry with one another because we can't make a child together?

MINISTER: No, I mean the other way about.

MR. W: You mean it could be psychosomatic? How could that be?

MINISTER: Well, it's not that simple, Mr. Wallace. It's not a matter of thoughts as much as emotions.

MR. W: We don't feel enough for one another!

MINISTER: On the contrary. I was thinking that maybe you are too close.

MR. W: Too close?

MRS. W: I understand. Some animals don't breed well in captivity.

MINISTER: Maybe you both aren't taking this marriage seriously enough.

MR. W: Not serious enough!

MRS. W: I think we are too serious.

MINISTER: What's the best way to make her playful?

MR. W: She's never playful!

MRS. W: That's not true. I have a very good sense of humor.

MINISTER: How does his seriousness serious you up?

MRS. W: He won't let me have any fun.

MINISTER: What happens when you tickle him?

MRS. W: He won't let me.

MINISTER: Well, this may sound crazy, but I think you're trying too hard. I would like to work with you separately and let's see if we can't break the shackles of this mutual captivity.

Over the course of the next several months the minister coached Mr. and Mrs. Wallace to work on their own differentiation of self, thus defocusing the fertility issue. Each was also coached to be more playful in their respective families of origin on precisely those issues that seemed most toxic.

Mr. Wallace, a pharmacist, kept his mother at a polite distance. He could not stand all her complaints. She always had something wrong with her, and he always would respond to such controlling efforts with impatient recommendations regarding medicines or doctors. He was encouraged to visit his mother without his wife and to exaggerate his mother's complaints in a way that would challenge her to take more responsibility for her own soma and would avoid his being forced to play her hypochondriacal games. On the next visit all he had to say was, "Let's go to dinner," and off she went about her stomach, her back, and her feet. He could hardly believe all the prescriptions and medical articles that immediately came to his mind, as if on some prerecorded tape message. He managed to contain his usual automatic playback of anxiety, however, and responded, "Mother, I don't want to alarm you, but you are talking about some of the seven warning signs of cancer."

He reported that she did everything he wanted that weekend. He was even able to beat her to the punch, playfully overprotecting her in advance. "Mother, it's only a few blocks but maybe we should take a taxi," or "I know how your stomach gets," or "Mother, I notice your back seems to be arching more when you walk." At the end of the visit, she hugged him, told him what a nice time they had had together and, as he left, called out, "Maybe you should have become a doctor, after all!"

Mrs. Wallace described her mother as totally unable to relax; she dutifully, but painfully, took care of her own mother, Mrs. Wallace's grandmother, age 85. She was encouraged to involve the third generation in her "therapy," to establish an independent relationship with her grandmother, and then to work at the three-generational triangle in as outlandish a way as possible.

At first, Mrs. Wallace found herself putting it off with all kinds of excuses, but finally she went home and visited grandma, alone, for the first time in her life. She still was going to play it straight until grandma herself blurted out, "Ain't it time you started having kids?" Before she realized it, Mrs. Wallace was telling her grandmother about her conception problems. All grandma would say was, "You're a female ain't ya?" Emboldened by the intimacy, she talked with grandma about the female in between them and asked her why her mother was so serious. They wound up having a ball. When mother found out about the visit, she became suspicious, but Mrs. Wallace avoided all the questions by responding, "We just talked about grandma's premarital sex life."

Over the next few months Mrs. Wallace continued to kid her mother in front of grandma (as if they were in cahoots), talking about mother as a child, and particularly kidding her about anything related to boys, dating, and sex.

As Mr. and Mrs. Wallace worked at being less serious (responsible?) in their families of origin, their relationship with one another, predictably, loosened up. Then Mr. Wallace received a sudden transfer to another town and the counseling (as well as the temperature charts) were interrupted. A year and a half went by. Then an envelope came. When the minister opened it, there was no letter enclosed, only a picture of a wide-eyed infant, with the words "thank you" ballooning from its lips.

Case 3: James Edwards came in to see his minister to discuss leaving his wife. Their 15-year-old marriage had gone steadily downhill the past 5 years. There was constant bickering and no physical intimacy. He had tried to leave several times. One of the reasons he had not was because of her constant poor health. During the past decade, Mrs. Edwards had been to doctors at various times for treatment of hiatal hernia, chronic vaginal bleeding that led to several D & Cs, lower back pain, pins-and-needles sensations in her legs, severe headaches, numerous infections in her nose and kidneys, and periodic flare-ups of cysts in her breasts. In addition, she was always tired and almost never went out by herself. Basically an attractive and competent woman, over the course of the marriage she had become more and more isolated. She

141

never took responsibility for initiating social events, had no friends, and got into frequent screaming matches with her children.

For his part, Mr. Edwards was a severe overfunctioner. He ran several offices for a real estate firm, was President of his local PTA, and a vestry member of his church. At home he was the keeper of the thermostat, always reminding everyone of their responsibilities. Whenever he read about a more efficient way to do something, he made sure to tack it to the refrigerator so that his wife could benefit from it.

Mr. Edwards was encouraged to view his wife's symptoms as symptomatic of their relationship, in part due to the inability of a far less articulate person to say no, but, more fundamentally, as the dysfunction that can result in an adaptive partner if there is no space left between them. It was emphasized to Mr. Edwards that what most tends to eliminate space is overfunctioning. He grasped the concept immediately, but added that it was more complicated. Once, when he had broken his leg, his wife's health improved 100%, but as soon as he was able to function independently again, she seemed to become sick overnight. "I had so much work to catch up on at that point, I know I didn't overfunction in her space. It's almost as though she's in my space, as though my functioning affects her even though it's not directed at her."

It was suggested that he test the hypothesis. He did. He made the most of his capacity for work, at the same time making sure not to overfunction around the house. She got sick. He also thought the same thing occurred with regard to moods, that if he was feeling great, she would either become very depressed, or precipitate an argument to bring him back down. He tested that hypothesis also. One day they happened to be shooting the breeze on their back porch and Mr. Edwards said, "You know, I've really been happy lately. Everything seems to be going well." He went on talking about some of the exciting things happening for him. His wife did not respond. There was no participation in his joy, but neither were there any putdowns.

Two days later, however, Mr. Edwards suddenly found himself embroiled with her in an unending donnybrook over the dishwasher. Suddenly, remembering what he had said two days previously, he quickly pulled out of the argument. But the incident convinced him that efforts to differentiate himself in the marriage would hardly be easy and might be beyond his power.

He continued for several months trying to stay out of her space while declining her invitations to step into hers. During this time, her health improved considerably. Eventually, he invited her to come to counseling with him. Ordinarily, she had refused to see any of her physical symptoms, other than fatigue, as having an emotional component. The counselor tried to focus her on issues in her family of origin, particularly on an older sister who had died when she was very young. But she never seemed very motivated to carry through with the suggestions.

About this time, Mr. Edwards became close to several divorced women, all of whom showed interest in him. He did not have an affair, but it raised his sights about relationships. Thus, as he continued trying in the marriage, the absence of reciprocity finally convinced him to give up. He remarried shortly after the divorce. After their separation, Mrs. Edwards went back to teaching, dated a few men, but never remarried. Most of her health problems, however, seemed to disappear with her marriage.

Case 4: When Ruth Miller's minister visited her in the hospital after her mastectomy she was caught off guard. Mrs. Miller requested that she visit her again so that they could plan her funeral, "at a time when my husband and children won't be around. I don't want them to know about it." Mrs. Miller had been a good housewife and mother. Her children had done well in school and her husband was respected in the community. They appeared to have an almost perfect marriage. It was almost, as one friend said, "as if they shared the same heart and brain."

When her minister arrived again, Ruth Miller, with almost no show of emotion, began to list her favorite hymns and some poetry she had selected. When the minister tried to get into "deeper things," Mrs. Miller put her off. When she tried to reassure her, all Mrs. Miller would say is, "It is God's will. I know it." When she tried to refute her theological position, Mrs. Miller seemed to stiffen. Her minister left sad and furious.

After much soul searching the minister decided to call Mr. Miller to tell him what was going on. After all, he was her parishioner too. To collude in this death vigil would deprive the family of important opportunities for dealing with their feelings and perhaps even for affecting the course of her illness. The minister, therefore, called Mr. Miller and received her second surprise.

MR. M: I'm sorry Mrs. Smith, but things have been very difficult on me lately. I just don't want to get into it right now.

MINISTER: But she's planning to die!

MR. M: Mrs. Smith, Ruth and I never discuss our religious beliefs; we have always honored and respected that private area.

MINISTER: I don't think you understand. This has very little to do with her religious beliefs, as you call them. Something else is happening.

MR. M: Well, if you want to discuss it on the phone a few minutes . . .

FAMILIES WITHIN THE CONGREGATION

MINISTER: I think it would go far better in my office. Couldn't you find some time? It's your wife's survival we're talking about.

MR. M: I appreciate the call, Mrs. Smith, and I know you mean well, but I just can't do it now. Perhaps in a few weeks.

Denial in a family can be more malignant than cancer. One way to beat denial is to outdeny it, through praise.

MINISTER: Ruth, I got to thinking about your request to discuss your funeral, and I must tell you that I rarely see a woman so young face death this bravely. I'm sure your kids will always remember you for the way you handled this period of your life.

MRS. M: I don't know what else to . . . (very heavy sobbing).

A decade previously, over a period of 18 months, Mrs. Miller's mother, her grandmother, and her aunt all died of cancer. All three were widowed at the time, and had fallen one by one, like dominoes. Realizing that she might have a genetic proclivity toward cancer, Mrs. Miller had waited her turn. From the time of that "all-fall-down" experience, she had devoted herself to her family, giving as much as she could in the years that remained available.

MINISTER: Ruth, do you know what the immune system is?

MRS. M: I think it has to do with how the body fights disease.

MINISTER: Right. And I think there is some relationship between the immune system and self.

MRS. M: But my mother, aunt, and grandmother were very strong.

MINISTER: Or they got their strength from the fact that they were all part of one organism.

MRS. M: I get mine from my family.

MINISTER: Maybe they get more from you.

MRS. M: They do rely on me. What are you getting at?

MINISTER: Ruth, there has been some new thinking about cancer, that the way people think about themselves and visualize their illness and the way others important to them think about their illness can have some effect on its course. I'm not promising you any cures, but . . .

MRS. M: I never think about myself.

MINISTER: Would you be willing to spend a week doing nothing but . . .

MRS. M: I once saw a book on the importance of "me" and I tried to look at who I was but, when I did that, there was nothing there.

MINISTER: Would you be willing to come in, say, a couple of times a month and just talk about "you"? We could also discuss your family of origin and try to understand what made it collapse.

MRS. M: I'd like that. Do you think I should come in with my husband?

MINISTER: I think things would go much better if you came alone.

Over the next few weeks, Mrs. Miller revealed that 6 months before her cancer was discovered her husband had had an affair. This in turn had come about 6 months after she had accepted a job offer as an office assistant in a local law firm, where she had in no time become the hub of the office, often working late and on occasion accompanying one of her bosses to important evening meetings. After her husband revealed his affair, she quit her job immediately and again became totally devoted to her family.

The matter of emotional interdependency was discussed with Ruth Miller with careful delineation of the difference between togetherness and stuck-togetherness. She was encouraged to do a family history. It showed an extraordinary degree of fusion between parent and child, and between spouse and spouse. There were several situations where one partner died right after the other, and the all-female death grouping that had existed between her grandmother, mother, and aunt, also surfaced elsewhere in the extended system. In the course of doing the history, Ruth Miller made contact with several cousins and as her strength returned, she told her husband that she was going to go back to work even if it meant his having another affair (He had actually started the old one up again around the time of her surgery.) This time when she went back to work he became severely depressed. By now, however, she had made many friends, was extremely content with her new work situation, and was making more plans for visiting her long-lost family. Somehow she was able to stay on course. He eventually recovered from what ailed him, and several years later the prognosis for her own recovery remained good.

Finally, lest the reader have visions about becoming a miracle worker, a brief warning about the devilish quality of physical symptoms. Physical disease often seems to be a form of perversity itself. When such contrariness surfaces in the course of efforts to heal "mental" illness, the worst that usually occurs is no change. In the context of physical illness, it can lead to no survival. To illustrate:

Unspoken Feelings: While her husband was in town, a woman in a small farming community let a friend take the children for a joyride in his

145

new crop duster. Mother watched in horror as the little plane stalled and nose-dived, killing all on board at the edge of their fields. About a year later, the wife was found to have multiple myeloma, a virulent and fatal form of bone cancer. She deteriorated rapidly, her skeleton fracturing, tubes in most of her openings.

Around this time the couple was asked if they would be willing to be interviewed by someone making videotapes of terminal conditions. They agreed. During the interviews it was discovered that neither husband nor wife had ever spoken to the other about the incident. The wife had never expressed publicly or privately any feeling about the tragedy, and the townspeople, evidently in an effort to spare their feelings, had always turned the other way, thus, inadvertently, isolating them more. Several months into the interviewing process, it was found that the wife's cancer had gone into remission!

It is quite possible that if someone had come to this woman and said straightforwardly, "We think there could be an emotional component in your cancer, and we would like you to consider therapy to bring some of this to the surface," it would not have worked! The modern healer—cleric or clinician—is never more the ancient exorcist, fighting unseen demons, than when the family symptom is physical.

6

When the Parent Becomes the Child

Mrs. Jones came in to see her minister for advice on nursing homes for her father. The minister was surprised to hear of his deterioration. He had always seen the "old man" as quite vital. Instead of just giving his parishioner a name to contact, therefore, he asked questions about the family. Father had two sisters but both had recently died, and he had been depressed ever since. Mother, on the other hand, had come into contact again with some old (widowed) friends from her youth, and had become revitalized. With her renewed energy, she had taken to hovering over her husband and monitoring his every move.

The minister suggested that if Mrs. Jones could get her father connected up with other relatives, and modify the infantilizing behavior of her mother, he might not need a nursing home at all. She liked the idea and, over a several month period, through letters, calls, and one or two visits, proceeded to reconnect her father with his surviving brother and nephew, and with two old, but close, friends whom he had not seen in recent years. In addition, Mrs. Jones responded to her father's deterioration herself with challenging responses, and managed to get her mother more invested elsewhere. The nursing home issue disappeared.

Everything that has been said thus far about family emotional systems, the identified patient, and physical pathology is applicable to aging and the aged, perhaps more so. As the aging process makes the personal characteristics of a person stand out, so the concepts of family theory become even more clear when the problem is located in an aged member. Also true in such situations is the previously described problem of members of the clergy being deluged with information and

147

expertise from the counseling disciplines. While the information being disseminated about the aged is useful, its encyclopedic volume can be overwhelming.

More important for the effectiveness of the clergy, however, is the fact that almost all the thinking about aging and the aged is drawn from an "individual model." The way problems tend to be conceptualized and solutions offered in this area of concern often isolate aging and the aged from the emotional processes that members of the clergy consistently encounter in their parishioner families.

The main importance of geriatric literature is that it can inform the clergy of various services and programs available, so that they can be more effective resource persons when aged congregation members, or more likely, members of their families, come in seeking help. Unfortunately, as with many well-intended approaches that target a particular group, one of the byproducts is to make that category of people "other." In many cases, therefore, the aged become the "identified helpless" of a community, with all that this connotes for any relational system.

AGING: A FAMILY SYMPTOM

The effort to help the aged outside the context of their own families contributes to the very process in families that advances aging. Similarly, the emphasis on communities rather than on families succumbs to the myth that individual growth is maximized by making persons independent of their families rather than better differentiated within those emotional systems. The process of aging often can be dealt with in a more fundamental manner if the approach works through an aged person's own family rather than through the community taking responsibility for that family.

Naturally, some do not have family and here the community must take its place. Here again, though, one must be wary of the myth that the family has broken down rather than gone underground. There is often far more potential for family involvement than appears. The aged members of a community who most need its assistance often are in such need not because they are aged, but because of their position in, or out of, their family. What can appear to be the symptom of an aged individual (senility, confusion, helplessness), when set in the perspective of family theory, could be a symptom of the emotional system of that person's family: sibling rivalry between that senior citizen's children, for example, or the preoccupation of those children with problems elsewhere. And all this does not begin to touch on the nursing home "ice floe" phenomenon as a family symptom. There is something uncanny about the similarity of families that institutionalize members as a way of dealing with unresolved issues, whether the family member institutionalized is a child, a spouse, or a parent.

It can often seem easier to take up the slack rather than try to involve the family. But when family resistance, either from relatives or from the aged parishioner, can be bypassed and aged individuals helped to connect up with their families, such efforts can fundamentally affect geriatric problems. Moreover, because a family approach to geriatric problems deals with systemic processes, unlike efforts that rely primarily on community resources, it tends to benefit more of the family than the "identified" aged member alone.

Where families are willing to accept an identified aged member as an integral part of their relationship system, and see the aging member's behavior as symptomatic of the family and the aged member's position within it, then "growing old" ceases to be simply an inexorable fate of biological deterioration. In fact, the very concept "old age" can then be recognized as less a condition than a diagnosis, that is, an identifying process that fixes perceptions.

Making aged persons an integral part of the family, however, means something far deeper than simply giving them responsibilities or including them at the dinner table. Solutions in the field of geriatrics tend too often to emphasize what might be termed "external" changes in the family environment to the exclusion (denial?) of changes in the "internal" environment of the family *emotional* system. The efforts to give aged members confidence or dignity, for example, by simply including them are often emotional and very weak splints at best. As with children or any physically weakened family member, the essential ingredients for a recipe of self-confidence and survival develop from being forced to face the challenges of existence within a context of belonging.

BENEFITS FOR THE CLERGY

There is a special professional benefit that accrues to clergy who take a family approach to the problems of aging. It has to do with the congregational family. To the extent that we are content to emphasize caretaking approaches to the elderly, we miss an excellent opportunity to affect, on the most primary level, our own relationships within our congregation.

The capacity of congregational members to view us objectively is directly related to the degree of differentiation they were able to achieve from their real parents. Much of the negative and superpositive "transference" that we receive from members of our congregational family is a direct result of the "baggage" they failed to leave at home. This is one of the major interlocking triangles that affects us. Therefore, any time we can coach them to deal with their "true" parents in growth-producing rather than caretaking ways, one of the by-products will be a lessening of their neurotic involvement in us, if not in the congregation itelf.

Naturally, the other side of the coin also exists, the so-called countertransference. Wherever we become involved in a mature parenting of our own parents (see Chapter 12), that process will always have salutary effects on our faith, our resolve, and the way we function with the families in our congregations.

When seen from the family systems point of view, therefore, the field of geriatrics ceases to become simply one more burden of responsibility and area of expertise. It is, rather, an extraordinary example of how the three families of the clergy interconnect, and how awareness of that connection offers a marvelous opportunity to bring benefits both to ourselves and to those we serve.

AGING AND THE INTERGENERATIONAL CYCLE

This chapter will describe how the same counseling and coaching approaches illustrated in regard to other family issues can be applied with equally beneficial results when the family problem surfaces in the elderly. Of all those family problems previously discussed, the one that turns out to be most similar is that found in child-focused families. Individual approaches to geriatrics emphasize treating the "hoary-headed" with respect and dignity. But the aged who function in ways that deserve such treatment are rarely the problem. Most of the problems associated with an aged family member tend to surface when that person is behaving like a child, and they tend to be perpetuated by the families who treat their elderly members like children. There is, in fact, some correlation between the capacity of parents to adopt growth-producing stands toward their children, and their capacity to function in similar ways toward their own parents. This is particularly true with regard to pain and anxiety.

There is, thus, often an intergenerational, vicious cycle in families concerned with aged members. Parents who tended to infantilize their children as they raised them are likely to receive a similar approach in return from their children who now must parent them. As with all vicious cycles in family life, however, the same interconnections that have a "negative" momentum, once they are understood and modified, they can show a positive acceleration. One may not be able to teach "old dogs" new tricks, but they will adapt when they have to, even if it means finally growing up.

Sometimes it is only when some aged family members become totally dependent on others that they can be forced to grow. Many of the most obstreperous aged are spoiled and always were spoiled. Their childish behavior is not simply a regression. Often they were too important to their own parents for the latter to take stands, and often they contracted marriages that perpetuated their immaturity. When their children become their parents, because these offspring have their own lives and their own children, they are sometimes more willing to take the kind of stand their grandparents failed to take. When children (now parents themselves) are able to, the growth-promoting process works the same way as it would with their own children, and doing it with their parents will increase their ability to define themselves to their own children. If, as was shown previously, involving a third generation in marital and child-focused problems contributes to fundamental change in those areas, then it follows that when the family problem surfaces in an aged member, any effective work done with that relationship must automatically contribute to reinforcing the health of all other family relationships.

Once again, crisis can be opportunity for the whole family. Whenever the generation "in the middle" is able to respond in growth-producing ways toward its elders, there is almost always a similar effect on their biological children. Indeed, sometimes the two can be combined, so that the positive effects on the aged member come as a by-product of efforts directed toward a child, and vice versa. And there is another reason that a family approach toward the problems of aging automatically affects the entire family. It brings us directly into confrontation with the unresolved issues of our own youth. It brings us four-square up against those basic requirements for maturity that one is always striving for when the family problem surfaces other than in the aged. The clergy, for all the reasons advanced thus far, stand out among the helping professionals as uniquely positioned to connect up the aged with their families, and to help "kids" take a family approach when their parents become their children.

FAMILY RESISTANCE

One other aspect of family process needs highlighting in the context of the aged, before illustrating a systems approach to the elderly: *family resistance*. Homeostatic resistance seems to be particularly accute in this area of family relational problems. Efforts on the part of motivated family members to challenge the elderly are invariably met with anxious, overprotective responses from other members, and from professionals as well.

Several factors combine to give family resistance in this area its particular rigidity. One is the sabotage naturally found in any systemic relationship pattern. With geriatric issues, however, that force is strenghtened by the fact that the relationship system has had a long time to set; family triangles have become patterned along the way; and, over time, many more interlocking triangles have developed.

A second factor has to do with the professional healing establishment. All physicians, nurses, psychologists, social workers had parents themselves. As members of the human family, they all have a significant amount of "un-worked-out-ness" in these relationships; their advice and suggestions on those issues, therefore, tend to contain a significant amount of anxiety, projection, and displacement, more so than with regard to matters affecting marriage or children. In perhaps no other area of family life do the unresolved emotional issues of professionals get so much in their own way.

A third factor contributing to family resistance is the body–soul connection described in the previous chapter, and the concomitant problems of physical diagnosis. There is more tendency to accept unquestioningly a psychological or physical diagnosis of an elderly person. The reason for this is somewhat related to the two resistance factors mentioned above, but it also has its own reason for being. It is just more logical to accept the fact that when aged people are confused it has to do with their aging, that is, their "natural" deterioration.

There is probably no other area of family life in which members are explained away to the same extent. Terms like "senility," Alzheimer's disease and "chronic brain syndrome" have extraordinary power to determine a person's role in the family. They seem to have more influence to fix other members' perceptions or to foster adaptive responses than similar terms used in other family crises, such as "depressed," "frigid," or "workaholic."

A Case Example: A middle-aged son went to visit his mother in a large institution. Not being familiar with the surroundings, he became confused on several occasions. He could not remember where he parked his car; he got lost in the maze of hallways on the way to and from the lavatory, and for a moment he could not remember on his way back to the car whether he had left his raincoat in his mother's room or in the hotel. He suddenly realized that if his mother had expressed similar confusion, they would all have attributed it to her condition.

WHEN THE PARENT BECOMES THE CHILD

Nowhere is the use of diagnostic terminology more pernicious: in the way it helps families avoid looking at their own contributions to the emotional process surfacing in the aged member; in the way it divorces physical conditions from their emotional setting; in the way it can give license to a symptomatic, aged member's tyranny over the other members, especially when the aged person is a "Mommy" or "Daddy"; or, in the way diagnosis promotes a plethora of comfort and caretaking so that the seeds of challenge necessary for growth and evolution never have a chance to sprout. All this, of course, is very similar to family situations in which parents hear their child diagnosed as "hyperactive," "retarded," or "learning disabled," and they can assume (1) the way the child is functioning must be due to his or her other "condition," rather than to the overlay of immaturity, and (2) the problem, therefore, is beyond the influence of the family. There can be no question that with the elderly there are situations in which the problem is beyond the capability of the family, but this is not nearly as true as often as it appears to be.

A Case Example: A man who was simultaneously working on problems with his highly energetic 7-year-old and his 70-year-old, obstreperous, contrary mother, said that the light suddenly dawned for him when on the same day a baby sitter, unable to keep up with his child, told him that he should take the boy to a doctor because he was "hyperactive," and a physician who was treating his mother advised him to put her in a nursing home because her erratic behavior was due to "chronic brain syndrome." With some perceptiveness, he wondered how his advisors were doing with their children and mother respectively.

It is a fact that our bodies wear out as they grow old. Aging cells observed in a laboratory lose their capacity for repair and defense. But those same cells, when treated as part of a whole human being, which in turn is part of a larger organism (the family), sometimes do it quicker and sometimes take longer. Individuals age at different rates. The matter of aging is not longevity, but vitality.

We are thus back to the two-variable concept of physical dysfunction discussed earlier, namely, that two conditions, one physical and one emotional, must be satisfied to determine why a given disease has become manifest at that particular point in a person's life. With aged members of a family, the physical variable has more influence. But that simply means that from the point of view of continued health or rehabilitation, more energy must be expended on the emotional variable to counterbalance the physical.

And this brings us full circle to the problems of family resistance. Precisely because more effort is needed to modify the emotional processes that influence aging, it is often more difficult to find a "coachable" family leader capable of persistent dedication, desire, motivation, stick-to-it-iveness, or any term used to explain that unexplainable quality that enables some to persevere in the face of sabotage and the opinions of others. Whatever it is, by its very nature it is a quality that is suspicious of the omniscience of and surrender inherent in diagnosis. We shall see later that when this same set of qualities is found in the clergy leader, his or her congregation, irrespective of age, is less likely to become "senile."

Described below are three examples of a family approach to pastoral care of the aged. Taken together they highlight the following crucial aspects of aging in the context of a family emotional system. These should be borne in mind in a systems approach to the elderly.

- The onset of senile or dysfunctional aspects of an aged person can often be correlated with other changes in the homeostasis of the family.
- Physical aspects of aging almost always contain an emotional component.
- Understanding of the role of multigenerational forces is crucial.
- Emphasis upon challenge rather than caretaking can break pathological triangulation.
- There will be reciprocal effects on other parts of the family, marriage, or children when a systems approach to aging is taken.
- There will be dramatic upswings in level of maturation in the family members most motivated to be coached in this approach toward their elders.

The first case example is that of Mrs. O'Connor, an only child, who came to the United States when she was 25. Her father had died when she was 3, and she was raised by her mother in the company of mother's own sisters, none of whom bore children. In the old country, all stayed very close to their mother. After Mrs. O'Connor met her husband and had two children, she brought her mother to America.

While her mother had never learned English very well, she did manage a fairly independent existence. The only difficult time in the family had come when Mrs. O'Connor's daughter was growing up. At one point she became very rebellious and experimented with "mind-blowing" substances. But Mrs. O'Connor had managed to take charge with a gentle firmness and the family came through none the worse for wear.

WHEN THE PARENT BECOMES THE CHILD

About a year after this daughter left home, Mrs. O'Connor went back to teaching school. Six months later, her mother began to complain about her health, her environment, and her son-in-law, but mostly about her daughter, who "no longer loved her." She began to ask her to chauffeur her around town. She became forgetful about her clothes, her appointments, and what she was cooking on the stove.

At this point Mrs. O'Connor sought help. She and her minister had had a long-term, ambivalent association, on the one hand, furthered by her diligent involvement in many church committees, and on the other hand, marred by her constant criticism of his preaching and preparation.

MRS. O'CONNOR: It's getting very difficult. She [her mother] asks me every morning when I'll be back, and later wants a complete account of the day. She tells me she's sick. Sometimes as I'm about to go out, I find she's crying.

MINISTER: What gets going in your head when she does that?

MRS. O'CONNOR: Guilt. It makes me feel very bad.

MINISTER: Is she so isolated?

MRS. O'CONNOR: No! She has friends. We live on a bus line. She knows how to find her way anywhere.

MINISTER: All this came on suddenly?

MRS. O'CONNOR: Seemed to. She used to be so independent. If she's not crying she follows me around. She's driving me nuts! Do you think it's Alzheimer's? I don't want to put her in a nursing home. I hate those places. But I can't take care of her. I mean I could, but I'd have to give up everything I've been waiting for. I thought finally with the kids out of the house . . .

MINISTER: (paradoxically siding with the guilt demon) But you're all she's got. Maybe you just have to put off . . .

MRS. O'CONNOR: Oh no! That's one thing I won't do. You know, this is all very familiar. My daughter started acting out when mother went back to Ireland for a while and I felt freed up. Now it's reversed. My daughter has left home this time, and just as I get going, it's my mother who's acting up.

MINISTER: What worked back then?

MRS. O'CONNOR: But it's very hard to talk that way to your own mother. On the other hand, one day I got so fed up with her shadowing that I told her she was nothing but a cry baby, slammed the door, and went to work. I wanted to call and apologize, but I was so mad I didn't. When I came back she was gone. I got scared, but she had only gone to a movie. And she came back like nothing happened.

MINISTER: How did you finally get your daughter to grow up?

MRS. O'CONNOR: I decided it was her or me.
MINISTER: Too bad you can't talk to your grandmother now.
MRS. O'CONNOR: Mother was the baby you know.

The minister then shifted the focus to mother's family. The genogram showed the intense symbiosis between Mrs. O'Connor and her own mother, and between her grandmother and her own family of origin. Mrs. O'Connor began to see the extent to which responsibility for her mother was the fallout of a multigenerational pattern. More than that, she began to realize that her mother had had other choices. She could have remarried. She could have had other children. If the chickens or lack of them had now come home to roost, mother had to take a large measure of responsibility for those earlier decisions.

Feeling freer, Mrs. O'Connor went into action with the same firm but gentle determination that had worked with her daughter. She also realized that, as with her daughter, her mother needed Mrs. O'Connor far more than Mrs. O'Connor needed her, and that meant she had the leverage for change.

She began by defining herself straightforwardly. "Mother, I have been waiting my entire life for the opportunity I now have. Nothing is going to detour me. It seems that you want more of me than I am prepared to give. I realize you are getting older, and weaker, and your memory is not as good, and your grandchildren are not around, but I can't fix that. In fact, things are going to get worse. I intend to put even more time and thought into my job. So if you feel you can't make it 'outside' maybe we should start thinking about a senior citizen community."

She suddenly had a fantasy of mother breaking a hip. Remembering a warning her minister had given her about symptoms for togetherness in contrary-acting family members when the differentiating member defines his or her self, she added, "And another thing, I would like you to live here, but only on the condition that you take care of yourself. If you get sick, or fall down, you'll just have to go into a nursing home." As dramatic as Mrs. O'Connor's speech was, so was the shift in her mother's functioning. It was almost as though the "old lady" had said, "Well, you win some and you lose some." (She eventually did have to go into a health care facility, but 7 years later.)

Mrs. O'Connor did not rest there, however. She contacted her relatives across the ocean and fostered more communication between her cousins and her mother, warned her grandchildren that if they wanted a grandmother they'd have to pay more attention to her, and continued the same attitude toward her mother that had worked so well with her daughter—one marked by the ability to say a very determined "no" but with a smile that also said "I love you."

WHEN THE PARENT BECOMES THE CHILD

Around this time, a group out to get rid of the minister remembered Mrs. O'Connor's critical attitudes and came to her expecting she would support them. To their shock, she dismissed them as immature and said she was too busy with her own professional development.

The second case example is about Henry Marvin, a self-made man with a reputation for industry, energy, a capacity to see a job through, and harping criticism of his minister: "He's a good pastor but . . ." Though the minister had made efforts to establish rapport with Henry, nothing had worked. Neither a defense of his own willingness to work hard nor praise of Mr. Marvin's contributions to the community ever seemed to quiet this parishioner down completely.

One day Mr. Marvin, in his usual very brusque and business-like manner, came to his minister for some suggestions about his father. Now an octogenarian, the old widower, who had been living independently, seemed to have been going downhill rapidly the past couple of months. He was losing weight and had become convinced that he had cancer in the same place as the cancer that had killed his own father. He held on to this belief despite the reassurances of several doctors. Always plunging straight ahead, Mr. Marvin wanted techniques for dealing with the old man like those the minister "had once mentioned in a sermon on the aged."

The minister tried unsuccessfully to get him to look at the larger relationship system. What else had been happening recently in the family? Mr. Marvin was impatient with such irrelevancies. At this point the minister found himself thinking about another parishioner. (When that happens it is generally a good rule-of-thumb to accept that there is some unrealized connection. It can often be useful simply to report the fantasy, disguising it, of course, so that the actual people involved will not be recognizable.) "I once saw a similar situation. An old man suddenly went downhill when the son, who did most of his caretaking, became involved with the IRS over some tax evasion issues. He didn't want to tell his father because he didn't want to worry him. Funny thing was, the distance he was creating between himself and his father in order not to spill the beans was increasing the father's anxiety more." Mr. Marvin sat silent for a moment and then said impatiently, "What's that got to do with me?" The minister replied, "I don't know, but I've thought about that situation twice while you were talking." Mr. Marvin started to leave, then suddenly collapsed back into his chair like a rapidly deflating balloon.

MR. MARVIN: You're right on the mark. It's my son. He beat the crap out of an airline employee, cussed him out publicly. Not only that, it could lead to a civil suit. I haven't slept in weeks, can't get it off my mind!

MINISTER: Would you be willing to tell your father?

MR. MARVIN: I don't want to worry him.

MINISTER: Maybe he could help.

MR. MARVIN: He'd just tell me, "I told you so."

MINISTER: Well my experience has been—I can't guarantee anything, of course—that parents tend to misjudge their own parents on issues such as these. The most critical parents often become helpful when asked for advice, even if it is an issue they have been critical about in the past.

MR. MARVIN: But he's so old.

MINISTER: That also means he's been around a long time.

MR. MARVIN: He always was good at these situations. But I'm afraid he won't be able to take it. He's withering as it is.

MINISTER: Nothing keeps the old folks around longer than the thought they are needed.

Mr. Marvin thanked the minister and left, still undecided. When he saw his father again several days later, he had not really planned to tell him. But by now he had become so anxious that he was on tranquilizers and stomach relaxants. When he looked at his father, he inadvertantly called him "Dad" instead of "Pop." Almost automatically father said, "What, son?"

Mr. Marvin cried in front of his father for the first time in his entire life, and let out the whole story between deep sobs. Said grandpa: "I figured something was going on. I'll be damned if I understand why you protect that kid the way you do. I never did that with you or your brother. Your mother (may she rest in peace) and I would have our greatest arguments over just this kind of thing. You know women, when it comes to their kids, particularly your brother. Did I ever tell you about my kid brother . . ."

The elder Mr. Marvin then went on to reveal a secret about Henry Marvin's highly respected uncle who, when he was 19, had gotten into trouble for trying to fence some jewelry two of his friends had stolen, and how his father, much to the consternation of his mother, refused to step in and use his influence, and how the only help he had offered his son was the names of some lawyers. And then the elder Mr. Marvin concluded: "They can't sue you, son, for what that rascal grandson of mine does. If I were you, I'd call that airline employee and tell him anything he and the police plan to do is all right with you."

Henry Marvin later reported that he suddenly felt the whole world was no longer his responsibility. He had never listened to advice before, from his minister, his attorney, his accountant, or, once, a psychologist; now he found himself listening, awed, and with rapt attention.

WHEN THE PARENT BECOMES THE CHILD

With almost no hesitation at all, Henry Marvin went to his son and gave him the name of a lawyer. When son pleaded helpless, father said, "It's your life, son. I don't know what you should do with it. Me, from here on I'm gonna worry about mine." Son, after almost nosediving into the ground with a splat, pulled himself up just in time. And father stayed on course, buoyed by a new, richer, warmer relationship with his own father that almost approached camaraderie before the old man died several years later. Needless to say, grandpa's cancer fantasies disappeared.

Several months after Mr. Marvin's turnaround encounter with his father the minister resigned to take a new post. Mr. Marvin asked to chair the testimonial committee, and his successor never experienced any hostility from him whatsoever.

The third case example is that of Mrs. Sampson, a woman of 55, who came in to see her priest after her divorce. Capable, and with a successful business of her own, she was having difficulty functioning and alternated between depression over her marital loss and anxiety over her parents; her children also did not seem to be handling the divorce well.

Her parents, both in their early 80s, lived in a retirement community a thousand miles away. They did not get along too well, were constantly bickering, and father seemed to be becoming more and more dependent. A major worry of Mrs. Sampson's was what would she ever do with her father if her mother died first. Her parents had a fused relationship. Mother overfunctioned severely, answered all phone calls, did all the grocery shopping by herself, and took sole responsibility for making social engagements. Father just seemed to drag along, and had no friends of his own. He certainly never took the initiative to do anything by or for himself.

Her own relationship with her parents was devoid of conflict, but it was not really close. She never felt she could lean on them and always saw them as encouraging her to be as independent as possible. Her younger sister, on the other hand, was very close and called them every week. Mrs. Sampson could talk with her mother, but said she had absolutely no relationship with her father, and could remember only one or two times in her entire life when she had had any kind of conversation with him, both times about money.

Concerned, however, about her own functioning and the effects of that functioning on them, she bought the notion that she should try to rework that triangle. A major problem was how to start something up with her father. She could never get him on the phone alone. She had written him letters, but he never replied. She had tried maneuvering the phone conversations, but mother always seemed to sabotage that. Finally, an opportunity arose for a major detriangling move.

One day Mrs. Sampson told the priest that her mother had been secretly giving her money over the years but that mother did not want father to know about this. Mrs. Sampson had dutifully colluded in this secret, always thinking, "I won't spend it. I'll keep putting it away and someday I'll give it back to both of them as a surprise." It was suggested that the furture was now! Mrs. Sampson then took the money and sent it to father with a note explaining what mother had been doing all these years. Father replied and a relationship began to form.

Over the next year, whenever mother tried to triangle Mrs. Sampson with negative comments about her lazy, obstinate husband, Mrs. Sampson passed them on to him "innocently." In addition, on her next visit she made sure to get father alone for walks, and for the first time in his life he began to talk about his childhood, his own parents, and a cut-off that had existed for years between him and his brother, over money! She also, as a result of this change with father, became more involved with cousins on his side of the family, many of whom she had not seen since she was a child. Several of them had been recently divorced and she found much in common to talk about.

Her relationship with her mother also began to change. Whereas previously she had seen her mother as merely someone she had to put up with, she now began to realize that many of her own ideas and much of her own drive came directly from her. The two women began to discuss contemporary moral issues of the day, particularly those related to the status of women.

As her relationship with her parents changed, she became less anxious about her own aloneness and was able to change her relationship with her children. She ceased making calls purposively, and writing letters designed only for their welfare. She spent a week with each, alone, taking care to devote the time they spent together to what they most had in common or liked to do best. Both children responded well. There were some hidden triangles with their father, and Mrs. Sampson also found herself more able to recognize them and avoid them. As a result, within a year both children made major changes. Son switched the focus of his thesis and produced a major work of publishable quality. Daughter gave up her menial job and her flakey boyfriend, and she applied for a more difficult position with a major corporation.

In her last session with the priest, Mrs. Sampson said, "You know, one of the most unusual by-products of the past few years has been the change in my parents. They don't argue anymore. My mother runs a special volunteer organization on 'gray power' and that involves her in many events that she can't take father to. She goes about without worrying over his health or his dinner. And father, that's the most amazing thing of all! Instead of continuing to go downhill, at 80, he's almost gone the other way. He gets up before mother, which is absolutely unheard of, has his own circle of cronies, and stands up to her when he disagrees, instead of passively sabotaging her plans. Now I worry what I am going to do with mother if he dies!"

Eventually, of course, all aged family members do die, sometimes after a long period of dying. Those events are also part of the family aging process and often involve the clergy even more intimately within the family. They will be discussed in the next chapter on a family systems view of rites of passage.

7

A Family Approach to Life-Cycle Ceremonies

It was the congregation's tradition to have the father bless the bar mitzvah child, but here was the maternal grandfather trying to take the place of his dead son-in-law. The boy's father had died 5 years ago during his older brother's bar mitzvah. The older brother had gone through with his part all right, but he never came into the synagogue again. Now he was back, sitting between his mother, still in mourning, and his 16-year-old sister, once an innocent, pleasant child, but now caught up in an undisciplined life of drugs and sex. Then I spotted the dead father's own aged mother. She had been sitting next to him when he keeled over at the older son's bar mitzvah.

Soon I realized that all the grandparents were bawling. I'd better do something quick, I thought. But I held back. This was a family event, I kept saying to myself. Like so many rites of passage, it was a way of marking change. So I psychologically nailed my shoes to the floor and did not intervene. After a while grandfather regained his composure. Here and there a sniffle, but not much more. He spoke easily now, mentioned his deceased son-in-law, and then directed his grandson to focus on his own future.

When the service was over, you could sense that something had happened. There was rejoicing. It was somewhat subdued, but it was clean of emotional holdovers. I don't really believe in spooks, or devils. But I think I was present at an exorcism.

Life-cycle ceremonies capture the healing processes of therapeutic encounter better than any other form of religious experience. Weddings, funerals, and the rites associated with birth and puberty are ancient in form, yet have the most modern results. "Rites of passage,"

162

were the first human efforts to deal with modern psychotherapy's major areas of concern: change and separation. They were the first modes of therapy, and originally, as well as today, they are really family therapy. In fact, both their antiquity and their context suggest that the original form of all therapy was family therapy. We seem to have lost sight of this fact because the emphasis in modern healing is on personality and psychodynamics. And this loss has deprived the clergy of valuable opportunities for understanding how family emotional processes operate during these significant moments, as well as how to take advantage of such opportunities to help families heal themselves, and how to encourage family involvement so as to heighten the spirituality of the occasion.

No other aspect of our duties so unifies our major responsibilities. At no other time do we operate so equally as priest (i.e., celebrant) and pastor. At no other time can we so effectively fulfill the pastoral part of our ministry without having to adopt modes and metaphors from outside our calling. And, at no other time are the two major dimensions of our healing potential so apparent: the uniqueness of our entrée into family life, and the power inherent in our community position.

But more than healing is involved. A family approach to life-cycle events also enhances the holiness inherent in the tradition, because religious values are far more likely to be heard when family process is working toward the success of the passage, rather than against it. After all, it is hard to get the message of consecration across at a baptism, a christening, or a bris if there has been intense conflict over the name to be bestowed. Working through the family emotional issues behind such conflicts will enhance the spirituality of the occasion.

This chapter, which concludes Section II, will present a family systems perspective of life-cycle celebrations. It will show how the ceremonies surrounding such nodal occasions in an individual's life may be conceived as family events. It will demonstrate how a family perspective offers practical ways to modify the stress usually accompanying such moments. And it will illustrate how a family systems view of rites of passage leads naturally to creative directions for evolving our own religious traditions without sacrificing the time-hallowed heritage of our past. All of this also applies to transitions in the congregational family as well as in the clergy's own interlocking personal family. If this chapter is about transitions, therefore, it is also a transitional chapter itself. Rites of passage may well be what all three of the clergy's families have most in common and what provides a major connection for their emotional interlock. (This will become more clear in the next two sections.)

The concept is highlighted here, however, as preparation for the coming chapters on the congregational family and our own. It is useful to realize that all that will be said in this chapter about separating, bonding, and the power of emotional process to override religious values in individual families is equally true regarding the parish family and the parsonage.

A FAMILY VIEW OF LIFE-CYCLE EVENTS

The convention in the social sciences has been to see rites of passage as individual events. The family has a secondary role; the family is a support system that participates in the customs and ceremonies provided by its culture in order to help the celebrated individual(s) to a new position in society. But, as with the individual model of "visitation," once the family is seen as *background* rather than *context*, pastoral services are reduced to helping families cope with their anxiety and their relatives, and the therapeutic power inherent in family process, as well as its sabotaging influence, is overlooked.

A family model of rites of passage creates a different perspective. When family systems concepts are applied to such nodal events, it becomes clear that, far from being an intermediary, it is the family itself that is going through the passage, rather than only some "identified" celebrant(s), and the family may actually go through more change than the focused member(s). This is precisely why rites of passage have so much therapeutic potential. They function as "hinges of time." All family relationship systems unlock during these periods. More doors open or close naturally between various family members than can be swung at other times, even after years of agonizing endeavors. And, as we will see in the next section, the same holds true for congregational families when they are in transition between spiritual leaders.

The major reason for this emotional fluidity is systemic. Life-cycle events are not as random as they often appear. They are almost always manifestations of deeper family processes that have been coming to fruition, often for long periods of time. It also appears to be true that families that go for long periods of time without rites of passage tend to be stuck, and as that stuckness has prevented the emergence of such rites, it has been intensified by their very absence.

Before illustrating how clergy may best utilize this family approach to specific celebrations of the human life cycle, it will be helpful first to clarify some misunderstandings about family life and nodal events, in particular, the current assumption that the family is breaking down, the generally held view that cultural traditions determine emotional functioning, and the conventional notion that the rite and the passage are one and the same.

THE "BREAKDOWN" OF THE FAMILY

Life-cycle events have the power of some futuristic "transporter" that can atomize relatives in one time zone and materialize them in another. Rites of passage are able to transcend both physical gaps and emotional gulfs. Perhaps no other aspect of family life provides better evidence that physical distance cannot be equated with emotional potential. As one groom reported, "I hadn't seen my cousin in years. I never expected anyone to come down from up there. They had just had a blizzard, and I knew their small airport would be snowed in. Well, he drives over a hundred miles to another city, catches a plane that requires two changes, and is the first one at the church." (This inverse ratio between travel miles and degree of punctuality is not unusual at family celebrations.)

The forces that determine which family members decide to come often have to do with emotional phenomena occurring in the family rather than the distance. In the case of the adventurous cousin, his mother and the groom's mother (sisters) had just "made up" for the first time in years, but the aunt was recovering from an illness and had to stay close to home. She actually lived 1000 miles closer to the wedding than the son she had delegated to take her place.

A similar instance involved overnight communication between family members living on three separate continents. A woman, before her son's naming, called her family in Ireland to check on the origins of the family name. The next morning she received a return call from her father, with whom she had not been on speaking terms since his second marriage, 5 years previously. He lived in Jerusalem!

One major reason that it is important not to correlate inversely physical distance of relatives with their emotional potential during rites of passage is that visits from "distant" family members can upset the homeostasis of that part of the system in which a life-cycle ceremony is taking place. The important "breakdown" to be associated with family gatherings is not that of the family; it is of that part of the family's homeostasis that was held in balance by the physical distance. Conversely, unitary, nuclear groupings that do not attend extended family events are often unable to do so because they are held in place by the gravitational pull of the togetherness forces within their own system. In other words, don't take it too personally if they don't show.

CULTURAL CAMOUFLAGE

A second misconception that inhibits seeing the family as the primary force during rites of passage is the widespread assumption that the customs and values of a family are directly determined by the culture to which it belongs. This is not quite accurate. No family practices all the customs and ceremonies of its cultural heritage. Family members tend to be selective from their cultural repertoire, and all families hear loudest those values in their culture that tend to prevent change, in other words, that support the family's own homeostasis.

This distinction between family background and family style has special significance for the job of the clergy. If we allow individual members who behave in extreme ways at family functions to justify their behavior with the explanation that it's a religious tradition, then we allow such cultural explanations to camouflage what is happening in the family. It then becomes very difficult to distinguish commitment from anxiety.

For example, a woman raised as a Catholic was about to marry a divorced man. Her father threatened to disinherit her. But her father was also known for disagreeing strongly with the church's opposition to birth control. He was a widower who had never adequately dealt with the sudden loss of his wife 2 years previously, and the prospective loss of his daughter brought the unresolved emotional residue of the other loss to the surface. Father had two younger brothers. It was suggested that the bride contact her uncles and tell them what was going on. Within 2 weeks father had switched to the point of saying he was coming to the wedding and would like to contribute to the expenses.

This father's opposition was not an example of a false religious value. On the contrary, it was precisely because the father's position was based on an important value in his tradition that it masked the emotional processes which were really fueling the interrelational conflict.

Similarly, a Methodist mother who, upon finding out that liquor was to be served at her son's wedding, suddenly refused to come. Her son was perplexed because, although she was devout, she had raised her children to seek their own religious identity. The son was encouraged to talk to mother's sister. She revealed that his grandfather, who had been very close to the groom's mother, had been alcoholic. In addition, his grandmother had reacted in a similar fashion at his mother's wedding, but the issue then was the minister. Once again, it is not that mother's values were wrong. On the contrary, it is precisely their authenticity in that religious tradition that provided the camouflage.

A third example is the Jewish parent who had shown little history of strong ethnic identification and who had not been in a synagogue in 20 years, but who, upon finding his child was going to marry a non-Jew, became an ardent defender of the faith overnight, reminding her daughter daily of the martyrdom of Auschwitz. Here too the parent's stand is based on a treasured and history-hallowed value in that tradition. But here also, when you have that kind of emotional intensity, there is almost always a multigenerational, family demon to be exorcised.

The emotional processes of a family always have the power to override the thinking processes necessary to establish authentic commitment. When clergy are able to uncover the cultural camouflage, therefore, they are not merely serving a pastoral need. Ultimately, such detection is in the service of honest religious conviction.

Clues are available for such detection. One is the degree of inconsistency in the reacting relative, for example, disagreement with the church on certain values and customs and zealous championing of others; or no previous history of concern over a matter and then suddenly avid championing. Another clue is the degree of emotionality in the reacting relative. Whether the issue is who sits next to whom at a wedding, or after whom a baby is to be named, if there is no deeper family issue involved, then the disagreeing relative will simply make a suggestion or be less happy over the occasion. When, however, that family member refuses to attend, stops communication, threatens disinheritance, constantly harasses with phone calls and letters, or actually tries to interfere by calling the minister, we can almost always assume that there is an important emotional triangle involving a third member of the family, usually the reacting relative's spouse or parent, dead or alive.

Where clergy can untilize the opportunity presented by such family life-cycle crises to foster increased mutual respect for the personal integrity of one another, the *religious* functioning of everyone actually reaches a higher level. Differentiation is always on the side of salvation.

PASSAGE AND CEREMONY

The third misconception that inhibits a family process view of life-cycle ceremonies is the assumption that the passage is the same as the ceremony. From the perspective of an emotional system, rites of passage begin six months to a year before, and end a similar length of time after the ceremony. After all, some people were married (emotionally) long before the ceremony, and some never emotionally leave home after it; some were "buried" before they died, while deceased others remain around to haunt for years. Indeed, only when we can see these passages as the year or more surrounding the ceremony can we understand that it is the family that is doing most of the changing, and that more members of the family than those being celebrated are going through the passage.

This time perspective can serve the clergy well in both their counseling and their officiating responsibilities. For example, let us say a family happens to be seeking help on some problem regarding a child, a marriage, a physical illness, or an aged person. If during the course of that counseling the family begins to go through a passage, then because of the loosening up of family relationship systems during such periods, the time is especially propitious for facilitating change even if the event seems totally unconnected with the focused problem. This is healing at its best. It is another example of what makes clergy "naturals" for doing family therapy, and what gives them more of a healing position despite less "professional" training or psychological knowledge.

From another direction, the concept that the passage is not merely the ceremony enhances the opportunity for involving family members creatively. There is no more clear-cut example of how process affects content. Involving relatives increases the spiritual message because such a procedure fits naturally with what the ceremony was supposed to have been all along, a family event. The family emotional process thus "gets behind" the message. Any time that we can be less the professional who is attempting to carry the entire family through the passage, and more the "coach" to the family who is carrying its own members through, we mobilize deep forces that will work naturally for its success. While some clergy may fear this approach will make them less important to the family or the congregation, the experience of those who have tried this approach is quite the opposite.

We will now reconnoiter the life cycle, beginning with a discussion of those nodal ceremonies common to almost all religious traditions: funerals, life-threatening illness, weddings, and births. I will then comment about several other nodal events that are not a part of the natural life cycle, but which also have effects upon, and reflect emotional processes within, family life: divorce, retirement, and geographical relocation. In Sections III and IV, the observations here will be applied to the effect these passages have on the congregational family and on our own.

DEATH AND FUNERALS

Death is the single most important event in family life. From an individual point of view it marks the end; from a family point of view it is often a beginning that initiates processes in the family that can continue for generations. More cut-offs begin and more reconciliations are accomplished during this passage. More shifts in responsibility occur. It is more likely that some family members will find new free-dom, and some will suddenly find themselves stuck. From the ceremo-nial point of view, the funeral also has more influence. It can affect the celebration of life-cycle events that follow in its "wake." A funeral coming before a wedding, a bar mitzvah, or a baptism can affect the whole tone of the later celebration, as well as influence who attends. That is not as likely to be true in the other direction. A funeral, generally not by invitation, is not as likely to be influenced by some other life-cycle ceremony that preceded it. Indeed, a funeral can give a subsequent event new importance for the entire family because the newly celebrated individual becomes the replacement for the family member who has just died.

CRISIS AS OPPORTUNITY

But if death has the most influence on a family, it also offers the most opportunity, particularly where the death is *expected*. Most families would prefer that their relatives die in their sleep. The terminal state, however, offers opportunities for intimacy and the working out of unresolved family issues that may not be possible at any other time. And no one is in a better position to facilitate such a process than members of the clergy. It will be seen later that the same is true when terminating a relationship with congregational families; the "terminal" period also offers an unusual opportunity for promoting emotional health. In fact, everything about to be said here regarding terminal illness foreshadows a strategy for terminating any relationship, per-sonal or professional.

Most advice given to clergy concerning terminal illness centers around comfort, helping the dying person to "die with dignity," or helping the family to cope with impending loss. As with a similar philosophy of visitation to the sick, this is a defensive position, rife with lost opportunities, a way of thinking that is overly concerned with tranquility and as is true of all such well-meant efforts, one that ultimately will attenuate family strengths rather than mobilize them. Most importantly, this individual focus tends to isolate the identified, dying member.

From a family systems point of view, grief and its components and aftershocks, sadness and pain over loss, difficulty in functioning, and the urge for replacement, all are the residue of the un-worked-out part of a relationship. When families can be encouraged to come together openly with the dying member, pernicious emotional processes that otherwise might have survived undeterred for generations, sometimes by means of a "hit-and-run" disinheriting will, can be thrown off track. (This is particularly true where the impending death of a loved one was being kept secret.)

All of this is also applicable to situations where individuals are biologically alive, but existentially dead, and are being kept alive in artificial ways. The burden of decision at such times for family members can be overwhelming. Also similar is the case where a dying person requests to die in order to avoid being a burden. All dilemmas surrounding "pulling the plug" have an extraordinary capacity to dissolve almost immediately when relatives in a decision-making capacity can be brought together with one another. In addition, family members who request that their "plug be pulled" are less likely to continue in that request when their relatives can be coached to say directly to them, "Don't die for us." In the event that the dying member continues in his or her death wish after open discussion with loved ones, the loved ones are left with less guilt, and the entire system is left with less residue. But to gain these benefits, it is necessary to understand that the rite of the funeral has already begun and to recognize that the entire family is going through the passage.

Similar benefits accrue from family sessions concerning "living wills," and other related issues such as donating one's body to science, which, as noble as that may be, often create situations that haunt and interfere with a smooth passage. Family involvement in the original decision lessens the effect of these impediments to the passage because, despite their being "individual" decisions, they are often related to family emotional processes operating at the time of decision. For instance, decisions to donate one's entire body to science, and sometimes the desire for cremation, can be indicative of a person's position in his or her family of origin. It would be too pat to always label it as a form of cut-off, but thinking about such decisions in a multigenerational context often reveals a lot of information helpful in counseling the family at such moments.

Offering to conduct family sessions around such decisions once again puts our counseling and celebrant functions together. We can, while everyone is still healthy, do more for their eventual grief work and the future family health than we could ever possibly do once the death has set certain processes in motion. The long-range healing power here is similar to, of all things, a family approach to premarital counseling!

The key to applying a family systems model to the death rite of passage is realizing that it is a member of a family, a part of a larger, living organism, who has died or is dying. This can help us see that the very term "dying" is somewhat illogical in the context of a systems

170

perspective. (We would not say someone is "deceasing.") There is no such thing as dying except as *part* of nature's grand systemic cycle. A family perspective, because it is organic in space and multigenerational in time, helps keep that living, eternal focus on death clear.

Philosophical issues such as "the right to die" or "dying with dignity" are of course important. But the capacity of family members and clergy counselors to function objectively on the basis of such values will depend on their first clearing the emotional system of unresolved issues. Doing it in that order will also augur a healthier future for the survivors.

One other advantage of treating the death rite of passage as a family happening is worth noting. When events conspire to prevent a family from dealing with terminal problems because the dying member has slipped into a coma, the individual model counseling approaches that emphasize individual adjustment to the "stages of death" will fail. They require that the family member be *compos mentis*. If he or she is comatose, or denying, or just plain hopelessly confused, the individual approach leaves little room to work through these issues. On the other hand, the family concepts of identified patient, homeostasis, and nuclear and extended family triangles offer concrete approaches for working them through even when the "dying" person is not able to participate in the counseling. And it is not out of the realm of possibility that in the course of such endeavors the changes made elsewhere in the family can modify the emotional processes affecting the identified, dying member.

Related here is the significance of burial to a family. Were death primarily an individual event, we would not see nearly as much concern, conflict, or intrafamilial struggle over such issues as the nature of the funeral, the style of the coffin, the site of the burial, or the disposal of the remains (or the property). As long as an individual's body is above ground, he or she is still a part of the family emotional system, whether or not he or she is biologically alive. As with the continuum of time periods regarding marriage and divorce (illustrated in Chapter 2), undue efforts to lengthen or shorten terminal periods always indicate important, unresolved issues in the family. The family is either desirous of rushing through the passage or fearful of entering into it.

TWO EXAMPLES

Here are two examples of a family approach to grief work that illustrate these principles. The first took place 2 years after an auto accident; the second, during the last stages of cancer. In the first, the minister failed to make use of his own triangled position in the parishioner family; in the second, the minister used that very position to affect the future grief and the future health of the entire family.

Exhuming a Tragedy: A man was killed in an 80-mile-an-hour, head-on collision. The wife's father told the minister that his son-in-law's body was a shambles but he did not want his daughter to know. He conspired with the minister to convince his daughter that the coffin would remain closed "on religious principles." The minister tried to compensate in his eulogy. Everyone said it was magnificent. Two years later, a new minister in the church was told about this poor widow who was still grieving over her poor husband. When the minister learned "in confidence" how the death had been handled, she told the family that it was extremely important that the woman be made to realize the truth. The parents were reluctant, but thought maybe their daughter could "handle" it now. The new minister, therefore, offered to conduct a counseling session in which the tragedy would be exhumed from the unconsciousness of the family. Shortly afterwards, the woman went back to work and later met a man she eventually married. Before her wedding, the minister, reminiscing with the bride, confessed that she had always wondered how the woman had not seen the obvious, that it hardly would have been possible for her first husband to have survived that accident unmangled. "It occurred to me," she said, "but I never said anything because I thought my father might not have been able to take it."

The notion that people might not be able to "take" the truth probably has more to do with the anxiety of the individuals who are thinking that way. This is true at almost any time. During the death rite of passage, secrets allow the demons an opening into the next generation.

The second case example will illustrate many aspects of clergy healing power that are available during the death rite of passage due to their position and entrée. These aspects are:

- Long-term association with the family.
- Facilitating the passage by acting as "coach" to the entire family rather than serving as a "substitute" for the family with the dying member (an individual model approach).
- Treating the crisis as an opportunity to affect the entire relationship system.
- Dealing with the debilitating effects of grief *before* the loss.
- Making the triangles that form around the clergyman or clergywoman perform therapeutically.

- Affecting physiological processes by affecting the emotional system of the family.
- Optimizing the possibility of long-term comfort by not anxiously rushing to supply a short-term balm.
- Approaching the overall emotional system in a way that does not require the dying person to be consciously involved.

Note also, that as the session goes on, although the issues of dying or grief are hardly touched directly at all, this is not denial! It is once again process and content. One does not have to be an expert in the psychodynamics of grief to derail the grief-spawning processes. All one has to do is ask questions. The following case is thus a good example of the fact that clergy do not have to "do" family therapy to facilitate change. Simply becoming a nonanxious part of the system, and refusing to be homogenized into its one-dimensional fusion, will force change. The nonanxious presence will have a disintegrating–reintegrating effect. The pieces, however, come back together differently.

Dying with Dignity: Roberta Hamilton called her minister in a state of great anxiety. She wanted "spiritual comfort" for her mother, Nora Storey, who had been dying of a brain tumor for several months, and who had recently gone into convulsions. Roberta had been coming into town weekly to sit by her mother's side and read poetry. Her mother, while sometimes alert, kept her eyes closed almost constantly.

In the hour of their desperate need, Mr. Storey had been grasping at straws, having called a minister of a different, far more mystical faith, the swami of a local Hindu meeting, and a specialist in "death counseling." The latter saw Mrs. Storey alone for a half hour then returned to the family sitting in the next room and said, "This woman wants to die, and I would like to show you how to make it easy for her to go." They told him not to come back.

The minister remembered that Mrs. Storey had sought him out once for marriage counseling, and how she had complained bitterly that her husband always victimized her with his selfish acts, but that he also was passively controlling if she tried to take any initiative. She seemed unwilling to enter into any prolonged efforts to change the marriage, however.

In addition, he remembered that the Storeys had gone through successive periods of rebelliousness with each of their daughters. There had been turmoil around Roberta's wedding regarding what role Mrs. Storey's own sisters and mother would play in the procession. Roberta's middle sister, Helen, the minister now found out, was living as a lesbian, and her youngest sister, Jerry, had been divorced twice, with two children born out of wedlock. Roberta was the only one of her siblings to complete college. She had a daughter; she also had an unhappy marriage.

The minister also learned of a recent shift in the triangle between Roberta and her parents. For years she had been bitter toward her "interfering" mother but had a reasonably friendly relationship with her father. Since the cancer diagnosis, things had become totally reversed. Roberta and her mother had become fast friends, as in the days before she was a teenager, while she and her father could not sit in the same room for 2 minutes without contradicting one another. The minister suggested a family session that would include all three sisters and father, in the room with mother.

MINISTER: (*at bedside of Mrs. Storey*) Hello, Mrs. Storey. Haven't seen you in years.

MRS. STOREY: It's been a long time.

MINISTER: Your daughter came to me saying you needed spiritual comfort, but I believe the family can be a stronger source of comfort, and I thought if we got together maybe I could help bring that about.

MRS. STOREY: That would be nice.

MINISTER: Mrs. Storey, I'm going to begin with you. What would you like to see come out of this meeting?

MRS. STOREY: (*who talked very softly and rarely opened her eyes*) I would like the fighting to stop.

MINISTER: How long has it been going on?

MRS. STOREY: A long time.

MINISTER: (*to Mr. Storey*) Does your wife's concern surprise you? I mean that what she wants most is for the fighting to stop?

MR. STOREY: No. She's always tried to keep the family together.

MINISTER: Has there really been so much fighting?

MR. STOREY: I know Roberta doesn't agree, but I don't think so.

ROBERTA: Sure, you always ducked the issues and let Mom fight them out.

MR. STOREY: (*to minister*) My daughter and I never saw eye to eye.

ROBERTA: (*also to minister*) I hate it when he gets so passive, he never would take stands except . . .

JERRY [sister]: Well you don't help, you know. You're always trying to be bossy. If it weren't for you, things would be a lot calmer around here.

ROBERTA: (*to minister*) Here we go again, I'm always to blame.

MINISTER: (*to Mrs. Storey, apparently asleep*) Is this the kind of stuff you were talking about?

MRS. STOREY: Yes.

MINISTER: Where have your thoughts been going, Helen?

HELEN [sister]: It's the same as always, though in the past Mother would be more at Dad.

MINISTER: (to Mrs. Storey) You gonna let her get away with that?

MRS. STOREY: It's true.

MINISTER: Mrs. Storey, would it be correct to say that one of the things that most preys on your mind is what will happen to this family when you die?

(This may be the crucial question to ask "dying" individuals in front of their families, not only for the effect it has on their capacity to die in peace, but also for its subsequent effects on the rest of the family.)

MRS. STOREY: (opening her eyes wide and speaking very firmly) I worry about that a great deal. I'm afraid the family will fall apart.

MINISTER: (to Mr. Storey) What would you say to that?

MR. STOREY: I have no intention of letting that happen. You'll see how we'll get along. (to minister) We fight, but we really care for one another.

ROBERTA: Money. The only way you know how to love is through money. There is so much that is not coming to the surface about him and Mom. They used to argue constantly about us. Mom wanted to discipline us and Dad would always undercut her.

MINISTER: Mrs. Storey, what would you say to that?

MRS. STOREY: She's right.

MR. STOREY: My wife and I did not always see eye to eye.

ROBERTA: Eye to eye! You wanted to poke hers out. They were in business together but fought constantly about every decision.

MR. STOREY: It's not like it used to be.

ROBERTA: Sure, you took away her power.

MINISTER: What do you mean?

ROBERTA: He took away the checkbook. She kept the records, and then suddenly he took them away.

MINISTER: (to Mrs. Storey) Was that a big thing?

MRS. STOREY: Very much so.

MINISTER: In what way?

MRS. STOREY: I no longer had any say.

MINISTER: Why did you let him do that?

MRS. STOREY: What could I do about it?

MINISTER: Well, from what I remember about you, you once really let me have it about one of my sermons on Vietnam, you're no pushover. Why didn't you fight?

MRS. STOREY: I don't know.

MR. STOREY: My wife and I talked about it. She understood why we were doing it that way.

(*Silence.*)

MINISTER: Mrs. Storey, I was wondering, you have one daughter who is a lesbian, one who is twice divorced and with two illegitimate children, and one bitter about her non-career, yet you've given them every opportunity. Are you going to leave this world disappointed?

MRS. STOREY: No.

MINISTER: You're not just saying that?

MRS. STOREY: No, we did fight a lot about what to do with them, although he was really more upset about them than I. But I'd come to realize that I shouldn't impose my values. They're all healthy, and maybe that's what counts most. They're not the biggest disappointment in my life.

MINISTER: There's something else?

ROBERTA: Her sisters, that's what really let her down. They used to live here. After grandma died a few years ago, they all agreed to stay together. Then one lost her husband and suddenly moved away. So my mother made the other sister promise to stay close, but last year she moved away also. That was very upsetting to Mom.

MINISTER: Sounds like keeping the family together has always been important to you.

MRS. STOREY: I got that from my mother. She always said, "That's all you can count on."

MINISTER: Seems you can't even count on that.

MR. STOREY: That's when I took the books away. She was too depressed and couldn't keep things straight.

MRS. STOREY: (*nodding*) I'm tired.

MINISTER: (*switching focus to sisters*) Jerry, I'd like to go back to what you were saying about your "bossy" oldest sister. How long have you perceived her that way?

JERRY: All my life.

MINISTER: Don't you know about oldest sisters? They're always trying to improve everyone else. It may be genetic.

HELEN: I think it's in her tongue, not her genes.

MINISTER: They sure don't appreciate you, Roberta. All you've been doing is trying to straighten them out and they think you don't like them.

During the rest of the session the minister used the crisis as an opportunity to catalyze more self-definition between Roberta and each of her sisters, bringing in father every now and then when things got too intense. Mrs. Storey slept through it. The minister then asked if they would like to meet again in a couple of weeks. They all agreed and said that the family hadn't been together like that since they were children.

Over the next several weeks father was seen alone and coached not to be afraid to take more stands in the family. The idea that family anxiety goes higher without a firm leader was presented to him, and he was encouraged not to be afraid to take stands with any of his daughters. On still another occasion, Mrs. Storey's two sisters visited, thinking it was the end, and Roberta brought them in to see the minister. In a vivid session, they revealed attitudes toward *their* "bossy" (dying) sister identical to those expressed by Roberta's sisters.

Mrs. Storey lived for 6 more months. When she died, the minister conducted a prefuneral meeting in which Helen asked to give the eulogy. In consultation with her sisters, Roberta chose to include Mrs. Storey's favorite poems.

After Mrs. Storey died, all the daughters began to make constructive moves about the life styles in which they had been stuck for several years. None of the changes were precipitous or reactive, all apparently were made after sober reflection. As Helen said, "One day I just started thinking differently."

Mr. Storey also made constructive changes. He sold the family business, moved to Florida, and remarried several years later, but maintained solid relationships with all his daughters, who called him regularly. It was emphasized in Chapter 3, regarding premarital counseling, and it will be reemphasized in the next section regarding congregational–clergy bonding, that the capacity of any new relationship to take depends primarily on how previous bonds were "terminated."

CRITICAL ILLNESS

Closely associated with the funeral rite of passage is critical illness, particularly where major surgery is involved. This "celebration" also contains "rites," in the operation "theater." Always present are the most consistently practiced rituals, easily recognized costumes, dramatic expectation of performance, preparation anxiety, and though the identified celebrant does not hear it, music, classical or country western, depending on the head surgeon's style. There is often even a representative of the Holy One, present in the shape of a heart–lung machine.

Those who endure such experiences often go through a "passage" as essential in its change-making capacity as any of the others described in this chapter. They often gain new outlooks on life, and sometimes fundamentally alter their behavior. This is particularly true to the extent that the person had to overcome severe challenges to his or her existence. Such changes must affect their families, their marriages, their parenting, their attitudes toward their clergy, or, in the other direction, the clergy's attitude toward their congregations. These passages also can be viewed and treated as family events.

In this "passage," the ideas and approaches mentioned in Chapter 5 concerning the family concept of physical illness dovetail with the family concept of rites of passages being explored here. Where families can be counseled before major surgery or during critical periods in the recuperation, the other family members can become aware that they also are going through a passage. In some hospitals a natural opportunity is created if it is their practice to make a presentation to the family about what to expect immediately after surgery and later.

An example of how surgery can be made into a family event is the very self-sufficient woman who had been encouraged to lean on her entire family before undergoing a 50–50 survival chance procedure. She was coached to get in touch with her siblings, uncles, aunts, and cousins, and tell them how scared she was. Uncharacteristically, she discussed her disease openly with all. They, in turn, all responded with great concern. Later she said, "It was as though I had the two hands of each of my relatives carrying me through." In the following months, she was able to develop relationships with these "distant" relatives, with consequent, differentiating effects in her own nuclear family.

It may be that treating severe illness as a rite of passage is one way to galvanize the family forces (mentioned in Chapter 5) that maximize recuperation, and, thus, to minimize the possibility that the funeral rites will be needed. After all, if the person were to die, the passage of the funeral would have actually begun before the surgery. In other words, at the beginning, of both of these passages, critical illness and funeral, the path is the same. Which fork is eventually taken may have much to do with how the family functions early on in the trip. Once again the clergy, by encouraging such family involvement, can contribute to physical healing processes without having to "play doctor."

It should be added here, as a foreshadowing of Section III, that congregational crises can also be viewed as life-threatening illness. While congregational families are somehow more likely to survive such illness, the condition of their future health as a vital organism is often determined by how the "family" gets together to handle this passage. In both cases, however, personal and professional, the family's capacity to come together in a salutary way depends primarily on the functioning of the family leader. This will be explored more fully in Chapter 9, where I will also describe my own experience with what was literally a life-threatening congregational illness.

FAMILY APPROACH TO LIFE-CYCLE CEREMONIES

MARRIAGE AND WEDDINGS

Along with funerals and weekly services, weddings absorb most of the clergy's ceremonial work. Awareness of the emotional processes in operation during this rite of passage can help explain and resolve many family conflicts. Similarly, the same focus can enable members of the clergy to involve family members in the ceremony and its preparation in a manner that not only facilitates the passage, but also heightens its spiritual message.

As described in Chapter 3, marriage has a major impact on the homeostasis of a family emotional system, and is itself always indicative of changes occurring in that balance. A wedding is like an iceberg: only one-eighth of the moving mass will be visible, but the process and decision usually have the impetus and momentum of generations of build-up. That is also why, once engagement has reached a certain point, it is as unstoppable as a similar point in orgasmic inevitability.

What generally happens when family issues come to the fore during this passage is a movement toward one of two extremes. Strong hostility may be vented, resulting in an elopement by the couple or a refusal to come to the wedding by the relatives. Sometimes the latter do come, as spoilers, refusing to enjoy themselves, and sometimes the couple getting married decides to appease the relatives: "They are the ones paying for it. I'll give in now, but once I'm married I will begin to take stands." Unfortunately, the appeasement usually sets a pattern "forever after," or the couple later uses physical distance to achieve emotional distance. It should be added, however, that sometimes a couple elopes *for* their parents, so that the parents won't have to become involved with *their* parents or extended families. In that context, people can also "elope" to baptisms, bar mitzvahs, and funerals. On the other hand, as the first example in Chapter 1 illustrated, and as the family approach to premarital counseling indicated (see Chapter 3), where a couple is willing to take advantage of premarital crisis in order to work at issues in their respective family systems, the extremes of distance and denial can be avoided.

IN-LAW PROBLEMS

The one emotional issue that has the most potential for disturbing a wedding celebration is nonacceptance of a future child-in-law. It deserves special mention. In its worst form, it creates a cut-off. Because cut-offs from extended family are almost always malignant in their enduring consequences for an emerging nuclear family, preventing them is one of the most fundamental forms of premarital counseling, even though it is not focused on the relationship of the couple.

The difficulty some families have going through the wedding rite of passage reminds one of the American Indian ritual of "running the gauntlet." It seems that in some families, in order to become a "brave," one has to pass among the entire "tribe" and allow everyone to take a swing.

There are three emotional coordinates that can always be used to plot the course of in-law reactions on the chart of the family's emotional system, and for creating therapeutic countermeasures as well. The third is the most important and, in some ways, makes the first two redundant because the first two usually follow as a result of the third.

1. There is little definition of self between the reacting relative and the person getting married. The reacting relative thus experiences the upcoming marriage as his or her own.
2. There are important, un-worked-out issues in the reacting relative's own marriage. Individuals who are satisfied in their own marriage rarely react *intensely* to another's.
3. The reacting relative is always caught in some important emotional triangle, usually a position of responsibility in his or her own family of origin.

When in-law issues arise during the marriage rite of passage, reasonableness rarely works in resolving them. Generally, efforts to calm a relative down by saying, "Dad, you were always so liberal," or "Mom, you always taught me that love was the important thing," are doomed to failure. Sometimes the bride or groom makes a special effort, goes home for a visit to "talk it out," and comes back thinking the trip was a success, only to find a letter or phone call which shows that everyone is back at ground zero. The ineffectiveness of such reasonable efforts is due to the fact that the issues are not *the issue.* All in-law issues before and after marriage are displacements. (See Chapter 10 for a comparison of relational issues in a religious, hierarchically extended family to in-law problems.)

Positions, philosophical or personal, can change when the emotional processes of a family change. But the attitudes of a family member will never change through a direct confrontation on ideological or cultural issues. On the contrary, these approaches always intensify the deeper emotional issues.

The first step, therefore, is to help the couple defocus the content issue and to address instead the emotional processes that are producing the symptom of extreme reaction. Through a combination of family history taking and straight teaching about family process, it is often possible to depersonalize the problem. The bride's or groom's own reactivity to their parents' emotionality can be reduced by showing them that they are the focus of a process that usually goes beyond even their parents. (The problem with parents is that they had parents.) The second step is to make the couple aware of how all efforts to bring their parents around, especially by trying to discuss the content of their objections, keep the focus (displacement) on them. Suggestions can then be made for interfering with the multigenerational transmission process that has been funneling its way down.

Where it is the parents who have come in to stop the child from "destroying" himself or herself (or want to triangle the minister into doing their dirty work), the goals are the same, although the counseling has to be more subtle. In those instances the effort should be made to switch the parents' focus from trying to stop the marriage, usually an impossible, counterproductive task anyway, to getting better definition between the parents and their child (as described in Chapter 4). Parents who succeed in this effort usually find that their child responds by drawing closer. The "child" then either breaks up the relationship (sometimes even after marriage) or forces his or her partner to grow. In the process, if the parents' focus can be switched to their own marriage, or their own family of origin, the objection, or at least the intensity, often wanes. This will be true no matter how traditional the parents are, or the basis of their position.

Actually, one of the most important bits of evidence for saying that it is the relationship system rather than the focused issue that causes in-law reaction is the fact that grandparents rarely object to the marriage of their grandchildren, even when they are more "old worldly." (Where parents claim their parents are upset, it is usually projection.) Grandparents, even when generally conservative in their thinking, are often useful allies. Involving them affects the unresolved emotional issues with their own children—the parents—that have been seeping down a generation or two and creating the problem around the wedding.

The bride or groom can catalyze this process with the following type of letter, written preferably to the grandparents, but sometimes to another family leader such as a parent, uncle, or aunt. That is, it must go to a family leader or a peer, such as a parent, uncle, or aunt.

Dear Grandfather and Grandmother [or Aunt, or Uncle]:

As you may have heard [they probably haven't] I am going to marry a Jew [a Catholic, a black, a Martian]. I would like to invite you to the wedding even though I know this probably goes so much against your principles that you feel you can't attend. I did want you to know, however. Also, I wondered if you could give me some advice. Your daughter [or kid sister, *but not "my mother"*] is absolutely off the wall about this. She keeps telling me this will be the end of our relationship, calls me every night, says if you found out you would drop dead, etc. I wondered if you could give me any information that would explain why she is behaving this way, or any advice on how to deal with her?

Generally the letter writer does not receive a direct answer; but the next time the bride or groom has spoken to his or her own parents, there is often a marked change. This approach has been found to work equally well in Christian or Jewish families. It will work as well in the future when the first Alpha Centurians arrive and earthling children are warned not to marry creatures who grew up in a different solar "system." It will be relatives in the same family positions who will react, and the same kind of families will produce intergalactic unions. It is important to remember that if the passage precipitated the crisis, the fact that the family was going through a "hinge of time" also potentiated these same therapeutic interventions. Attempted at other times, when the family's set of relationships was more locked in, they would be far less likely to affect the homeostasis of its emotional system so fundamentally.

THE LIGHTER SIDE

There is, of course, also a lighter (more humorous) side to the wedding ceremony, for example, the perseverating concern with etiquette, the stupidity of some of the gifts, the jealousy of who gets seated with whom. Once again, though, when viewed in family process terms, these little things are sometimes more significant than we think. Sometimes the significance is blatant, like the mother who, during the wedding, whispers to the bride as she partakes of the ceremonial wine, "Not too much now, dear." Similarly, a humorous but often significant warning signal is when the parent makes the initial contact with the minister, either because son "works," or because daughter lives in Alaska and "it would be a long distance call."

Sometimes the awareness (unconscious?) of family process is uncanny. A man who was marrying a woman with a 5-year-old daughter turned to the little girl immediately after the pronouncement and also gave the child a ring. At some level, he knew what he was doing; in terms of family theory he really did marry *both* of them, not only his bride.

Appreciating the lighter side of weddings, can also be a powerful medicine in the repertoire of the clergy during this passage, especially when families are not light enough. As mentioned in Chapter 2, anxiousness and seriousness are blood brothers, if not Siamese twins, and a cleric's capacity to be playful or paradoxical at serious moments can be just the right antidote. For example, just before the ceremony, when met with a barrage of questions about "what do we do, when, if, while? etc.," no amount of reassuring responses to the content of the questions will usually help reduce the basic level of nervousness over the impending transition. Serious answers at such times tend to enervate everyone because they encourage a process of more serious, content questions. A more "comforting" process response can be: "Look, if anything goes wrong, we'll just start over, just as we did at the rehearsal," or "Don't worry, we'll just take it from the top." Such "looseness" on the part of the minister facilitates what a wedding is supposed to do, foster separation. Of course, if the clergyman or clergywoman is too anxious, such a response may come off as sarcastic. It will make everyone more uptight and defeat the wedding's purpose. In that case, he or she had better stick to the content of the questions.

Another way in which playfulness can facilitate the wedding passage is when the couple comes in for their first premarital interview. No matter how they appear, the couple is always nervous and, therefore, tends to be serious. The seriousness of many of the questions they will be asked, while well-meaning, often "jacks up" the anxiety in the room and inhibits the transition toward which they are bound. Playfulness at the beginning of the first interview can also set the stage for smoothing the entire passage and enabling the couple to respond more easily later to some of those serious questions. For example:

MINISTER: How long have you both known each other?

BRIDE/GROOM: Two months [two years].

MINISTER: What took you so long?

BRIDE/GROOM: Don't look at me! [or sometimes getting right to it:] I was waiting for him [her] to make up my mind.

MINISTER: (*usually to bride, but sometimes ludicrously to groom*) How did you finally trap him [her]?

BRIDE/GROOM: I used nets [or a secret potion, or if they are very uptight:] Look, we just came in here to get married!

MINISTER: (*to the other partner*) How did you get her [him] to trap you?

At the very least, the playful approach will establish camaraderie very quickly. At the worst, it will be a litmus test for determining the emotional acidity of the system. Sometimes it will bring hidden issues to the surface more quickly than the most seriously prepared questionnaire, and it allows the cleric an entrée as "coach" to the family (which has the real transitional power), rather than placing on the minister the whole burden for the success of the marriage.

PREPARATIONS AND PASSAGE

Even where there is no family crisis during the marriage rite of passage, the bride's and groom's families can be involved in a manner that will facilitate the passage, that is, the separation. This can be done by including them at the ceremony as well as in the preparations for it.

Little has been written about how the tiresome, practical details of wedding preparations actually afford an opportunity to abet and ease the impending separation between parents and their child, perhaps even more so than at the ceremony. Where these matters are not handled well, of course, this is usually symptomatic of the difficulty the family is having with the impending separation. (In Chapter 10 it will be shown that when clergy and their congregational partners are leaving each other for another, there, too, the way in which administrative details are handled can foster a cleaner "break.")

A very competent mother found herself appalled at her daughter's choices regarding gown, food, and invitations. Daughter was also expecting her to help in arranging these details. The notion of content and process was explained to this mother, as well as the concept that much disengagement could be accomplished during the engagement period. If, therefore, she could allow herself to become involved without taking over, feeling free to express her own taste while still allowing her daughter to make her own ("tasteless") decisions, that kind of nonanxious presence, while appearing to be only administrative, would facilitate the separation that the wedding ceremony is designed to mark.

From the other direction, when it is the bride who comes in distraught about mother's interference, and they are coming to loggerheads over many details, and daughter is making the whole thing into a fight for independence, the following paradoxical note from daughter has similar effects on the separation process:

> Mother, I have come to realize how important all these details are to you, so I have decided to send you a list of 100 different aspects of the wedding. I would appreciate it if you would look all these over carefully and give me your first and second choice on each:
>
> 1. Do you want the knives placed next to the spoons in the traditional way or would you prefer the revisionist fashion of placing the knife at a 45-degree angle to the fork?
> 100. Enclosed are 50 typefaces and a color chart for the invitations. Could you rank them in order of your preference?
>
> Take your time with this. I want you to be pleased.
>
> Your loving daughter,

FAMILY APPROACH TO LIFE-CYCLE CEREMONIES

BIRTH (BAPTISM, BRIS)

The third natural rite of passage celebrated by all religious traditions is the birth of a child. From an individual therapy point of view, it obviously marks the beginning. It is discussed after funerals and weddings because, in the life of a family, it comes in the middle of things; and it sometimes culminates more than it initiates. As with other nodal events, the significance of birth to a family, and the future position of the celebrated, has to do with what has been happening a year either side of the *event*, which is not the birth date, but the gestation period. The important period, therefore, is from a year before conception to a year after the birth. Sometimes, because of the replacement phenomenon, the emotional processes that culminate in a birth may have been percolating for generations.

Thus, while birth itself is a very short passage, in family terms it can be the longest and, as with other passages, this nodal event always indicates the system is in flux. Understanding birth in terms of family emotional process can help clergy in both their counseling and ceremonial functioning during this passage. (In the next section it will be shown that when a new church or synagogue partner is to be chosen, inquiring into the circumstances of its birth can be important information.)

EFFECT ON THE FAMILY

If the atmosphere before some weddings is reminiscent of the American Indian gauntlet rite, what happens in some families during pregnancy reminds one of the celestial portents in Shakespeare or in the Testaments that presage a significant advent.

Birth can have an immediate impact on the family. The sudden emotional investment in the newborn (or the fetus) can break up a previously stable marriage. It can give a mother more (false) security for facing life, her husband, or her own mother. It can result in a sibling of the newborn becoming ill, depressed, or dysfunctional. In one family, for example, a very adaptive wife became extremely self-possessed as soon as she felt the baby within her. Her autocratic, apparently independent husband developed almost overnight a fatty (benign) tumor.

Some similar disruption of homeostasis may be suspected where fathers are killed in auto accidents or run away during their wives' pregnancies. Also similar are those situations where a new mother leaves her husband, and goes back to live with her own mother, sometimes giving the grandchild to the grandmother to raise (in exchange for her own freedom?). This last example of multigenerational process hints that some similar triangle exists in cases of postpartum depression. Mothers who become severely depressed after the birth of a child may be suspected of being locked in a triangle with dependent husband and dependent (or unavailable) mother.

But these negative effects of the birth are not caused by the actual birth itself. It is rather that a new family member is joining a system whose stability was precarious to begin with. Generally, at the time of a birth, the more free-floating anxiety that exists, the more unresolved emotional attachment, the more distance between the parents, the more triangled an older sibling in the parents' relationship, then the more likely the "blessed event" will either upset the balance of things or bring about a new homeostasis. In the former case, tensions and symptom(s) will eventually surface; in the latter, the newborn may be the one who will eventually suffer years later when it tries to get out of homeostatic patterns it had unwittingly stabilized by its entrance. A family approach to the life cycle suggests that a postpartum depression of mother can be deferred for 20 years and then show up in the child when it tries to separate (become more a-*part*).

A MULTIGENERATIONAL VIEW OF CONCEPTION

Just as decisions to marry can be deeply embedded in the emotional processes of the family, so also can "decisions" to have children. An extraordinary number of "accidents" (conceptions) can be seen as far from serendipitous when viewed in the context of the parents' nuclear and extended families around the time of conception. For example, children who come long after a family has been completed tend to assume they were accidents. But they usually come as a replacement—perhaps to fill a hole in mother's empty nest. What percentage of the human race was planned in any generation? What matters is not whether or not a child was conceived with conscious planning, but whether or not the parents decided to have the pregnancy continue to term, and whether or not they decided to "adopt" this accident as their own and not to give it away. Even the Egyptians knew about abortion; that option, despite legal and theological objections, has always been available to our species.

Actually, an abortion can function as a family rite of passage in all the same ways as a birth, and with all the pejorative consequences that we saw in secrecy surrounding death. As previously mentioned, women's issues related to the reproductive cycle have uncanny connections

186

to multigenerational roots. If a woman who is having an abortion will discuss the event with her parents, particularly her mother, but also her grandmother, preferably before, but at least after this life-cycle change, then turning abortion into a family rite of passage will often give it the quality of an exorcism.

Conversely, the inability to conceive can also be set into a family context. Given two sisters from the same family where one is having difficulty conceiving and the other difficulty not conceiving, the odds that the former is in a responsible position in the extended family are extremely high. In either case, family approaches that rework those women's positions in their family of origin can change the destiny of their ovaries. An illustration of how deeply rooted in family history birth phenomena can be is the following case of the Hoffmans.

Dead Issues: As a pediatrician, Dr. Hoffman kept delaying the state of parenthood, saying that the marriage was not stable enough. Sessions that discussed every disagreement in their marriage from sex and money to working hours and the thermostat did not change his opinion. A history of his family revealed the following. He had had an older brother who died shortly after he was born, although he knew neither that child's name nor where he was buried. In addition, his younger brother had lost a child to the mysterious SIDS (sudden infant death syndrome). Neither event was ever discussed in the family, and Dr. Hoffman was extremely reluctant to trouble his parents by bringing up "dead issues."

Further history taking showed family trauma around the incident of birth for two more generations. Father's mother had been disgraced for a child born out-of-wedlock and then mysteriously given away. His mother's great-grandmother had died after the birth of her daughter, his grandmother. As Dr. Hoffman became more aware of this multigenerational shockwave he became better able to deal openly with his parents over the loss of their child and grandchild. As the anxiety in the family subsided, he found himself wanting to care for a child of his own.

NAMING CEREMONIES

All of these emotional processes surrounding birth can surface innocently in the choosing of a name. While members of the clergy may not wish to become involved in uncovering these connections every time they help a family celebrate a newborn, just the realization that multigenerational proceses are always in the background can be helpful in understanding the family conflicts that sometimes surface around the celebrating ceremonies of a christening or a bris. With this event especially, it goes without saying that the actual ceremony is hardly the rite of passage. When a child is adopted, these processes are often more evident, and the opportunties they present for bringing change to the family can also be greater because the mother does not have to be concerned with her own physical health while waiting to hear from the agency. During an emotional gestation period, she often can be freer to work at family triangles.

To the extent that clergy wish to involve family members in naming ceremonies (one minister does this by having the grandparents choose and read the Scripture passage), some knowledge of the family history, in particular who the child might be replacing one or more generations back, can put the religious and emotional aspects of the event into a mutually beneficial relationship.

In all events, parents should be discouraged from "eloping" to a naming ceremony. When parents do stand alone at the baptismal font, or before the Ark, their own parents, dead or alive, are always there also, sitting on their shoulders. Far more ancestors than angels can stand on the head of the proverbial pin at such moments.

MODERN PASSAGES

Funerals, weddings, and birth ceremonies have been rites of passages as long as the human species has had a tribal culture. Modern society seems to be producing three other nodal points of consequence for the life cycle: divorce, retirement, and geographical uprooting. While members of the clergy are less likely to become involved in them ceremonially, they do have significance for a family and they also can be symptomatic of flux in a family's emotional system. Thus, even though clergy do not have the same opportunity to help families in their congregations mark these significant time periods, awareness of the emotional processes that surround them can help develop a deeper understanding of what they are experiencing during such nodal periods. And, where these modern passages do occur during some natural (or ancient) rite of passage, it can be extremely useful to have this additional information about the family emotional processes characteristic of these modern happenings. It should be emphasized, however, that these three are not *biologically* connected to the life cycle. They may not, therefore, have the same automatic power for change as the others, unless they come about as residuals of the former events, for example, when divorce comes within a year after an important death, or the geographical relocation soon after the marriage. While they may hint that the time is ripe for change in the family, it is well to keep in mind that in and of themselves they are not natural family phenomena, with all the power for healing that implies.

DIVORCE

Among these nonbiological nodal points in life, divorce would seem to portend the most family change. Several religious groups have had or are experimenting with the creation of a divorce ceremony, but they tend to focus on the *individuals* being divorced. If rites of passage are family events, it may be that for many families only a second marriage or a funeral can really complete this passage.

A general principle can be drawn, however, as to when clergy participation in this passage can be useful. To the extent that a divorce comes about because the rite of passage of marriage did not do its work (i.e., bring about disengagement from families of origin), then the divorce is not likely to bring real change, because the triangles in the family of origin are still stuck. In these situations, well-meaning efforts by the clergy will be limited in their effects. On the other hand, to the extent that the divorce is a result of recent changes with respect to family of origin that, in turn, unbalanced the marriage, then the divorce is more likely to offer opportunity. Here the clergy's entrée is more likely to be helpful.

In either case, if parishioners, who come in during this period with fears of loneliness, instability, adjustment of their children, loss of moorings, etc. (the focus of most of the self-help books on divorce) can instead be focused on relationships with family of origin, and they often are more motivated to do so at this time, then clergy can make divorce a rite of passage in the fullest sense of the term. (They can also do so for themselves by involving their own families of origin when they are experiencing divorce from a congregation that has become emotionally important.)

RETIREMENT

Retirement may have more ramifications for family life than has been realized, although military chaplains don't have to be told this fact. The number of divorces that occur after early service retirement is quite high. A useful rule of thumb to keep in mind here is: Where a marriage has been balanced by mother being intensely involved in the children, and father with his work system (which becomes a sort of extended family), his retirement often unbalances his nuclear family, particularly if he now tries to reenter it and finds himself excluded, or seeks a replacement for the work system in the form of an extramarital relationship. This phenomenon is not limited to the military and their work relationship system. (In Section III, parallels will be drawn to the clergy's own work-family balance.)

Retirement can also unbalance the family homeostasis in other ways. In one case a couple who had been engaged for 5 years "decided" to get married when retirement made their parents closer. At the other end of the continuum, retirement itself can appear to advance aging and dysfunction, but there is almost always a family component in the process. The general rule is: If, at the time of retirement of one family member, another is in search of a replacement for an intense interdependency, senile processes will develop in the newly retired member far more rapidly than had he or she still been involved in the "extended system" of the work family.

GEOGRAPHICAL CHANGE

Geographical uprooting can also have important consequences for a family, especially to the extent that it means leaving an emotionally important house or community. The latter is particularly true concerning the aged. Also crucial is the extent to which a move changes the balance of a marriage, for example, taking a spouse farther away from his or her family, which can then result in either partner freeing up more or becoming more dependent. On the other hand, when couples move nearer to an area in which both extended systems reside, if the balance of their marriage was a by-product of the previous distance from these families, the marriage can blow apart in months.

Should religion try to create ceremonies to mark such events so as to enable families to become more aware of their portent? I suspect that while such ceremonies might be helpful in some cases, their effectiveness will be limited by the fact that divorce, retirement, and geographical relocation are not part of the natural life cycle and tend to serve more as triggers for or symptoms of triangles or problems in the family emotional system rather than as vehicles for their expression.

Finally, a link to the next section on the congregational family and its transitions: If rabbis, ministers, and priests would keep a file of family genograms and notes on how their various families function during rites of passage, they would immeasurably increase their successors' ability to serve those same families in the future. This approach helps keep the life cycle from becoming a vicious cycle.

THE CONGREGATION AS A FAMILY SYSTEM

8

Family Process and Organizational Life

Eight months after Mr. Smith's congregation celebrated a testimonial to him for 10 years of selfless dedication, the vestry presented their pastor with a detailed critique of his functioning. Mr. Smith was floored. He thought everything was going well. He was extremely hurt; he had been trying harder than ever and was almost at the point of exhaustion. He quickly gathered a small group around him. The leader of this clique was particularly articulate and seemed to carry the day. But the following autumn, the criticisms began again, openly and surreptitiously. Mr. Smith took his case to the forum of the pulpit, but when few seemed to rise to his defense this time, he resigned, bitter and tired.

Efforts to understand Mr. Smith's all too familiar experience in terms of individual-model psychodynamics might explain the congregation's hostility in terms of its unrealistic attitudes toward an authority figure; or the pastor's burnout in terms of character traits that made him respond in a maladaptive manner. The divorce between Mr. Smith and his congregation could then be seen as the result of personality conflicts, or "incompatibility." As with any "marriage" problem, family theory creates a different perspective for such troubled "families."

Mr. Smith and his wife had met and married while he was at the seminary. They had a child soon after, and their marriage became balanced by his intense involvement in his studies and his wife's reciprocal involvement in their child, a condition furthered by her distance from her own family of origin. After his ordination, they had a second child, but the emotional balance of their marriage continued along the same parallel paths of intensity: Mrs. Smith's investment in their eldest child, and the transfer of Mr. Smith's emotional energy from his

193

studies to his congregation, who, of course, responded to all this attention with adoration. As is the spiral nature of systems, the pastor's continued intense investment in his flock developed into a continuing adaptation to the mother–child axis, and that axis, in turn, was reciprocally fixed by Mr. Smith's intense relationship with his "paramour," the congregation.

Then, in the 10th year of his congregational tenure, the homeostasis of his personal family went "out of whack." Their eldest, a compliant member of the marital triangle until then, went into a full-blown adolescent rebellion. Because of the nature of the Smith family balance, this daughter's natural efforts to separate were particularly threatening to mother. It was the first time in 14 years of a very placid marriage that any family problems had arisen. Though Mr. Smith had always been a "good family man," he was now drawn into his family far more deeply than had ever occurred before. As he became more involved in his personal family, he unwittingly began to withdraw emotional energy from his other "family," and the homeostasis there also became unbalanced. Predictably, those in that system who were most tied into him emotionally sensed the pull-out immediately, and reacted with the kind of intense criticism that can always be understood as a "symptom for togetherness." Unaware of what was happening on the emotional process level, Mr. Smith took his congregational partner's criticism too seriously. He responded defensively by trying harder to please, or to explain the use of his time and role. This was ineffective because the content of the comments (quality of sermons, amount of visitations to the sick, time spent in office, etc.) was like pus coming out of a wound and, as usually happens in such circumstances, ignoring the source of the infection not only fails to cure the wound, it often allows the inflammation to spread.

Further investigation showed that the leader of the opposition had recently become extremely stressed by changes in the homeostasis of her own extended family (mother and sister), which left her "out in the cold." Furthermore, the articulate congregant who had won Mr. Smith his earlier, momentary victory was a major business competitor of that woman's husband. (In a very similar congregational family, the emotional frenzy became whipped up to the point that someone physically attacked the minister. It later turned out that the respective leaders of the opposing factions had once had an affair!)

A family systems approach to the marriage of Mr. Smith and his congregation would have encouraged the pastor to become less reactive to (anxious about) the content of the specific charges leveled against him, and to try to deal with the underlying emotional processes instead by doing some of the following: to get some emotional distance from the two major, interlocking emotional systems, his family and his congregation; to try to maintain a nonanxious presence with both by reducing his own anxiety about being the one who must satisfy both groups; to shift responsibility for the "problem" to other members of the congregational family in a way that would not polarize; to keep up his own personal level of functioning by shifting his energy to doing what he enjoyed and was good at; and to seek an opportunity in the future to focus those members who were most "hostile" (i.e., intense toward him) onto unresolved issues in their own families, perhaps during some celebration of a rite of passage.

CONGREGATIONAL FAMILY PROCESS

Everything that has been said thus far about emotional process in personal families is equally applicable to emotional process in churches, synagogues, rectories (which function as nuclear systems), and hierarchies (which function as extended systems). These too are families. They function as organic structures in their own right, according to the rules and models of family life described in Chapters 1 and 2. But religious institutions not only function like families, they also contain families. Indeed, they often derive their very structure from families. Thus, emotional process in religious organizations not only mirrors emotional process in personal families, but also, both types of family systems plug into one another. That is a major reason why unresolved issues in any of the clergy's three families can produce symptoms in one of the others, and why within that emotional interlock often lies the key to knowledge or to further stress.

This section of the book will develop a family systems view of organized religious life. It will draw upon the models and thinking previously applied to marriage and parenting in order to create a family framework for the clergy's professional life, a framework that not only continues to clarify their counseling position but also benefits their administrative functioning, their leadership, and their own personal health.

A family approach to organized religious life touches upon major personal and practical issues in the professional life of the clergy. With regard to personal issues, it has relevance for the dilemmas of intimacy, expectations, privacy, being a model or being oneself, refreshment, feelings of competence, adequacy, and isolation, etc. It can even be applied to crises in personal faith. The family approach can also be extended to preaching.

195

CONGREGATION AS A FAMILY SYSTEM

Professionally, as Mr. Smith's situation illustrated, family systems theory offers new perspectives and approaches for clergy–congregational problems and the stress experienced by clergy at such times. In addition, because the family approach is based on an organic model, it offers a way of thinking about this kind of "marital counseling" that is far less blaming and far less polarizing. A systems approach, as always, tends to redistribute the guilt and to take the sting out of toxic issues.

Just as it is possible to bring change in an acting-out child by focusing mother on her relationship with her own mother, change in a dysfunctional spouse by working instead with the partner, or change in the rate of increasing senility by connecting the aged up with their siblings, it is also possible to bring change to a congregational family problem by focusing on unresolved issues in the personal families of the clergy or lay leaders, rather than on issues in the session, the vestry, or the board of trustees.

Similarly, it is possible to modify the intensity of clergy–congregational relational issues by teaching ministers to recognize how they may be unwittingly "snookered" into unresolved problems in their parishioners' personal families, or between factions in the congregational family itself, or into issues that could have been passed down in that emotional system for generations. This is particularly true when the congregation was born out of a split, or a revolt in another congregational family. In those cases, it has become a multigenerational transmission process that will not be changed by the introduction of new blood, lay or ordained. Such unresolved issues tend to affect the atmosphere because they are the still active background radiation from the big bang of that congregation's creation.

Nor does the range of application of the family model end there. As will be seen in Chapter 10, analogies to "creative divorce" lead to strategies for breaking up clergy–congregational marriages so that the least amount of "baggage" will be carried into their next relationships. Analogies to the problems of blended or reconstituted families create effective strategies for how to function when first entering a congregational family with a long established relationship system. Analogies to terminal illness can help reduce the suffering and conflict when congregations are to be merged.

With regard to burnout, family systems theory also makes a major contribution to understanding and modifying the emotional processes in clergy–congregational relationships. Efforts to deal with burnout that are based on the individual model run the risk of adding more burden to the enervated professional because they convey the message that the problem originates or is located in his or her own psyche. The focus tends to be on the burned-out professional's personality, conflicts, or feelings. A family systems view of burnout sees the enervated clergyman or clergywoman as the "identified burnout," as the symptom-bearer of the relationship system of his or her congregational family. It asks: "What kind of congregational families are most likely to burn out their spiritual leaders? And how can clergy learn to function in such systems so that they are less likely to become the symptom-bearers for their congregations?"

This section of the book is divided into three chapters. This chapter will create a framework for learning how work systems can be understood in terms of family process and will conclude by showing how such a framework explains burnout as a "family" phenomenon. In Chapter 9, this framework will be used to develop a concept of leadership that maximizes the capacity of family leaders to stay on course, retain integrity, and avoid enervation, despite the sabotaging dependency of our followers. In Chapter 10, the family systems framework will be applied to entering and leaving a post and to the "extended family" of hierarchical relations. Family systems strategies for such events link each member of our profession in a mutually helpful way with our fellow "siblings" within our brotherhoods, our sisterhoods, and the newly emerging brother–sisterhoods. Last but not least, a family approach to entering and leaving posts offers sound criteria for deciding when to "divorce" and how to select a new "mate" for the next "hitch."

FAMILY THEORY AND WORK SYSTEMS

Family theory can be applied to all work systems, depending primarily on two factors: (1) the degree of emotional interdependency in that relationship system and (2) the extent to which its business is "life." A family business, for example, will mirror in its own system the emotional processes going on in the family that runs it. (This is also true of small-town churches.) Indeed it is almost impossible to bring change to a troubled family if the various members are also involved with one another in a family business because the economic relationships often lock into the personal interdependencies. This may also be a major reason why family businesses rarely last more than a few generations. But even where there is little or no personal family involvement, work systems that deal with the basic stresses of life, particularly medical or law partnerships, labor unions, psychiatric clinics or hospitals, and to a lesser extent school systems (but especially private schools), all are particularly susceptible to the rules of family process, including those rules that govern who in the family is likely to become ill. Of all work systems, however, the one that functions most like a family is the church or synagogue. This is true in part because it is so difficult for clergy to distinguish home life from professional life (whether or not there is a parsonage and whether or not the spouse is deeply invested), and partly because the intensity with which some lay people become invested in their religious institutions makes the church or synagogue a prime arena for the displacement of important, unresolved family issues. Interlocking emotional triangles between personal family issues and congregational family issues are the natural consequence of such displacement.

To appreciate what is being emphasized here, it is important to point out that this model of work systems is not simply saying that they have an "impact" on the family or vice versa. Obviously, if someone loses a job or is made irritable at work, that event will affect the family. If someone has had a bad night at home, that can lead to a bad day at the office. But the concept of "impact" suggests two different, discrete entities that influence one another from outside each other's space, as might occur in a crash between two boulders, two trains, or two billiard balls. This is A-causes-B linear thinking again.

The model being developed here is more analogous to electricity. The deepest effects that work systems and family systems have on one another come from the fact that they both run on the same current, if not the identical energy source. The influence is internal rather than external. They are plugged into one another and *their respective states of homeostasis join in a new overall balance.*

Some might object at this point that in a work system the "family" members change more frequently, and they are not really related. This view misunderstands the nature of organic systems. As has been shown, they have their own organizing principles inherent in their structures, principles that go beyond the nature of their parts. After all, even with a personal family, emotional process is passed down to new people who did not know the family members several "generations" back, and who were around when processes now affecting the third, fourth, or even the fifth generation began.

Similarly, even with the human organism, when it comes to the transmission of malignant processes, we may ask in what does cancer reside. The cells of the human body change rapidly from day to day and do almost a complete turnover every couple of years. It should not be surprising, therefore, that with families and congregations also, if there is a cancer in the system, the change-over in "cells" from year to year or from generation to generation will not necessarily effect a change in a malignant process. This is also why the transfusion of "new blood" or the performing of "major operations" rarely gets to the fundamental (systemic) problem.

Before applying a family systems model to synagogues and churches, here are several examples of its application to a variety of secular work systems. Six major family systems concepts previously discussed will then be explored as they relate specifically to religious institutions. As will be seen, the models and rules of family process are so transferable to religious organizational life that it could easily appear that the second part of this book gave rise to the first.

A Nursery School: A small volunteer nursery school was having problems with membership. Morale was poor and they recently had been beset with several acting-out children, something that had been absent almost totally in the past. Investigation of the overall relationship system showed that the six women who had organized the school, and who still administered the network and planned its programs, had almost no other interests. They tended to spend all their spare time together, sometimes including their husbands, and talked almost exclusively about the school when they met. At a meeting with the general membership, the problems of fusion according to the family model were discussed. Subsequently, the leaders made efforts to deemphasize the significance of the school in their personal lives. Some of them seemed to be simply waiting for "permission"; others found it very difficult. But within months of the differentiating efforts, enthusiasm returned and discipline problems with the children diminished.

A Law Firm: A prestigious law firm found itself in the midst of a "young Turk" revolt of the junior partners. The issue was the election of one of the new attorneys to junior partner status. According to the "family" rules, no one could be elected to junior status without the agreement of all three senior, founding partners. Two objected to the young man in question. Several of the junior partners threatened to leave the "family" and take their clients with them. The senior partners were perplexed. All law firms run on similar principles; the junior partners knew the setup when they joined. The firm had been growing nicely and the particular member who had become the *cause célèbre* was known to be disliked by some of those who most championed his cause.

One senior partner had been in family therapy with regard to one of his children. He reflected on that experience and perspectives. First, he noticed that over the previous half year, all three senior partners had become emotionally invested elsewhere. One had recently married; another, after a bitter divorce, had taken to the golf courses of Florida. And he himself, with all four children finally out of the home, had bought an old house in Spain that he and his wife were rebuilding, and that had become the all-consuming passion of their lives.

In addition, the offices of the other two senior partners were on a different floor. He realized quickly that one of the three partners would have to become more personally involved in the firm–family. He knew, however, that neither of his partners really understood what had to be done. He decided, therefore, to get back into the work triangles, but with a limited type of involvement. He held two parties at his home. The first was just for the attorneys. They were encouraged to speak frankly, and off the record. He made no effort to defend things, but let the discussions bring him back into the system. To the second party he also invited the spouses as well as the supporting staff. This time he made sure to defocus the serious aspect, spent the evening working at one-to-one relationships, and tried hard to keep things light through playfulness and paradox.

Involved once more in the relationship system of his own professional "family," he used the triangles that formed around him, between the junior partners and his senior-partner colleagues, to encourage further differentiation throughout the firm. He functioned primarily as the passive relay, simply reporting to the other senior partners, without comment, what the junior partners were saying about them: "By the way, I was talking with Ed Forsythe the other day and, would you believe, he thinks your reputation is built on rumor!" The expectable response was: "How can he say that? Everyone knows I. . . ." He interrupts: "Hey, I didn't say he was right. Just thought you ought to know what he thinks."

Eventually the junior and senior partners (first and second generations?) began to talk directly to one another. Only one junior partner left the "family," and the firm soon began to live up to its reputation once more.

A Medical Partnership: Four doctors joined in an obstetrical practice, but one of them did not carry his weight. He failed to cover his assigned duty times; he did not bring new patients into the practice; and he was very rigid about the advice he gave his patients. One of the other physicians took up the slack. When he eventually became more stressed by the load, he seemed to change at home, and his wife began to get on him about the office. His response was, "The poor guy has a lot of problems at home with his kids, and he needs the income badly."

His wife became increasingly fed up, said that she, in effect, had to compensate for the other wife's failures, and continued to pressure her husband to change. He, however, resented her interference and seemed to respond by giving even more time to the practice, which his colleagues, especially the underfunctioning one, took advantage of. The doctor's wife was taught about triangles. She pulled out of her husband's professional life and worked more on her own differentiation, especially around issues that arose when her mother became ill. The doctor began to stand up to his colleagues. The underfunctioning doctor became very depressed, went to a therapist, learned to take stands in his own family, and not only became a more responsible member of his medical partnership but also the quality of his health care improved.

A Nursing Staff: Olga Kinny took over as director of nursing for a large suburban hospital only to find ineptness at every turn. The five assistant directors rarely had much to do with one another, and each was used to doing things as she pleased. Within the first week, every one of these assistant directors triangled Olga by giving her negative reports about the others or by praising her in comparison to her predecessor. During the second week, several of the head nurses below them on the organizational chart also created triangles with their "siblings."

Olga, who had been receiving coaching for problems at home with her passive husband and nonfunctioning sons, decided to take a clear, well-defined leadership position in her work family. She spelled out clearly to her assistant directors her expectations for an efficient, well-run hospital. She also rearranged their offices so that they would be nearer to their own spheres of responsibility.

Within the week, one assistant went over Olga's head to ask for training money; another went to the hospital administrator and complained; and a third had an absolute tantrum when Olga pointed out that several of her wards were not operating according to procedure. Olga, however, stayed on course and dealt with all the flak with paradox and challenge When one assistant director told her she was moving too fast, she responded, "Wait 'til you see me when I go full speed." She consistently told everyone that while she would listen to what they had to say, she had a responsibility to be in charge and would help anyone find a position elsewhere if they felt they "couldn't hack it." She also had the good sense to watch her flank, and made sure to keep open her communication lines with "Father," the hospital administrator.

After 3 months, one assistant director went back to her home town; the one who had triangled her with the hospital administrator wrote a stinging letter of resignation; and a third decided to go back to school. Within 6 months Olga had replenished her team, and a study showed that convalescent stays in the hospital were shorter. There was also some indication that the amount of drugs being administered had decreased. In addition, during this period her husband, whom she had tried unsuccessfully for years to involve with their irresponsible sons, began to take firmer stands with them.

CONGREGATION AS A FAMILY SYSTEM

The most familiar aspects of family life, such as fusion, sibling rivalry, interlocking triangles, playing off parents, sabotage of a well-defined leader, and problems of entering and leaving, are part and parcel of organizational life. This is not just a cute analogy. In fact, it is no analogy at all. It is the exact same thing. Efforts have been made in recent years to compare family life *to* politics, but such comparisons have it backwards. For where else did the human race learn to function like that? The emotional structure of "organ"-izations replicates the emotional structure of the organisms we call families because, frankly, it's the only way we know how to do it.

RELIGIOUS ORGANIZATIONS

When family theory is applied to religious work systems, six basic family concepts have particular relevance: homeostasis, process and content, the nonanxious presence, overfunctioning, triangles, and symptom-bearer (identified patient). Each will now be described, first in the general context of religious organizational life and then with regard to the three major issues mentioned previously: burnout (this chapter), leadership (Chapter 9), and entering and leaving a post (Chapter 10). As in personal families, all these concepts are interrelated; discussion of any one serves as an introduction to the others.

HOMEOSTASIS

The concept of homeostasis can be helpful in understanding well-known problems of change found in all religious institutions. It also helps explain the changing nature of lay members' personalities when they assume positions of leadership, or of the clergy, when they assume leadership in a hierarchy. One of the most universal experiences of clergy everywhere is that things can appear to be going smoothly when suddenly there is "trouble in paradise." A related phenomenon is how things can appear to have quieted down "once and for all" only to surface again and again. As mentioned earlier, efforts to bring about change by dealing only with symptoms (content), rather than process, never will achieve lasting changes in an organic system. Problems will recycle unless the balancing factors in the homeostasis of the system shift.

As we saw in Section I, family issues rarely surface spontaneously, and even when they appear to, they do not have to continue on to malignant thresholds. This is also true of congregational family efforts to "get the minister." Whether the particular issue is criticism of clergy functioning, a problem related to administration, adequate salary, a sabbatical, or a theological matter, when such issues subtly surface, and with great intensity, or when they won't go away despite numerous, reasonable efforts to compromise with the more vociferous, then the issues under dispute are not the issues. In churches or synagogues the underlying homeostatic forces are sometimes more difficult to identify because they tend to be camouflaged in religious terminology.

The concept of homeostasis can be very useful in detecting such underlying forces and in evaluating whether or not a given change is really systemic. Again the questions "Why now?" "What has gone out of balance?" are extraordinarily pertinent. As with personal families, the focus ought to be on recent changes elsewhere in the emotional system, either in the families of key leaders or within the congregation itself. Some of the major changes that can promote "issues" are:

1. Changes in the family of the spiritual leader.

a. Birth, death, illness, divorce, hospitalization, affair or other marital problem, psychotherapy (particularly psychoanalysis or its termination), child acting out or leaving home, aged parent's needs, a problem in the extended family of the minister or his or her spouse.

b. Professional change in the life of the spiritual leader, for example, personal advancement, studying for or earning new degree, dedicated involvement in community project, new responsibilities in extended faith system, extension of contract, granting of tenure, change in location of office.

2. Changes similar to 1a and 1b in the personal or professional lives of key lay leaders or other congregational members intensely involved in the issues that have arisen.

3. Changes in the long-term constituency of the parish: racial, professional, philosophical, average age, etc.

In congregations that have long been run by a few families, the conflict in the congregation can, as in a family business, appear to be about new ideas or a change in philosophy, but the intensity can really reflect personal issues in those families, particularly intergenerational problems between father and son. For example, a small wine-importing establishment was family owned. Father, mother, and son all worked closely together. Father, an old-world sort, had slowly and patiently built the business up by means of his charm and taste. One of the first things the son did when he "took over" was to computerize the inventory. There followed a struggle for control of the company stock that pitted father against son, mother against daughter, and it almost destroyed the firm. A similar dispute almost destroyed a small church when the son of a previous leader tried to substitute pledge cards for passing the plate.

4. Changes in the church family's own professional leadership.

a. Hiring, firing, or the resignation of a key professional person (especially the administrative secretary).

b. Rise or elimination of interpersonal conflict between two professional leaders.

5. Changes in the *extended* family of the church hierarchy or the parish system.

a. Death or retirement of a founder, builder, or charismatic organizer.

b. Restructuring of the hierarchy or reorganization of the regions or parish system (decentralizing, recentralizing, creating more or fewer subgroupings).

c. If a church or synagogue is part of an ethnic group, general anxiety in that "extended" system can escalate anxiety over specific issues in the various "nuclear" congregational groupings.

Such homeostatic changes do not necessarily "cause" problems themselves. All are able to, however, in the presence of some combination of the others. Also, homeostatic changes do not have to produce obviously connected problems. A struggle between two members of a hierarchy over a theological matter, for example, does not have to result in a symptom that is theological. On the other hand, a theological symptom can be the content issue produced by some interpersonal disruption elsewhere in the system. As with personal marriages, the differences partners "differ" over do not *cause* the differing.

Similarly, no issue merely by the nature of its content is automatically more virulent than another. Congregations can be rent asunder or fire their ministers over the same issue that, under other homeostatic conditions, will go quietly away. Not every minister has to resign because of impolitic remarks or indiscretions. Pastors have been fired over the mere suspicion of an affair or the violation of a practice, and they have also been able to stay on after an affair has been revealed or even after evidence of teenage molestation has become public. It is almost never the issue *per se* that is destructive but, rather, the overall homeostatic conditions that give to any issue its destructive potential.

Another way that the concept of homeostasis can be helpful in understanding congregational family systems is that it supplies clues to the source of intensity. As with rites of passage, severe intensity over an otherwise authentic religious issue strongly suggests an unresolved emotional issue in the nuclear or extended family of the complainer. It can be equally true of the clergy's intensity. Here is an example of each.

A heated struggle developed between a female minister and the head of the women's auxiliary over this clergywoman's stands on a number of women's issues. Every nodal point in the fight—its onset, its climax, and its conclusion—coincided with a similar nodal point in the life of the lay leader's daughter: her initial involvement with a man, the time she first brought him home, the engagement, and the breakup of the engagement.

In a midwestern city one synagogue wanted to share space and teachers with another. It had originally broken away from the other 30 years previously. None of the present lay leaders had been involved in that earlier tiff, and some had not even been born. The leaders of the older congregation agreed; then, suddenly, their rabbi carried on as though a pact had been made with Satan. He launched a vituperative attack on the younger congregation's attitude to tradition and threatened to write a letter to all the members of his own group. His father had been the rabbi 30 years previously when the two congregations split!

It would be interesting to see what the effects would be on congregational families that were conceived in the womb of another if years after the "break" they would go out of their way to join with the "parent" system in some cooperative project and stop the cut-off that often results from such splits. The same could be said for entire faith systems, of course. The effect of cut-offs in religious systems is similar to their impact on personal families—they always leave live wires loosely flapping about.

One other, subtle quality of congregational homeostasis is worth noting. Clergy whose congregations include many members in therapy may find the flock constantly changing their stand on issues in the congregation, or suddenly changing in the way they relate to their minister as they resolve transference issues with their therapists. This can be quite disconcerting for the minister and for the congregational emotional system, particularly if those lay persons are significantly involved. The suspicion exists here that such shifts do not tend to be quite as abrupt when the parishioners are in family therapy.

PROCESS AND CONTENT

The capacity of clergymen and clergywomen to keep their minds on homeostatic changes in the emotional process of their congregational families depends largely on their ability to identify the content issues such homeostasis promotes. Table 8-1 presents a list of such issues when the focus is on the spiritual leader. As with marriage problems, the total number of differences that all the churches and synagogues in

TABLE 8–1. Content Issues When the Focus is on the Clergy

Preaching	Personal preferences	Personal qualities	Family members	Congregational administration	Availability for	Theological attitudes
Preparation	Grooming	Warmth	How spouse:	Budget (any item)	Pastoral duties	Prayers chosen
Delivery	Attire	Enthusiasm	dresses	Time spent in:	Adult education	Order of prayers
Content	Home	Good listener	drinks	office	Sick visitations	
	Car	Accessibility	drives	visitations	Choir	Texts selected
	Vacations	Good relations with:	acts	committees	Fund raising	Music chosen
	Spending	both sexes	looks	community	Retreats	Rites administered
	Hobbies	all ages	dances		Sunday school curriculum	
	Friends	families	prays		Teacher training	Traditions observed
	Politics	singles	sings		Officiation at ceremonies	
			cooks		Recruiting new members	
			How children behave in:			
			school			
			church			
			home			
			community			

the universe have ever had with their minister is relatively small and finite. And as with marital conflict, peace attained by focusing on these content issues is not likely to last. The effort here is not to whitewash the clergy, but to emphasize once again that when the relationship system of a family is in balance, such issues are handled rationally through discussion and the democratic process. But when they achieve such intensity that a "family" becomes polarized and threatens to split, then the issues are more likely to be false issues and will never be totally resolved by increased efforts at articulate reasoning, no less the conspiracies of "behind-the-pulpit politicking."

DEFOCUSING CONTENT

The capacity of clergy to spot content issues for the red herrings they really are, whether or not the focus is on the clergy member personally, is doubly advantageous. First, it can enable us to reduce our anxiety about such symptoms, thus making us less defensive even when we have a large personal or philosophical stake in what the congregation decides, or when our own survival as a spiritual leader is in the balance. Much of the criticism directed at spiritual leaders is henpecking, pure and simple. It can never be made to go away permanently by trying harder to please. Despite the time-bomb quality of the emotionality, it is usually rather harmless in itself and will tend to self-destruct if there is no defensive feedback to keep it ticking.

Sometimes, however, the content issue *is* symptomatic of a continuing malignant process. A second advantage, therefore, of being able to distinguish content from process is that it prevents the "fake-outs" of apparent, symptomatic change. As with personal families, to the extent a symptom goes away because the complaining party was appeased, or where issues are resolved in isolation from other changes in the system, such change is not likely to last.

An Illusion of Change: A minister was resented by a handful of congregants from the very beginning of his ministry. His predecessor had been their pet. He, in contrast, had been selected by the "new guard" after internecine conflict in the congregation. They urged him to make a number of rapid changes. After 3 years, the "old guard" counterattacked (over a theological position) and lost again. The pastor made a public attempt at reconciliation, and publicly praised their contributions to the congregation again and again. *Things calmed down, but the minister, had never made the younger lay leaders responsible for the problem* in their own congregational family. In other words, he remained in the triangle. Five years later the congregation decided to move and needed the contributions of these six older families. As their price, the latter exacted a new spiritual leader.

Every time members of a congregation begin to concentrate on their minister's *"performance,"* there is a good chance they are displacing something from their own personal lives. All of this feeds back to what was said in Chapter 4 concerning child focus. When ministers accept that displacement (by getting lost in the content of the charges), they not only become the identified focus of the congregation, as in all such "family" situations, but they also permit the others not to have to face themselves. Perhaps the most apropos example of the failure of content focus to bring systemic change is the following story.

A Test of Faith: A dedicated minister, whose wife had left him for another man, began to date a divorced woman in the church. He was himself legally separated but not divorced. A small group began a terrific attack on his morals. At first the leadership said, "Don't pay attention," and he agreed. Then they said, "Just date her discreetly," and he agreed. Then they said, "Better not date her until your own divorce," and he agreed. They finally demanded a public confession, and not being "a man for all seasons," he agreed again. When contract time came around, they "beheaded" him anyway.

NONANXIOUS PRESENCE

The benefits of being a nonanxious presence in counseling situations or within one's own personal family have already been described. Maintaining a similar presence in a religious organizational family also distributes benefits throughout that type of system. In fact, the capacity of members of the clergy to contain their own anxiety regarding congregational matters, both those not related to them, as well as those where they become the identified focus, may be the most significant capability in their arsenal. Not only can such capacity enable religious leaders to be more clear-headed about solutions and more adroit in triangles but, because of the systemic effect that a leader's functioning always has on an entire organism, a nonanxious presence will modify anxiety throughout the entire congregation. And that aspect of family leadership, as we will see in the next chapter, can sometimes do more to resolve issues than the ability to come up with good (content) solutions.

To change metaphors, members of the clergy function as transformers in an electrical circuit. To the extent we are anxious ourselves, then, when anxiety in the congregation permeates our being, it becomes potentiated and feeds back into the congregational family at a higher voltage. But to the extent we can recognize and contain our own anxiety, then we function as step-down transformers, or perhaps circuit breakers. In that case, our presence, far from escalating emotional potential, actually serves to diminish its "zapping" effect. This idea will be illustrated in the next chapter.

Two aspects of the nonanxious presence that are worth highlighting here are the value of playfulness and the dangers of diagnosis. Both come together in a new way regarding anxiety in religious institutions. As emphasized in Chapter 2, anxiety's major tone is seriousness, often an affliction in itself. It is always content-oriented. Its major antidote is playfulness, especially with those for whom we feel too responsible. This is obvious in parent–child relationships, but it is even more crucial when the responsibility is for another's salvation, much less the survival of an entire group.

The capacity of clergy to be paradoxical, challenging (rather than saving), earthy, sometimes crazy, and even "devilish," often can do more to loosen knots in a congregational relationship system than the most well-meaning "serious" efforts. Again, this is not because being paradoxical affects the content in the heads of others (reverse psychology), but because the act of being playful frees others by forcing them out of their serious "games."

Taking the Other Side: A rabbi came into his Sunday school one morning to find teachers, parents, and the religious school principal terribly uspet by the fact that a mischievous 11-year-old had transliterated the well-known Anglo-Saxon word for "feces" into its equivalent Hebrew phonetics. There was to be an important celebration that day, and it was clear that the wrong tone had been set from the beginning. Instead of entering the discussion going on about the psychological and religious import of the child's action, the rabbi noticed that the child had spelled the word mistakenly, with a long vowel instead of a short one. The rabbi ignored the content of the situation, berated the kid for not paying more attention to phonetic details, and then told him that he could only join the festivities after he had spelled it right 100 times! Process superseded content and celebration carried the day.

The exact opposite of playful functioning, that which is most likely to heighten the seriousness in a system, is diagnostic thinking. As previously emphasized, diagnostic categories are inherently antisystemic. They tend to increase polarization. With congregational families, as with personal families, focusing on the personality of someone with whom one had a close relationship tends to hinder objectivity and to make the system paranoid. Diagnosis intensifies anxiety, and is its natural manifestation as well.

The categories of playfulness and diagnosis, therefore, can provide us with accurate measurements of how well we are functioning in our efforts to maintain a nonanxious presence. As long as we find ourselves able to stay loose about content issues in the congregation, or about the content of charges directed against us, this is a strong suggestion we are doing well. But if we find ourselves thinking about the members of our congregations in diagnostic categories, that is firm evidence we are not.

The Loyal Opposition: One very outspoken, controversial minister was finally able to reduce his own anxiety when he began to think of his detractors as the "loyal opposition." As pompous as the phrase sounds, it helped him stay out of a polarizing position with other members of the congregation who in the past got "togetherness" with him by "loyally" attacking the attackers. By conveying that he thought their attacks on him were a sign of *duty* rather than *subversion*, he eliminated almost completely from his own behavior the anxious feedback that is necessary to sustain chronic conditions.

Hostile congregational environments never victimize automatically. The response of clergy to their environment is almost always the main factor that determines how harmful it will be. To the extent that we can reduce our anxiety with such awareness, the less likely it is that we will go to the extremes of prematurely capitulating, victim-like, or overreacting in an "autoimmune," self-destructive response.

One important distinction must be made, however, between family systems and work systems. In a family system, efforts to reduce anxiety by dealing only with process and totally avoiding content issues, even if it makes others more upset for a while, generally will lead to fundamental change in the long run. A work system, however, can kick us out before change comes about. In a work family, therefore, it is sometimes necessary to touch upon content to some extent so as not to create so much havoc that we lose our jobs.

OVERFUNCTIONING

Playing Hero: A minister who had served a parish for many years left disillusioned. Repeatedly, members of the congregation he thought agreed with him philosophically, and who were members only because he was the minister, failed to support him on important matters in the church. Moreover, on several occasions when a different group tried to oust him, his supporters did not rise to his defense as aggressively as he had expected they would. "Sometimes," he reported, "I felt like the classic cowboy hired by the cowardly townspeople to rid them of the desperados, but who wouldn't take risks even when the very person they hired to save them was in trouble."

During the next year, after he had left, he happened to meet several of his former parishioners. Each of them told him how much he was missed, and how the church wasn't the same without him. "Where were they when I needed them?" he asked.

One of the most universal complaints from clergy of all faiths is the feeling of being stuck with all the responsibility. (Compare Moses's complaints in Numbers 11:11ff.) This can extend from ideas for programming to turning out the lights in the office. All this focus on getting the other to take responsibility has a "familiar" ring. It echoes the sound of parents or spouses caught in an overfunctioning position in their families. The results in a congregational family are similar: It is never possible to make others responsible by trying to make them responsible, because the very act of trying to make others responsible is preempting their responsibility. What rarely occurs to those in the overfunctioning position is that in any type of family the rest of the system may be underfunctioning as an adaptive response! In other words, it has become a familial, homeostatic correction to an extreme position. No one remembers the overfunctioner's birthday; he or she is less likely to be forgiven for mistakes. In any family, he or she gets no balance of credit on which to draw. As one, long-experienced, government bureaucrat noted, "If we need to get something done quickly, we never give it to the person with the cleanest desk, but always to the staff member with the most cluttered desk."

Sometimes the problems of overfunctioning come from someone supposedly outside of the work system, as when a retired or emeritus minister stays too much in the picture. While some clergy in that position can enjoy the honored state, some can't let go, and they (or in some cases their spouses) remain too involved in the relationship system. Here, if the incumbent minister can contain his or her anxiety about the retired minister's anxious interference, perhaps by paradoxically loading him up for more involvement and quoting him publicly at every turn, there is a high likelihood that the emeritus will become more "retiring."

Overfunctioning in any system is an anxious response in both senses of the word, "anxious" as in anticipatory and "anxious" as in *fearful*. In a congregational family, it will result in the same kinds of fusion that it produces in marriage or in parenting. In any emotional system these effects can be quite profound. For if overfunctioning is a manifestation of anxiety, it will serve to promote it as well. If it is a

211

manifestation of dependency, it is also a force for its creation. And if in smaller organisms the resulting loss of differentiation cultivates self-destroying forms of symbiosis, among human organisms its analogical creations are cults and cultic thinking.

Overfunctioning is, in a sense, both model and message, the mode by which clergy inadvertently teach parents and spouses to hang onto others rather than to let them go, to focus on others rather than themselves, to be obsessed with the salvation of others rather than their own. But it is really more complex than mere message or modeling. As indicated, congregational family and personal family systems are interconnected. Therefore, fusion in the relationships of clergy and their congregations will foster fusion in the relationships of congregants and their families.

A style of "family leadership" less prone to overfunctioning will be explored in the next chapter, and its relationship to burnout will be discussed shortly, but one aspect of that broader emotional phenomenon can be emphasized here. One of the subtlest yet most fundamental effects of overfunctioning is spiritual. It destroys the spiritual quality of the overfunctioner. Several ministers and rabbis have reported, after switching professions: "Now I can go back to being a good Christian/ Jew; now I can enjoy prayers and the Holy Days again."

TRIANGLES

The concept of an emotional triangle has equal relevance for family systems and for congregational systems. It also helps explain their connection. And in both systems, it is the previously described over-functioner who is more likely to get caught in their sharp angles. All the rules of an emotional triangle described in Chapter 1 apply here. As triangles in an extended family can perpetuate triangles in personal families, so triangles in personal families can perpetuate triangles in work systems.

We will see how this principle operates from the perspective of the clergy's own nuclear and extended families in Section IV. And in Chapter 9 we will see how the concept of an emotional triangle can enable leaders to free themselves from the enervating resistance of their followers. Similarly, we will see in Chapter 10 how the triangle concept can be useful in understanding the binds that await us on entering a new post, or the unexpected and apparently unrelated changes that often occur on leaving an old position. Another important benefit of the concept of an emotional triangle is that it can teach process approaches for dealing with content issues, as, for example, the following triangle involving three members of the same staff.

212

STAFF TRIANGLES

A-rhythmia: A congregation hired a new choir director who knew little about church music but who was a whiz at inspiring a choir. The minister, who loved music, began to spend a great deal of time with her so that he could apply her skills to enrich the service. In the middle of the year, the Sunday school director launched an attack on this woman's knowledge of hymns, saying that her rhythm was constantly inappropriate. No amount of pointing out that those factors were less important than her ability to involve people had any success. The minister learned about emotional triangles, began spending more resource time with the Sunday school director, and the "a-rhythmia" disappeared.

An Allergic Reaction: Another staff triangle involved an assistant minister's wife who was gadflying about the congregation stirring up all kinds of problems with her outspoken opinions. The senior minister was extremely perturbed but reluctant to talk to his colleague's wife. Then his own wife created an interlocking triangle by pushing him to do something about it. The senior minister began to have chronic headaches that were diagnosed as an allergic reaction, but they did not go away no matter what antihistamines he took. It was suggested that he get out of the middle by making his assistant responsible for his own wife: "Son, you've been doing a good job here, and we would like to keep you on; but, frankly, your wife is getting to be more trouble than you're worth. If you can handle her, you can stay. If not, I'll be glad to give you a glowing recommendation." The wife went back to school, the assistant minister stayed on, and the senior minister ceased taking medication.

The staff triangle can also be with the previous pastor if the latter keeps sending his church bulletin back to members in his former congregation.

PARISHIONER TRIANGLES

It is not only in staff relations, however, that triangles surface. Triangles between members of our congregations, although perhaps less overtly disruptive of daily pastoral duties, can take their toll in the long run.

Woman to minister after she had dropped him off at home, following a meeting: "Mr. Williams, I just want you to know that there are some members of this congregation who are out to get you, but I'm on your side." Or: "A lot of us think you have great potential, but couldn't you get your wife to come to meetings more often?" Or: "We always come to you, rather than your associate rabbi, when we need comfort. He's a good speaker, but we find you much easier to talk to."

A priest, after coming to understand triangles, found a cartoon which ke kept on his door. It showed a couple leaving church, and as the wife is shaking the minister's hand, she says: "You certainly got my husband's number."

Superpositive triangles can be equally pernicious. One rabbi reported that a woman president of his Board had worked her way up the congregational family ladder and had alienated many other "sibling" members along the way. When she got to the top, she invariably praised the rabbi at every opportunity. Every time she did so, he found it more difficult to keep up good relationships with other members of the congregation. He finally had to ask her to stop giving him so much credit.

And then there are the vicarious triangles, not of atonement but of excuses for inaction: "No, we don't keep Lent ourselves, but we certainly expect our minister to." For Lent you can substitute: Passover, kosher, monogamous, honest, empathic, moral, sober, etc.

TRIANGLES AND LIFE-CYCLE EVENTS

One of the most fertile areas for the sprouting of triangles between clergy and their families are the highly anxious periods surrounding life-cycle ceremonies. This can be before or after the ceremony.

A good example of *before* the ceremony is divorced parents, both still members of the parish, who come to their minister before the wedding of their daughter. Mother wants her new husband to walk down the aisle and father says, "Then I won't come," and both say, "Solve it for us, minister."

An example of *after* is when the daughter comes up to minister after her father's funeral and confides that she is "kidnapping" mother to go back to her home town with her, but "Don't tell my brother," who is a member of minister's congregation, of course.

And here is one example that coincided with the entire rite of passage and wound up involving the entire congregational family as well.

A Note from the Past: A woman with a terminal condition gave her minister a letter with specific instructions for her funeral, emphasizing that she desired absolutely no eulogy, nor personal remarks, nor family involvement. She had told her minister that her husband knew about the note, so the minister did not bother to show it to him (which would have been the right detriangling move that might have affected the eventual mourning).

When the woman died, her husband asked to see the note. It turned out that she had not shown it to him, only informed him of its existence. As is characteristic of the state of grief, the family said, "We must follow her wishes." The clergywoman was, therefore, totally unable to convince the family that they should do what was best for the survivors. But the effects of the triangling did not end there. As the minister drove over to conduct the funeral, she found she was also triangled with the rest of the congregational family. The note was preventing her from fulfilling her duty to aid their mourning. She found herself carrying on a monologue with the deceased woman, cursing her for the bind she had put her in.

As she mounted the pulpit for the service, she suddenly realized what to do. She read the note to the congregational family. At that moment, she said, her hostility evaporated like a mist, and she was able to perform the funeral according to the woman's wishes. After the service, the triangle had predictably shifted; the congregation was absolutely furious at the deceased.

Whether B and C in Figure 8-1 represent two pastors, two other staff members, two members of the minister's family, two congregational families or issues, or one each from any of these categories, if the pastor (A) functions according to Diagram I, which represents taking responsibility for their relationship, rather than as in Diagram II, which represents individualizing his or her relationship with each of the other two parts of the triangle, he or she is "asking for it." As one wily octogenarian, who had survived more than 50 years in congregational foxholes, advised: "If the bullet doesn't have your name on it, get out of its way."

And this brings us to the sixth family process concept useful to a systems understanding of congregational life, the idea of the symptom-bearer.

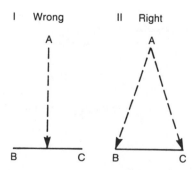

FIGURE 8-1. Clergy response to triangling efforts.

IDENTIFIED PATIENT

In recent years, the notion of burnout has become popular as a way of explaining the state of exhaustion and dysfunction experienced by well-intentioned individuals who lose their energy and persistence. It is more likely to occur to people whose job involves a great deal of nurturing, although it can happen to individuals in the most ruthless corporations. Generally, it is less likely to occur to "idea-people" than to "people-people." And it may aptly describe the state of some mothers, fathers, spouses, and grown children who get themselves in similarly stressful family positions. Since studies of stress indicate that the worst possible combination of work conditions is high-performance demand, combined with little control over the situation, the position of the clergy may, by nature, be dangerous to health.

BURNOUT AND THE INDIVIDUAL MODEL

The individual model tends to see burnout as a symptom of the ener-vated person. Many programs for recuperation have been created by burnout specialists to help individuals replenish their strength, their vigor, and their verve. They tend to overlook, however, the transplant metaphor (see Chapter 1). Resting and refreshment do not change triangles. Furthermore, because these programs focus on the burned-out "family" member, they can actually add to his or her burden if such individuals are inclined to be soul searchers to begin with. The inade-quacy of individual-based remedies for clergy burnout is highlighted by the following list of suggestions a mental health association published for coping with stress. They appear along with some parenthetical retorts that appropriately could be made by the clergy of any faith:

- Find an outlet for working off stress. (The increased complaints would increase my stress.)
- Talk to someone about your worries. (Who would understand whom I could also trust?)
- Learn to accept what you cannot change. (But my whole purpose and training in life is to strive for change!)
- Try to balance the time between work and recreation. (My work is too close to home to allow that.)
- Be sure to get sufficient rest and sleep. (You mean get out of town or cut my telephone cord?)
- Do one thing at a time instead of trying to tackle all of your tasks at once. (I'd be fired on the spot!)

- Get out and make yourself available instead of sitting alone and feeling sorry for yourself. (If only I had time to be alone!)
- Do something for others. (Are you kidding?)

A SYSTEMS VIEW OF BURNOUT

It is possible to take a family systems approach to burnout. In such a view, the burned-out professional is seen as the "identified burnout," and the focus will be the overloading system. A family approach to burnout also broadens the perspective. Not only can the physical or spiritual exhaustion of the minister be considered burnout, but, because of the interlocking nature of all the clergy's families, so can an alcoholic spouse or a delinquent child. Depending on the structure of the minister's own family, nuclear family symptoms can be produced by congregational emotional forces that in other clergy families surface only in the religious leader.

A family model of burnout asks what are the characteristics of a congregational family emotional system most likely to burn out its spiritual leader or promote symptoms in his or her nuclear family. Here are five that all congregations and parishes satisfy to some extent:

1. Degree of isolation between the congregation and other congregations in its own faith community or in its local community.
2. Degree of distance between the lay leadership and the general membership.
3. The extent to which the lay leadership allows the congregation to pre-empt its entire emotional life (no other friends or social networks).
4. The degree to which the lay leadership has intense interdependent relationships with one another beyond their congregational functioning, such as being related through blood, marriage, or business.
5. The inability of the lay leadership, particularly the "president" or the senior warden, to take well-defined positions, independent of the complainers.

To the extent any congregation, parish, or hierarchy can be accurately described by this set of characteristics, and to the extent its spiritual leader tends to overfunction, to that extent will he or she be stressed. Spiritual leaders in such systems will inescapably become caught up in the emotional triangle spin-off that such systems produce.

Ministers will consequently dysfunction in whatever ways they are prone to dysfunction when they are triangled, that is, stressed.

Some congregations (using the individual approach) tend to see points, not triangles. You might hear a congregation member say, "He drank heavily before he took the post." Or, "I happen to know that she had a lesbian affair even before she was ordained." Or, "They also had problems with their kid in his former congregation." Or, "I heard he seduced a teenager 10 years ago." This is the same attitude taken toward marital problems: He or she entered the relationship with that problem from the past. The answer to this reductive approach, as mentioned in Chapter 2, is that humans are programmed for more pathology than could possibly become manifest in a lifetime. The question is not what did they bring into the relationship, but why are they manifesting a symptom now? They don't do it every day. Certainly, each family member in any system must take responsibility for his or her own behavior, but to try to understand problems only in terms of their personality exonerates the system. Worse than that, it increases the burden and the guilt of the symptom-bearer.

One of the most astounding facts about organized religious life in America is the extent to which professional clergy organizations and hierarchies permit religious institutions to get away with blaming all crashes on "pilot error." By focusing well-meaning efforts to help burned-out members on the burned-out members themselves, they inadvertently support the system and, in the process, miss a special opportunity to understand what makes many congregations tick (and miss beats) as they do.

All faith communities have congregations that have reputations for being "pills" or "plums." Little or no work has been done to ask what goes into that difference. Perhaps it is simply ignorance of the family model that has prevented such studies. Whatever the reason, members of the clergy who come to understand in what ways the relationship system of a congregational family can itself be pathogenic can learn how to avoid becoming the symptom-bearer for that system, and how to develop criteria for choosing the right "family" to begin with. This latter notion will be developed further in Chapter 10.

Finally, a comment needs to be made in this systems context about martyrdom. There are a number of clergy of all faiths who, rather than burning out, almost seem to relish abuse, either emotionally or in their physical surroundings. If they are Christian, they might see themselves as emulating Jesus on the cross. If they are Jewish, they might justify their suffering by recalling the martyrs of Jewish history. In both cases this is sheer theological camouflage for an ineffective immune system. In any family, taking the suffering for others, or being willing to suffer because of the suffering of others, is absolutely irresponsible if it enables others to avoid facing their own suffering! Indeed, the effects of that type of self-abnegation can only increase others' guilt!

As one minister with an extremely kind but passive husband put it, "I used to believe a martyr was someone who went around taking everyone else's pain without complaint and refusing praise for his actions. I now realize that is not a martyr; that's a saint. A martyr is someone who's willing to live with a saint."

9

Leadership and Self in a
Congregational Family

In a medium-size city, the two most prominent ministers in town died within months of one another. Both had served their "flocks" for more than 25 years. Although one had been far more charismatic, his congregation dwindled and disappeared overnight. The other, an old, established, if less vibrant, "family," mourned, selected a successor, and continued with little loss of functioning. Some said the survival of one church and the disintegration of the other was due to the structure of their respective organizations. The second had tradition and roots. It thus had its own impetus for survival and was better prepared to withstand the loss of a leader.

There was another view, however: namely, that it was the functioning of these leaders that had affected the survival of their respective families. A different style of leadership might have enabled the younger church to continue after the loss of the leader, while a different style of leadership in the other, despite its established structure, might have made survival there more difficult.

This chapter, which will apply family systems thinking to leadership, takes its cue from the second perspective. It will champion the vital importance of a leader, not only to any family's nature and functioning, but also to its ultimate survival. These effects are inextricably connected: The effects of loss on any family depend primarily on the functioning of its leader at that moment, but when the loss is of the leader, the effect is primarily a result of how the leader functioned before he or she was lost. In emphasizing the crucial significance of leaders, however, the purpose is not to burden the clergy with unbearable responsibility. On the contrary, family systems thinking leads to a leadership style that is far less burdensome than is usually assumed, even though it considers leaders to be more important than is usually assumed.

It will be the thesis of this chapter that the overall health and functioning of any organization depend primarily on one or two people at the top, and that this is true whether the relationship system is a personal family, a sports team, an orchestra, a congregation, a religious hierarchy, or an entire nation. But the reason for that connection is not some mechanistic, trickle-down, domino effect. It is, rather, that leadership in families, like leadership in any flock, swarm, or herd, is essentially an organic, perhaps even biological, phenomenon. And an organism tends to function best when its "head" is well differentiated. The key to successful spiritual leadership, therefore, with success understood not only as moving people toward a goal, but also in terms of the survival of the family (and its leader), has more to do with the leader's capacity for self-definition than with the ability to motivate others.

THE POSITION AT THE TOP

Some of the strongest evidence for the vital importance of leadership comes from an area of our civilization we would not normally connect with religious life, namely, sports. On the one hand, no segment of our culture appears to be more dependent on individual performance; on the other hand, the most successful teams do not necessarily consist of players with the best individual records. The missing factor is often labeled "teamwork." If, however, we try to understand just what goes into the chemistry of teamwork, the idea becomes elusive.

The concept of teamwork also fails to explain slumps, streaks, or that remarkably randomly appearing phenomenon, injuries, all of which could also be part of the teamwork chemistry. The family systems concepts of homeostasis and identified patient suggest that slumps, streaks, and injuries could be symptoms of emotional process in the team, and the logic of the theory suggests that this would be true with all teams, not just those whose business is sports.

One other clue to the fact that something systemic is at work in the overall performance of a team is that there does not seem to be an automatic correlation between how a player played on one team and how he or she will function when "transplanted" to the next. Sometimes there is a correlation, but then it may be that one of the other players who had been functioning well in the past is having a "bad season," or has been injured.

Of particular note here is an event that occurred in 1972 when the owners of the Baltimore Colts and Los Angeles Rams traded entire football teams. It is the only instance of the trading of whole teams rather than a few players. One could say that the teams weren't traded at all; it was the owners, the people at the top, who were transplanted. Both of these teams almost immediately traded personalities, and these transformations lasted more than a decade! The characteristics of both these sports "families" went with the people at the top! If the day ever comes when heads can be transplanted, will it be more accurate to say that the heads were exchanged or the bodies?

Congregations and parishes also have reputations for being "winners" or "losers." They also are quick to blame or praise their "coach" for their own successes or slumps—emotional or membership—often with some justification. And they also fail to ask how the "owners" of the team might be contributing. There are some owners who can make things very difficult, but in the vast majority of situations the functioning of the church or synagogue team depends primarily on the functioning of the "coach." What is rarely realized, however, and this may be true even with sports and symphonies, is that the key to successful coaches is less a matter of how they "handle" the players than how they handle themselves.

This chapter will be divided into three parts. The first part will discuss two types of resistance that are the bane of all who occupy the position at the top, no matter what type of family they are leading. Then it will show that the push–pull methods generally developed for trying to overcome such resistance tend to triangle and enervate the leaders because they are based on a personality model when the resistance is really a systemic phenomenon. The second part will describe a family systems approach to leadership that is far less susceptible to such binds. It will be called "leadership through self-differentiation." Its major characteristic is that it does not create the usual dichotomy between a family and its leader but, instead, it conceptualizes the problems of resistance in terms of an organic model that emphasizes a continuous connection between a "head" and the "body politic." The third part will describe two congregational family histories and the application to them of leadership through self-differentiation. From a more personal perspective, the first history describes my own efforts to detriangle myself from a leadership position in a congregational family I had served for many years when, after I began to burn out, the congregation appeared to be on the verge of collapse. The second describes my efforts to teach this family systems model to a congregation from a different faith community (actually a composite of several), where I had the opportunity to coach both the "team" and its "coach."

As in Chapter 5, the depth, range, and ramifications of this chapter go well beyond one more bailiwick in the clergy's sphere of responsibility. All that will be said here about leadership in congregational families can be retroactively applied to leadership triangles in personal families, whether the focus is marriage, children, or the elderly. And looking ahead to Section IV, it is also relevant to the problems of leadership for clergy in their own personal families.

THE PARADOXICAL TRIANGLES OF RESISTANCE

There is something remarkably similar about the efforts of all family leaders to change their followers, whether it is a parent trying to motivate a child to do homework, a spouse trying to motivate a partner to change a habit, a healer trying to motivate a patient to take care of himself or herself, members of the clergy trying to motivate members of the congregation to attend more often, or even an entire family trying to change the mind of one of its members. In all such situations, the motivators function as though their followers did not know what is good for them and, furthermore, would never change were it not for their efforts. Teachers, salesmen, and therapists also tend to think this way. In addition, leaders tend to assume that if they have failed to change the heads of their followers, it is because they, the leaders, did not try hard enough. Almost universally, therefore, they respond to lack of change by trying harder to push, pull, tug, kick, shove, threaten, convince, arm-twist, charm, entice, cajole, seduce, induce guilt, shout louder, or be more eloquent. The resulting treadmill of trying harder is usually energized by an absolute belief in the "power of the word." Even when such efforts are successful, change tends to be short-lived and enervating because continued success depends so much on the continued triangulation of the leader between his or her followers, and some goal. It rarely occurs to the people at the top, at home or at work, that because of the nature of emotional triangles, some threshold has been reached so that further efforts not only will fail to bring change, but also will be converted into forces that stabilize the *status quo*. One major effect of this power conversion is that it gives leverage to the follower. In system after system, it is the most dependent who are calling the shots. On the other hand, as will be seen later, those same triangular processes that subvert the "word," once they are recognized, can be turned to the leader's favor.

But the paradox of counterproductivity when one tries to be overly productive is not the only aspect of leadership triangles with which all family leaders struggle. Successful leadership depends not only on the ability to overcome inertial passivity, but it also must be able to avoid being sidetracked by active sabotage. Another paradox facing people at the top is the predictable fact that followers will work to throw them off course precisely when they are functioning at their

223

best. It is probably a good rule of thumb that whenever you are feeling real good about things, watch out! This automatic, mindless resistance of followers is hardly limited to religious institutions. It is prevalent in all kinds of human families and is, if anything, usually evidence that the leader has been functioning well. An understanding of this second paradoxical characteristic of leadership triangles may be more crucial to successful leadership than getting people going in the first place. Indeed, learning how to deal effectively with this aspect of leadership may be more important than vision, intelligence, wisdom, perspicacity, self-starting ability, personality, persistence, or the right motivational techniques.

Interestingly, this second paradoxical characteristic of leadership triangles—active sabotage—is identical in both the political and counseling processes. And that suggests that there is something basic to all human efforts to change or to resist being changed, irrespective of the context. In the therapeutic form of the paradox, the counselee comes in and says, "I have such and such a problem. I want you to help me with it but . . ."—this is the part of the contract that is never spelled out— "I will do everything I can to prevent you from succeeding." When this kind of resistance shows up in the counseling process, it tends to be attributed to the client's personality conflicts and seems proof that the person is "screwed up" because he or she wouldn't otherwise have sought help.

However, exactly the same paradoxical resistance shows up in political leadership, and, therefore, cannot be so easily explained away as simply a quirk or a neurotic tendency. And political contracts contain the same unwritten clause. People choose leaders because they promise to lead them to a happier or more fruitful state, but after the election, the followers invariably function, either individually or in concert, to frustrate their leaders' efforts. This is as true with Congress as with the Presidium; in Parliament as in any church or synagogue.

This similarity in the political and the counseling contracts not only suggests that the triangles of "family" leadership are rooted in some fundamental aspect of the human phenomenon rather than in the specific context; it also suggests that a leadership approach that could successfully keep the leader detriangled would have equal significance for any type of emotional system.

LEADERSHIP AND THE CHARISMA-CONSENSUS CONTINUUM

Almost all approaches to the aims of leadership—for example, promoting the welfare of a community and moving that community toward a mutually desired goal—falls somewhere along a continuum marked at one end by charisma and at the other by consensus. The focus of charisma tends to be on the personality of the leader; the focus of consensus tends to be on the will of the followers. Each approach has its advantages and disadvantages. Neither, despite the fact that they come from diametrically opposite directions, tends to be very successful in resolving the aforementioned paradoxes of leadership triangles: (1) that continued efforts to change others tends to prevent change and (2) that followers tend to increase their resistance precisely when their leader is functioning best. A major reason that the charisma and consensus approaches to leadership are so ineffective in resolving these paradoxical aspects of the leadership triangle is that they are both based on an individual model, where the paradoxes are essentially due to homeostatic phenomena (and not to personality conflicts). The family approach to leadership, precisely because it is systemic, offers a more effective, less enervating way of dealing with such resistance to change because it considers the paradoxes of resistance not as something blocking effective leadership but, rather, as part and parcel of the leadership process itself. From the point of view of leadership through self-differentiation, the resistance in leadership triangles is not simply some obstacle to be overcome. It is, rather, the key to the kingdom.

The specific manner in which family systems theory deals with such resistance, however, cannot be separated from other basic elements in its overall theory of leadership. Before explaining this organic approach more fully, therefore, it is important to explore further the thinking that is characteristic of the charisma and consensus leadership philosophies, as well as some of their pitfalls. This will help delineate the problems of leadership that are universal to all families and provide a background for sharpening the contrast between the individual-model approach and the family systems approach.

CHARISMA

Those who champion the charismatic approach to leadership try to make the most out of that indefinable, magnetic, personally attractive quality that is exuded by certain people. While anyone in a leadership position may have all of these qualities attributed to him or her, most individuals in leadership positions do possess some. Charisma does not seem to be a "trait" that can be taught, only cultivated; and if the evidence from ethology is relevant, the quality of charisma might even have a genetic component. The charismatic style of leadership can bring about dramatic changes: It can unify disparate elements within a system, infect with contagious enthusiasm, galvanize a family into quick action, take an emotional system that has been down in the doldrums and lift it rapidly to great heights, and in a short period of time produce an efficient organization that moves as one toward a clearly articulated goal. It seems to work best, however, when the relationship system is despondent, helpless, confused, and hungry for change; and it seems to be most appealing when the family members are in need of a stimulator beyond themselves. Demagoguery, whether it is political, religious, or therapeutic, is always most attractive in a "depression."

Some of the problems with a charismatic approach are as follows: (1) It can polarize as well as unify because the emphasis on the personality of the leader tends to personalize the issues facing the family, with the result that emotions and issues become harder to separate from one another. (2) It can create polarization between the family itself and all other relationship systems. Where charismatic leadership does succeed in unifying a family, the results tend toward homogeneity. The group, thus, often comes to define itself by opposition to other groups. This paranoid quality is the major emotional characteristic of all cults, whether they are religious, therapeutic, or political. (3) Leadership by charisma has difficulty with succession. Families or historical movements that become too dependent on their leaders tend to lose their purpose after the loss of such leaders. Sometimes another replacement can be found, but this will rarely continue for more than two or three "generations," and, as is always the case with the replacement phenomenon, when an unresolved issue that has long been avoided finally does surface, it will usually be all the more severe. (4) Leadership by charimsa ultimately is not healthy for the leader. He or she is perpetually forced to overfunction, most constantly balance all the triangles, and, in the long run, paradoxically finds that his or her functiioning has become dependent on having a family to lead. For all these reasons, and more, the charismatic leader remains in a chronic state of stress. (5) While charismatic leaders tend to be individualistic themselves, because of the high degree of emotional interdependency their style fosters, they tend to create clones among their followers rather than individuals. By some perverse logic, *individuality cannot be replicated by cloning, no matter how individualistic the organism that is being copied.*

This last point is most important when it comes to leadership in religious or personal families. If one is a political leader whose main goal is to stay in power, or a sales manager who has a proven technique for creating a successful sales force, the cloning effect of charisma is not a problem. On the contrary, it is the leader's dream. But the leader of a religious or personal family must be concerned with the growth process that goes beyond "votes" and "sales." Effective leadership in religious and personal family organizations, paradoxically, must be wary of too slavishly following the leader.

CONSENSUS

A counterpoint to the charisma philosophy of leadership is consensus. The strategies at this end of the leadership continuum, while designed to avoid the dilemmas of the opposite extreme, often wind up with similar effects. The basic emphasis in the consensus approach is on the will of the group. Consensus is prepared to wait longer for "results," being more concerned with the development of a cohesive infrastructure. It tends to value peace over progress and personal relationships (feelings) over ideas. It abhors polarization. In such a setting, the individualism of a leader is more likely to create anxiety than reduce it. Since the will of the group is supposed to develop out of its own personality, rather than come down from the top, the function of the leader becomes more that of a resource person or an "enabler."

Some of the basic problems with the consensus approach to leadership are as follows: (1) The family led by consensus will tend to be less imaginative. The major creative ideas of our species have tended to come from individuals rather than groups. Prophets are far more likely to hear "the call" in the wilderness. The muse rarely strikes the artist in a crowd. The world's most important ideas, philosophical, religious, and scientific, have tended to come to people in their own solitude. It is not that the consensus approach gives people less time to be alone but, rather, that it discourages the initiative to be solitary. (2) Leaderless groups are more easily panicked and the anxiety tends to cascade. The circuit-breaker effect of self is missing in an undifferentiated crowd. For all its advantages over autocracy, democracy can have a more difficult time dealing with anxiety when there is no self-differentiated individual who can say, "Here I stand!" (3) Emphasis on consensus gives strength to the extremists. They can continue to push the carrot of unity further out on the togetherness stick as the price of their cooperation. In some absurd turnaround, when the main goal of a family is consensus, they actually make it harder to achieve that goal because they put themselves in the position of being blackmailed by those least willing to cooperate. This is as true in marriage as in the vestry. (4) Consensus is no guarantee against xenophobia or polarization. The paranoid dangers of emotional interdependency enumerated in the charismatic approach are also present in consensus approach. An emotional system led by consensus can become equally cultic. Paradoxically, as a consensus-based approach to family leadership nears its goal, the degree of emotional fusion that results is likely to create or exacerbate the very problems its approach was designed to avoid.

LEADERSHIP THROUGH SELF-DIFFERENTIATION

In any field of endeavor, when different approaches produce similar results, something basic to the philosophy and methods of that field must be questioned. Some apparently fundamental division between these approaches is probably a false dichotomy. Change in such circumstances requires not "trying harder" to define the distinctions but rather rethinking the basic conceptualization that produced those seemingly opposing philosophies to begin with. Family theory does exactly that with the concept of self in leadership. The false dichotomy in the charisma–consensus continuum is the division between the relationship system of a family and the self of its leader, between a body and its head (soul). Thinking about leadership on a charisma–consensus continuum tends to go either in the direction of a leader who stands out from the group or in the direction of a leader who blends himself or herself in with the group. Criticism of leadership failures tends to go in the direction of a leader who has exerted himself or herself too much or a leader who has exerted himself or herself too little.

In contrast, a family systems perspective does not create this polarity between leader and follower. Instead, it focuses on the organic nature of their relationship as constituent parts of the same organism. Avoided once more is linear thinking where A causes B, that is, where a leader motivates a follower or a follower resists a leader. Instead of viewing the interactions of leaders and followers as the impact each has upon the other, a family systems concept of leadership looks at how they function as *part* of one another. The family systems approach to leadership thus comes in at a tangent to the charisma–consensus continuum. At times it can appear to resemble either end, but its thinking is at a different level of inquiry. For example, like the charisma approach, it recognizes the importance of personal leadership, but it emphasizes the leader's *position* in the system rather than his or her personality. The responsibility of the leader therefore ceases to be the entire family, a heavy load indeed, and becomes, instead *the position of leadership.* Like the consensus approach, a family systems theory of leadership does not belittle the importance of an organization's coherence. But, because it distinguishes between togetherness and stuck-togetherness, it refuses to purchase the intactness of the group at the cost of the self-integrity of its members. Consensus, while it is an important accessory, is not considered a style of life.

The basic concept of leadership through self-differentiation is this: If a leader will take primary responsibility for his or her own position as "head" and work to define his or her own goals and self, while *staying in touch* with the rest of the organism, there is a more than reasonable chance that the body will follow. There may be initial resistance but, if the leader can stay in touch with the resisters, the body will usually go along.

This emphasis on a leader's self-differentiation is not to be confused with *independence* or some kind of selfish individuality. On the contrary, we are talking here about the ability of a leader to be a self while still remaining a part of the system. It is the most difficult thing in the world in any family. And yet, when accomplished, the process will convert the dependency that is the source of most sabotage to the leader's favor instead.

There are three distinct but interrelated components to leadership through self-differentiation, keeping in mind that successful leadership means not only moving a family toward its goals but also maximizing its functioning, as well as the health and survival of both the family and its leader. First and foremost, the leader must stay in touch. The concept is basically organic: For any part of an organism to have a continuous or lasting effect, it obviously must stay connected. This is not nearly as easy as it may seem. Remaining connected becomes increasingly difficult in direct proportion to the leader's success at defining his or her own being (the second component). It is far easier for a head to remain attached if it is content to merge its "self" with the body. Any leader can stay in touch if he or she does not try to stand out. The trick, as we shall see shortly, is to be able to differentiate self and still remain in touch despite the body's efforts to counter such differentiation.

The second central component is the capacity and willingness of the leader to take nonreactive, clearly conceived, and clearly defined positions. Again, this is easier to accomplish in isolation when the leader is not in touch with (or beholden to) the rest of the system. It is difficult even to think out such positions while attached, much less to function on the basis of those positions while still connected. Yet, and this is crucial, the functioning of any organism, often its survival, and certainly its evolution are directly dependent on the capacity of its "head" to do precisely that. *Define self and continue to stay in touch.* Note here, with regard to safeguarding against sabotage, that the leader is not trying to define the followers, only himself or herself. The triangle-potentiating approaches of motivating their "minds," or overcoming their resistance are thus bypassed; *it is their need for a head that will move them.* As was said, it is hardly that simple. The better self-defined followers will follow the lead of the leader and respond to his or her differentiation by taking their own nonreactive positions, which is not necessarily the same as simply agreeing. The more dependent followers, however, will initially react and try to retriangle the leader. (See Chapter 1, on the litmus paper test for assessing the capacity of various congregants to following a well-differentiated leader.)

It is here that we come to the importance of the third component in a family systems approach to leadership, the capacity to deal with the sabotage. The more poorly differentiated members of a family will be quickest to feel the pull-out when the head of the family tries to emerge from the undifferentiated state of the organism. What they feel will be at the deepest cellular level, because they have fused with their leader. It is almost as though they experience part of their own self being ripped away. Their response is unthinking, automatic, and always serious. It by-passes the "conscious" and is more biological than the "unconscious." It is like a twitch. It is instantaneous and, as with differentiation efforts in any marriage, the specific nature of the response tends to be that which succeeded in triangling the leader in the past, a reflexive effort to reestablish the old homeostasis.

But the leader cannot expect his or her followers to "understand." He or she, after all, is the leader. Here is the moment of truth; will the leader have the capacity to maintain his or her differentiation? This is not the same as being unwilling to compromise or move back a little. A reciprocal, unthinking "twitch" on a leader's part will cause him or her to forget both goals and purpose. It will return the organism to its previously undifferentiated state, and no evolution will result. Similarly, any leader can maintain his or her position by taking a rigid dogmatic stand or by cutting himself or herself off, but from that moment on, the leader is no longer a leader, only a head. Furthermore, cutting off perpetuates triangles, despite the illusion that it makes them disappear. It is in the capacity of the leader to maintain a position and still stay in touch that the organism's potential growth resides. Crucial here is the leader's capacity to distinguish process from content, and the ability to be playful, that is, not serious or anxiously helpful. Many leaders have the capacity to stay in touch, fewer leaders have the capacity to differentiate their selves, fewest have the capacity to remain connected while maintaining self-differentiation. It is the most difficult part of leading a family, personal or congregational. It may be important to note here that because the concept of leadership through self-differentiation is an organic one, size is not an important factor. The head of an elephant has as much influence on its body as the head of a chinchilla. Actually, while churches and synagogues may differ widely in size of their congregations, they are remarkably similar in the number of lay leadership positions.

SELF-DIFFERENTIATION AND THE TRIANGLES OF RESISTANCE

Leadership through self-differentiation has a significantly different effect on the paradoxes of resistance than do the models of leadership through charisma or consensus. It eliminates the leverage of the dependent; it reduces conflict of wills; and it accomplishes these without increasing the potential for cloning.

The Leverage of the Dependent

A husband who was once asked, "Why do the dependent in any system seem to be in charge?" answered, "Because they have more investment in relationships." They are, thus, always ahead of the leader in this respect. While the better differentiated members of any family are putting more time into developing their own self, the more dependent are becoming experts on how to keep the better differentiated close, that is, less well-differentiated. (These are also the family members quickest to see themselves as victimized and, *ipso facto*, quickest to sue.)

Leadership through self-differentiation turns the tables. As long as the leader is trying to change his or her followers, the latter are in the "cat-bird's seat." As long as the head, or the rest of the body, makes its functioning dependent on the other's functioning, the organism is in their control. But when the leader is concentrating on where he or she is "headed," the effects of that dependency are reversed. It is the dependents who now feel the pressure. The ball is in their court. The need of the more dependent for a leader now encourages them to follow through because they now fear losing the game by default! The same emotional interdependency that requires all flocks and herds to have leaders in order to function effectively is now put to the service of leadership. The triangle remains but the power flow shifts. It is the leader who may now become the *resistant* one as he or she, instead of having to work to change others, now works to resist their efforts to change him or her back! Not easy, but far less stressful since it is a position inherently less susceptible to overfunctioning, sabotage, or burnout.

Some may regard this as manipulation or as acting unilaterally. But if leaders want progress, in choosing between the poles of individuality and togetherness, they had better err in the direction of the former, lest they be the ones who are manipulated. Some may think this borders on narcissism, but those who cannot distinguish self-differentiation from narcissism have no comprehension of the dilemmas or the value of leadership. They have confused pathology with power and the healing potential of properly self-conceived power. When spiritual leaders must defend time-hallowed traditions from the onslaught of contemporary backsliding and erosion, all the while jeopardizing their jobs, health, families, and resolve, it is time for a healthy infusion of what those who fear such strength mistake for narcissism, or they are not very likely to survive. But unilateralism is less likely to be narcissistic if the leader is also taking care to remain connected. That is once again the difference between *differentiation* and "in-dependence." It is independence or autonomy, without staying in touch, that is most likely to end in divorce.

Reduction of Conflict of Wills

Because leadership through self-differentiation focuses on the self-expression of the leader, it tends to sidestep the conflict of wills that is so often a by-product of the charisma and consensus approaches. It thus tends to avoid the different, yet twinned, results typical of such conflict: polarization or cultic togetherness. After all, what creates polarization is not the actual content of the issue on which a family "splits." It is rather the emotional processes that foster conflict of wills (efforts to convert one another). To the extent a leader can contain his or her own reactiveness to the reactivity of followers, principally by focusing on self-functioning rather than by trying to change the functioning of others, intensity tends to wane, and polarization or a cut-off that, like a tango, always takes two, is less likely to be the result.

From another angle, what creates cultic togetherness in a family is either the leader surrendering his or her will to the group, which deprives the entire system of the leaven of individuation, or the leader successfully exerting his or her will over the will of the followers, and then using the fostered emotional interdependency to keep the family "unified." Where the leader's primary concern is self-differentiation neither of these extremes is as likely to result.

Sometimes leadership through self-differentiation can appear to have a homogenizing effect if it keeps the followers following, but it tends to be a *differentiated* following. For, as long as the choice to follow or quit has been allowed, the leader has *challenged* the followers to define themselves, in particular, to decide whether to go along, quit, or find a new leader. Since a self is always more attractive than a "no-self," in an atmosphere free of emotional coercion, whether that follower is child, spouse, or member of the congregation, he or she is far more likely to follow (after struggle and sabotage, perhaps) rather than quit, provided that the leader remains connected.

Disciples versus Clones

The notion of differentiated following has important theological consequences. Were the problems of family leadership simply a matter of getting congregational members to go along, then the will of the leader and the right motivational techniques would be the paramount factors in overcoming resistance. But, as mentioned earlier, for personal families and religious families, there is also the matter of "soul."

It is perhaps only when this balance between achieving goals and promoting growth is emphasized that the full value of leadership through self-differentiation can be appreciated, because it lines up the leader with what has worked throughout the ages to advance the evolution of our species and the image of our Creator. It is formation through the self-actualizing process of response to challenge rather than turning out copies from a mold. A leader (parent or spiritual) who is simply out to replicate his or her followers, as successful as the outcomes might appear, would be like a god who clones his or her image.

This means, of course, that leaders have an obligation, to their family (following), to their Creator, and to their species, to keep working at their own self-differentiation. That, indeed, is leadership's basic challenge. When leaders accept that challenge, they automatically challenge their followers to do the same and, thus, maximize the process of self-differentiation throughout the entire family. (Perhaps it was the first god in an ancient pantheon to accept that challenge who succeeded in creating monotheism.)

The leader who accepts this model of leadership not only creates in God's image, he or she images God's model for creation. The evolution of our species, physically and morally, has been as dependent on the development of its strengths as on the elimination of its weaknesses. Leadership through self-differentiation thus puts the leader more on the side of the continuing evolution of our species than does leadership by charisma or consensus. It is focused on the preservation of our species' strengths *as carried by, that is, embodied in, the leader*, whether originally implanted within the species by biological imperative or divine interference (or divine interference by means of biological imperative).

Obviously, this is not a philosophy that opposes care and concern for others. The nature of the human phenomenon is that the more differentiated the self (i.e., the connected self), the more natural such care and concern becomes. It tends, however, to be a more objective caring and concern for others when it is derived from an attitude that also maintains caring and concern for oneself. It is in this sense that being "self-ish" is in the service of the family. And it is in this sense, most of all, that in any family, human or divine, the functioning of the members depends primarily on the functioning (which includes the thinking) of the being "at the top."

For the clergy especially, leadership capacity is often enriched or hindered by their position in the hierarchy of their own family of origin. Just how the triangles in these two systems link up will be described in the next section. Here, first, are two examples of the application of leadership through self-differentiation to congregational families.

CONGREGATIONAL LEADERSHIP THROUGH SELF-DIFFERENTIATION

In 1974, a congregation that I had led from its inception in 1964 nearly collapsed as a result of decreasing leadership on my part over the previous few years. What follows is a description of my efforts to get that family going again without repeating the mistake of making its functioning so dependent on my functioning.

A LEADERSHIP CRISIS IN A SYNAGOGUE

The congregation was begun in 1964 by 20 families, most of whom had belonged to another congregation that I had served for the previous 5 years. All had gone well in my previous "match" (1959–1964) for the first 2 years, and then took a sharp drop after I was married during the 3rd year. By the 5th year, that first congregation was rent with dissension that eventually resulted in a huge fight and my expulsion. Throughout that period I had been in psychoanalysis.

The initial arrangement in '64 was that I would be part-time. At first, my other occupation was as a community relations specialist for the White House on matters relating to fair housing. But for the most part, I did family counseling. We all thought that the part-time idea would reduce the well-known intensity of clergy–congregational relationships, most of the congregation having experienced the bitterness of the recent "divorce."

For the first 6 years everything in our new "family" went uphill. Many creative ideas and innovative programs were introduced; the pioneering attitude created camaraderie. All business meetings were marked by a looseness that manifested itself in the humor and playful character of the dialogue between the members themselves and with the rabbi. In the 7th year, tired from two jobs that had both become larger, I asked for a sabbatical and was shocked by the members' refusal. In the 8th year the request was made again; it was met with comments that this "unaffiliated" group that did not have its own building (we rented space in a church) needed its rabbi around more than others.

Much like a disaffected marriage partner reacting to the overdependency of a spouse, I continued to go through the motions. But I became increasingly bored. My emotional energy went more into my training for, and practice of, family psychotherapy. Unwittingly, I was pulling myself out of the relationship system of the congregation. And then, as in a marriage, my "partner" responded to my withdrawal by henpecking. I came under more and more criticism, and the general tone of the whole congregation went "serious." Most of those in lay leadership positions at that point had originally gravitated toward one another during a congregational retreat, and, shades of courtship and marriage, had developed false expectations during the intensity of that weekend about how close a relationship they could always expect to have with their spiritual leader. Many of these same members now wanted me to leave, and some wanted to "merge" the congregation out of existence. By the 10th year, board meetings were marked by a terrible seriousness over the smallest points, great pessimism about the congregation's future, and the kind of increasing collective anxiety that bordered on outright panic.

At this point, some of the board members, who were not as totally caught up in the emotional maelstrom, came to me and said: "Frankly, we do not think the congregation can survive [this critical illness] unless you assume the kind of leadership role you had in the early years." I wanted more time to write, and I knew their suggestion meant at least 1 full year's effort and probably 2. Moreover, to get it started, I would have to get past the hostility in the present lay leadership, and I wondered what was the point if the symptom was bound to recycle when I became overworked again.

After several days of inner turmoil, I decided to try it. I had invested a lot of effort over the years and I did not want the whole decade ending with a massive failure. In addition, I had just begun to formulate the possible application of family systems ideas to organizational "family" life. Here was an opportunity, I thought, to put my beliefs to the test, though I had no idea at the time that with congregational families also, critical illness could become a rite of passage with all that portends for change in a family.

Since I was becoming aware at this time of the interlocking triangles concept, I also made sure to discuss with my wife how reinvolvement in the congregational family could affect our nuclear family. After all, the congregation's own homeostasis had been disturbed by my emotional energy being directed away from them. Awareness of this rebalancing would not guarantee calm at home, but it certainly would help us to weather the expectable storms.

There were also some homeostatic changes that occurred around this time in my family of origin which may have affected my new leadership style. My initial decision to go into the rabbinate was connected to my relationship with my grandmother. I was born 6 months before her husband died, and shortly thereafter my maternal grandmother came to live with us, and we kind of "grew up together." She became the primary influence on my Jewish identity, her father, my great-grandfather, having been a Jewish scholar in Europe. Since I had just made major changes in my relationship with my mother around the time the congregation verged on collapse, I believe that my reentry into the congregation came at a time when I was freer to function differently. The universality of this type of interlocking connection for all clergy will be explored further in Chapter 12.

The Process of Change

The first step, as I saw it, was to create an opportunity that would immediately get me back in touch with the relationship system of the congregational family. I accomplished this by personally phoning almost 80 percent of the congregation and inviting four or five couples at a time to small parlor meetings at my house. At each of these meetings I began by talking about the crisis in the congregation, what I perceived my own role to be in the development of the crisis, and invited everyone to speak his or her mind. Some of this, of course, came up spontaneously in each invitational phone call.

At every meeting I sat with a large yellow pad and made notes of every critical comment and helpful suggestion. As the meetings went on, I was able to inform later groups of what had been said at previous meetings and found that, in the notetaking process, I myself was beginning to get new ideas, which I also included. After the last gathering, I put all my notes into coherent order, and a week before the annual congregational meeting, when it would decide on its own future, I sent out a 24-page report so that those who had come to the earlier meetings would be as informed as those who came to the later ones. In effect, I used my position in the relationship system to catalyze self-definition in much the same manner as described previously in Chapter 3.

In only one way did I consciously try to manipulate this process. At the small meetings I had made sure that families who were extremist in their views on the saving of money, or on the hopelessness of the future, were not overrepresented in any group because I believed that they would reinforce each other's anxiety and carry some of the less extreme members. The purpose of these meetings had not been to promote catharsis. That would have been manipulation, as well as taking away an important stimulus for change—pain! I had begun to realize that the quicker leaders (or therapists) are to relieve their followers' pain, the less real change they will bring to the system. Catharsis can be a very manipulative way of preserving the *status quo*.

My meetings with the general membership, however, were only one part of the process. There was still the board of trustees, about equally divided on whether or not to recommend an end to the congregation. If I had lost touch with the larger congregation, so had this part of the family. After a few of the at-home meetings, I could see that the vast majority of the congregation wanted itself to survive, but I wished to avoid the kind of split and bitterness that I had come to see as the "original sin" for the creation of new congregations. Any recommendation to end the congregation would have been defeated at the annual meeting, but it seemed almost as important not to have such a recommendation come from the board. I therefore did the following with that portion of the congregational family.

At the next board meeting, I announced my renewed commitment to keep the congregation functioning and told them about the small parlor meetings I had begun. (Some of the board members, of course, had already been called.) At this meeting, which was to approve the budget for the next year, the mood was one of deep pessimism. Everyone kept looking for an item to cut; everyone kept worrying how the membership was going down and how the deficit would get bigger. As each person spoke, the dreary atmosphere thickened and the anxiety increased. Any effort on my part to suggest that cutting this or that item would hurt the quality of programs was futile.

When everyone was through cutting and pruning, I said I wanted to make a different suggestion. Instead of defending the budget against the cuts, I paradoxically suggested that the original budget be *increased* by 25 percent. I told them that I thought their solution was defensive and could only lead to self-defeating consequences. Since I was now doing what they complained I hadn't done—exert leadership—it would never work without (I pulled the word from nowhere) an "aggressive" budget. To my utter shock, the dominoes stopped falling, and one by one everyone agreed, though everyone was also unwilling to take responsibility for such a recommendation. The final result was the preparation of two different budgets that were then mailed out to the congregation for the membership to decide. It is interesting to compare the board's failure to take a stand with Eisenhower's responsible act after deciding to proceed with "Operation Overlord." He sat down as the other officers (who were divided in their views) left the room and reportedly scribbled a telegram something like this: "Allied forces attempted a landing today in Normandy and were repulsed with heavy losses. The full responsibility for that decision rests on my shoulders alone." That telegram represents the kind of responsible leadership that helps assure success. This board was just not up to it.

I was now beginning to conceive of the congregation in terms of a nuclear family (the board) and an extended system (the membership). I knew from my work with troubled families that if members of a nuclear family will change their relationship with members of the extended system, a change in their relationships with one another will follow.

I therefore set about trying to change the emotional climate within the board by creating triangles either between myself and two board members or between myself, a member of the nuclear (board) family, and a member of the extended system at large. I also started to feed back anger. While I am not opposed to confrontation, I think it is rarely effective in bringing lasting change. Also, I did not want to increase polarization with emotional confrontations. What I did, therefore, was to use the congregation's gossip system to tell one member how angry I was about the behavior of another. I avoided commenting on personality. The one word I kept using over and over was *irresponsible*. Months later, people told me how they had never seen me so angry, and all seemed to be able to say it in a way that showed they had not reacted in kind to my anger but only had been motivated by it. My message about responsibility was thus heard.

There was still, however, a key decision to be taken by the board on whether or not to recommend the continuance of the congregation and/or my leadership. This nuclear group was evenly divided, but too many of those on the continuance side were silent types, all the vocal opinions coming from the dissolution side. In addition, the president, the man at the top, while a very liberal thinker and one who tried to be fair, was simply too weak to carry the day. His liberalism, which strove for consensus, always gave strength to the extremists on the board. He obviously did not realize that reasonableness is a highly inadequate tool for change in anxious systems. Since in my family counseling practice I was increasingly successful in effecting change by not seeing the whole family together and never bothering to see those most resistant to change, I made no attempt to deal with the board as a group, or to assuage the hostility, and in some cases downright pathology, of some of the members. Instead, I singled out those who I thought had strength, and went to them individually. I told them how important I thought it was, despite the fact that it was not usually their style, to speak up and circuit-break the kind of anxious feedback that tends to get going "in this family."

I also tried to do this with the man "at the top." He tried to be cordial, but the more we spoke, the more provocative he became, slipping in such comments as, "Ed, didn't all this happen to you at a previous congregation?" I managed to dodge all this content and get to my process reason for wanting to see him. I said something like this: "I know you pride yourself on being fair and keeping an open mind, but I believe a leader has an obligation to speak his position. I believe that if you run that meeting as you envision democracy is run, by letting everyone speak his mind without taking a position yourself, the congregation will be split." "For," I added, "I believe that in times of high anxiety, a consensus approach is absolutely pernicious." He responded that he had never thought of things that way, but he did not seem particularly convinced.

It was later reported to me that at the crucial board meeting, after giving everyone a chance to speak, he got up and said: "I don't know how the rest of you are going to vote, and I'm not going to try to change your minds, but as for me, given what the rabbi has already begun, I don't see how we can fail to give him the opportunity." Whereupon, the man at the top having defined himself, one of the typically silent members of the board, stood up and said, "I think this focus on Ed Friedman is bullshit. He's not the problem; it's the board that has the problem."

At the annual general membership meeting, the whole package, program and budget, passed with one dissenting vote (cast by the vice president in line for the presidency who had been passed over by the new nominating committee).

At the last of the parlor get-togethers, just before the annual meeting of the entire congregation family, one of the members had said to me, "Things are starting to look good. I sure hope they accept it." My response then was: "This is the 17th small meeting; we've involved 75 percent of the congregation; there's no more *they*."

One incident that occurred during this period is worth noting because of the light it sheds on the interlocking of family emotional processes. A very rigid member of the board, who was most paranoid about the future of the congregational family, had been having severe difficulties with his own family. During this period, his (adaptive) wife's mother died, and when I went to pay a condolence call I could see immediately that this woman, now relieved of the dependency of her mother, was going to function more independently. Deciding that I should not let my personal feelings about her husband interfere, I told her that if they wanted to get a grasp on the kind of emotional processes that could be released by this change in their family system, I would be glad to give them the benefit of my counseling experience.

It was the stupidest thing I could have done. I had no way of knowing how my message would get relayed to his part of the triangle and how she might use me in her marital struggle. All I know is that he came to the next board meeting with his hostility increased tenfold. Luckily, it worked against him because everyone was aghast at his intensity.

I did one other thing during those days that probably should be mentioned because it runs so contrary to the preservation-of-togetherness instinct of leaders in crisis. Whenever I saw one of the members who had been most critical of my functioning at a congregational gathering, I went out of my way to express precisely those positions in which I believed most strongly and with which he or she most disagreed. I did not do it in pointed ways but always as a self-expression of my own views on life. Most of the ten or so families comprising this group quietly left the congregation, and joined others more to their style.

The New Family System

At the annual meeting, a key statement echoing the president's remark to the board was, "If the rabbi is willing to commit himself this much, we have got to back him." While that comment helped galvanize the membership into a community, it was also a trap. I wanted them to function for themselves, not for me. To accomplish a leadership style that would avoid this pitfall, for the rest of the year I concentrated on three things: (1) I stayed in touch with the relationship system, for example, weekly or biweekly contacts with all lay leaders (committee chairmen, board members, and other influential members). (2) At every public opportunity I kept defining myself: what I believed, where I stood, what I would do and not do. (3) I made every effort not to rush in and take up the slack when things faltered, but, rather, tried to "defect in place." And here we come full circle to what created the problem originally. I had learned that this works only if one can default and at the same time stay in the relationship system. It is defaulting by withdrawal that is likely to produce collapse.

I think it is fair to say that I never "did" so little while getting so much credit for all the congregation's accomplishments. Whereas in the previous years I had been responding to all the critical comments by trying harder, at times to the point of exhaustion, now I was "doing" much less of the things I had hitherto been criticized for, yet being praised for everything that was happening. Talk about process and content!

At the end of that year, another process occurred that I had failed to accomplish through years of content focusing. As part of the renewal going on in the congregation, the constitution was being rewritten. I had always felt that it did not protect the rabbi sufficiently. I myself was particularly sensitive to the issue because of my own bitter experience with my first congregation in which the constitution had stated that for the rabbi to continue from year to year, two-thirds (not a simple majority) of the board had to agree, irrespective of the wishes of the congregation. That provision, in turn, had been conceived as a direct result of that congregation's previous experience with what they had thought to be a constitution that gave another rabbi too much power, a rabbi they had failed to expel. This year I had been too focused elsewhere to become very involved in the consitutional revision process, making only some innocuous suggestions when asked about the rabbi clause. To my utter shock, the congregation passed without incident a section so strong as almost to install me as emperor. And it came at a time when I no longer seemed to care!

The following year was extraordinary in two respects. First, the enthusiasm and playfulness of the earlier years was back. Everyone was looser in his or her relationships, and the programming was more imaginative than I had ever seen. We also seemed to have a new perspective on ourselves and our surroundings. Previously, we had not done very much to make ourselves better known in the community. We did a lot of that all year, and the following autumn the congregation grew by almost 40 percent. Talk about rites of passage!

The second extraordinary feature of that year consisted of two events that could have sent any congregation into a severe crisis, certainly one that was already tottering. They also illustrate dramatically the primacy of process over content.

First, the budget deficit reached one-third of the total budget. Second, a key officer, who was doing a terrific job, suddenly became erratic, left his wife, and within a month wound up in a psychiatric hospital, from which he continued to try to lead the congregation through random phone calls. Since general anxiety was low, neither event caused more than a ripple. With regard to the deficit, the board, laughing all the way about our demise, called a congregational meeting, announced the need for an immediate assessment, and raised dues for the coming year. Few people came to the meeting, and the assessment passed without objection. Everyone gave willingly.

The officer's dysfunction was more complicated. Board members did not want to assume his responsibility in case he might suddenly reappear and try to change their directions. Several (therapists) on the board began worrying that we would be undercutting his confidence by taking away his job. At this point I took a position. I said I thought the board's primary responsibility was the survival of the congregation. Several lawyers picked it up from there and the transition was smooth. (After leaving town for a while, the officer returned the following year and came back to a leadership position.) *In an emotional atmosphere that is calm and positive, issues that under other circumstances could be lethal are handled objectively.* That is true with all families.

Five years later I resigned from the congregation in order to have more time to write. The story will be picked up again at that point in the next chapter, which describes the application of family systems theory to congregational family transitions. Finally, one other incident is worth noting since it reflects on the interlocking triangles that always exist between the clergy's congregational and personal families. My daughter, aged 11 at the time, had always received nearly perfect marks in spelling, although her understanding of the reading material did not always come easily. During this period when I was learning how to focus more on process than on content, I suddenly realized that her marks in spelling had gone down, but that her grades in reading comprehension had soared.

A LEADERSHIP CRISIS IN A CHURCH

The Fellowship of Reconciliation Church had become deeply disturbed over its spiritual stagnation. Once known for its leadership in civic causes, it seemed to have grown fatigued. The lay leadership had always enjoyed the friendliest of relationships, but back-biting and distancing had become rampant. Their minister, John Love, was in great pain because he could not explain what had happened. Try as he would, through stimulating sermons or taking up more of the slack, nothing had any lasting effect. In addition, he found himself having more personal difficulties with some of his parishioners.

Presented here will be three aspects of the "therapeutic" endeavor: (1) a description of the emotional history of this "family," including relevant facts in the personal lives of the minister, his wife, and two important members; (2) a verbatim transcript of one of the "family therapy" sessions I conducted that dramatizes the emotional processes between board members and their minister and between board members and board members; and (3) therapeutic coaching to promote differentiation between minister and wife, the latter with regard to her family of origin, the former with regard to all of his "functions."

Family History

The Fellowship of Reconciliation was begun 15 years prior to its crisis when two small groups in town merged after they had simultaneously lost their ministers. Soon after, Mr. Love, a native of the community, came to town directly from the seminary, and the two hit it off from the start. The first decade was Nirvana. The times cried out for a strong voice on Vietnam and civil rights, and their minister was eloquent on both. The times were also ripe for sensitivity to personal relationships, and the minister here too was a leader in "being open." He prided himself on being direct and encouraged others to be so with him. They had been considering buying a building when the minister personally inherited a five-acre site on the edge of the city. Never imagining that things could be different, he donated it lock, stock, and barrel to the congregation, with the sole request that he be allowed to live there.

Mrs. Love was also involved in the church, emotionally, physically, and intellectually. Her philosophical involvement came from her father, also a minister, who had founded a similar church in another city, and whose writings had deeply influenced her husband.

The vestry contained 15 members, nine individuals and three couples; almost all had been members from the beginning. They were close generally and often socialized outside the congregation. One of the members who had become critical of Mr. Love had had a romantic involvement with one of the other board members before she married her present husband, also on the board. The two male members got on famously.

Two years previous to the present crisis, Mrs. Love's venerable father died, and 1 year later the Loves had a baby after years of unsuccessful efforts.

As a way of introducing the lay leaders to systemic thinking about congregational family problems in a nonpointed way, it was arranged for me to give a general talk on family process before the entire congregation. The presentation was directed at general family problems but laid the theoretical basis for our work together. Two weeks after that presentation, the vestry had its first "family therapy" session.

A Congregational Family Session

AUTHOR: I understand you all have been together a long time, and that many of you are perplexed as to how things got this way. My own experience is that one can't pick up an entire family and just move it; one has to start with the individual relationships, the dyads, and triads. Definition on that level eventually works similar changes throughout the larger system. So really we can begin anywhere.

LISA: Well, I'll start. John, I feel extreme anger toward you. The other day when I was questioning your salary, what I was after was what do we pay you for? You say it's spiritual leadership, but I think it's your administrative functioning—but—it's your response (*almost in tears*). The way you answered was so condescending, "It's in the charter, you know." I resent being treated that way.

MRS. LOVE: (*to the rescue*) Lisa, you're taking that out of context. When John referred to the charter, he was . . .

243

AUTHOR: (*rescuing the rescuer*) Mrs. Love, what would John do without you to rescue him from these aggressive females?

(*General laughter.*)

MRS. LOVE: You're right. He's quite capable of fighting his own battles.

LISA: What I resent is the inference that you make all the sacrifices. I'm doing it too. I'm a prime note holder, you know. There's too much dependency on John. We are all expected to give too much. We oversacrifice, and still we're not pure enough.

AUTHOR: Lisa, why does John have so much power to "condescend" you?

LISA: I pick it up with a fine-tooth comb, but it is particularly him. He's been too self-sacrificing.

JOE: This is a sleeping giant. We're terribly dependent on him, but he's dependent too, only he never owns up to it.

AL: We've been trying to transfer power to a committee, and it's unnerved us all. I tried to make one small point the other day and I got attacked by the whole group. But I agree with Lisa, John doesn't make it easier with his "holier than thou" attitude.

AUTHOR: Could you give an example?

AL: John, you deserve compassion but not special treatment.

BILL: I agree.

HARRIET: He expects too much from us.

AUTHOR: (*paradoxically*) Well, after what he did for this church how could any of you ever compare the gifts of your own hands and spirit?

SEVERAL: Boy, did you hit it! . . . That's what we were talking about the other night. . . . Now we're down to it! . . . Sometimes I think that myself.

AUTHOR: (*intended playfully*) Well, if it's such a burden, why not give it back?

HARRIET: That's a terrific question. I would feel incredible relief. I wouldn't have to spend my lifetime making up for it.

JOE: It would be possible to be clean again.

AUTHOR: He could rent it out to you on some semicommercial basis.

AL: He's the spiritual leader; he can't do that.

AUTHOR: What I'm really after is why does it follow that because John was so magnanimous, everyone has to treat him with kid gloves.

JOE: That's not the only issue. Maybe it's not even the real issue. I'm afraid he might shatter.

AUTHOR: How does he convey such fragility?

JOE: He's always hurt. He claims he's open, but somehow when he says it, it's very guilting.

AUTHOR: How does he convey this "hurt"?

JOE: He says so. But it's more—like the other night. Things got hot and heavy and afterwards he said he wasn't feeling well, and went home early.

HARRIET: I felt bad. I said to myself, God what did we do? He has a right to be hurt, but I hear, "you did it to me." At least, John, if you said, "I'm P.O.'d," then there'd be a chance.

AUTHOR: You know, it's difficult to verify feelings of others. Body language and voice tones are pretty slippery stuff; you never can be sure what you might be reading into the other's mind. So I was wondering what would happen if the next time you perceived John to be blaming, you responded with something like, "If you're hurt now, John, wait till you see what I've got planned next week."

(Dead, stupified silence.)

LISA: I can't even deal with the concept.

JOE: If we did that, "See what I do to you next week," it would be overwhelming sin. The resulting self-condemnation would be unbearable.

AUTHOR: Well, you could always lower his salary while you were saying it.

AL: It's not only that John wants special status; we want him to have it.

AUTHOR: John, how do you handle this double message? "We don't think the spiritual leader should get special treatment, but we rely on him being special."

JOHN: I don't know, but I'm working on it.

AUTHOR: Good luck.

AL: I see John as 10 feet tall. It's very threatening. I see him as punishing.

AUTHOR: You could put a 3-year-old in the White House and he's got the "aura."

AL: That's not the problem. The problem is his bewilderment. John, we want you to be special, but you also want it. You love it! So stop being so damn bewildered by it.

JOHN: I feel trapped. I'm beginning to wonder if this leadership trip is worth it. But I don't know how to get out of it. When they talk about me that way, it doesn't sound like me.

AUTHOR: But they say you love it.

JOHN: Sometimes I do. Sometimes I want to be 10 feet tall. I guess I wish I could have one without the other.

AUTHOR: If you figure that out you can bottle it.

AL: I don't know if this helps, but I've been feeling depressed and torn, and when you said, "Give the inheritance back," I felt a ray of hope. The obligation is overwhelming.

AUTHOR: How much of the burden is financial and how much emotional? I mean, is it the drain or resources?

HARRIET: Both.

AUTHOR: Well, if it's financial, sell it. And if it's emotional, what are the other issues?

JOE: We have to deal with the emotional ones first. John, when you said that part of you wants to be 10 feet tall, that was terribly releasing. It was a ray of sanity. If you had said only the first half, I'd have gone away feeling nuts. You owned it.

AUTHOR: Any of you got an idea about what in your own background makes it so important to have John "own it"?

LISA: I do. My mother sacrificed all her life. I could never repay it, even if I made that the goal of my entire life. She never got angry and said "Stop!"

JOHN: But I don't see myself as sacrificing. It's the way I live, and I love it.

LISA: Well, I'll never feel I could do enough.

AUTHOR: Isn't it amazing how little control we have of the ways we "control" others. You know, the stuff going on here is absolutely universal. Ever read Golding's *Lord of the Flies*? Sweet naive kids sent to a small out-of-the-way island to avoid an imminent nuclear holocaust, and they recreate in that idyllic setting the same society as their adults.

HARRIET: You mean, "*Love* is not enough?"

AUTHOR: "Lord of the Flies" in Hebrew is *Baal-zvuv*—Beelzebub.

AL: That's really scary. After protesting Vietnam—on the verge of our own Vietnam.

AUTHOR: Al, you were talking about John's humility but saying he always sounded like a victim. Did the rest of you hear it that way also?

SEVERAL: Not at all.

JOE: I did. John, I have trouble experiencing you as vulnerable.

AUTHOR: Well, which would you all prefer, that he be more humble or that he be more arrogant?

AL: Depends on who you are talking to.

HARRIET: And when.

LISA: My heart goes out to him more easily when he is more vulnerable. Yet I know he's holding this place together. I want him to be—5 feet 10 and a half!

HARRIET: But if he comes down to size, we'll fall apart; the future of this church depends on him.

AUTHOR: I'd like to switch directions for the remaining time. We've been focusing on this family's problems from the point of view of the kids and their parent. I was wondering how the "sibling" relationship might be affecting this family also.

HARRIET: Al, last year you were saying many of the same things John is saying now.

JOE: Maybe we need a victim.

BARBARA: I feel frightened when you want to shift the focus like this. I never was close to my sister; the only togetherness we got was by talking about our parents. Now that mother is dead we hardly ever talk at all.

AUTHOR: Usually when two talk about a third they're uncomfortable with one another. Of course, if people didn't have presidents and ministers to "cat" about, there'd be an awful lot of dull cocktail parties.

JOE: Well, there's no denying we've had our issues with one another—romance, jealousy, money, jealousy, being close to John, jealousy.

AL: If John leaves we'd fall apart. It would be anarchy—we'd shoot off into space. He's the antichaos figure.

JOE: He's right. We tried to meet without him, but after a few sessions the cohesion fell apart . . .

LISA: I'm furious! Look what just happened: you guys are afraid; Barbara started us on a new track. We were going to talk about our relationships with one another and you shot it back to John.

AUTHOR: I think it's striking how much easier it is for all of you to be articulate when you are expressing your feelings about John than when you are talking to one another. My suggestion—if you are willing—is to have another meeting like this one in a couple of weeks but without "Mom" and "Dad," just the "sibs."

Coaching the Ministerial Nuclear Family

In the sessions with Mr. and Mrs. Love, the emphasis was on their own emotional interdependencies, what the coming of their baby meant for the homeostasis in their nuclear family, and the effect of this shift on the congregational family. Mr. Love said he thought he could do without all her investment, but Mrs. Love did not find it that easy to disengage. Mrs. Love was seen separately in an effort to help her refocus her energies.

The youngest of three, her whole demeanor sparked serious sympathy. She was encouraged to enjoy her new motherhood, and let her

247

husband worry about their other "baby." She found, however, that she felt too responsible for other people's dilemmas. She attributed this to the very critical attitudes of her own mother, an impatient woman with impossible standards. She was encouraged to stop trying to prove herself to mother and, when the latter became critical, to try in some playful way to take credit for her actions rather than defending them. As it happened, Mrs. Love was going home for a visit. Sure enough, when the plane was late, mother's first remarks were that she had an extremely busy schedule and all she needed was for her daughter's plane to be late. Immediately Mrs. Love felt the need to justify herself. Somehow she realized the absurdity of taking responsibility for the airline. Then she saw the pilot passing by, took her mother by the hand, went over to him, and said, "Sir, my mother is all upset about our plane being late. Would you please tell her it was not my fault?" The pilot must have understood the whole scene in a glance because he responded without pause. "Frankly, Madam, your daughter is a lousy navigator!" The curve of mother's criticism went flat. They had a ball all weekend. In direct proportion to Mrs. Love's ability to have a more mature and more fun-filled relationship with her mother, she became less responsible for her husband's responsibilities.

As Mrs. Love found herself less needy of her husband's needs, he predictably went into a funk. He began to question again whether or not to stay with the church or the cloth. He began to drink and his general functioning level suffered. He was, therefore, focused on the fusion in his marriage, how it came about, and what Mrs. Love's differentiation of self could mean. He began to close the distance between himself and his own family of origin, whom he rarely visited. He was encouraged to engage his elderly parents and his siblings in discussions about raising children, particularly about how responsible a parent has to be, and what the right mix of leniency and discipline should be. Everyone in his family responded with the notion that caring was all-important, except his kid brother who said, "*Discipline!*" He came away thinking, "I never realized how incredibly self-sacrificing my whole family is. I always saw it simply as glue." As he became aware that he had parented his congregation much as his elders had parented him, he began to develop a less load-bearing approach to his congregational charges.

At first, several of them reacted intensely to his more differentiated leadership, and in their own sessions together began to say that Mr. Love didn't care any more. Most, however, were able to see that the new distance was better for all. Within the next few months, two of the lay leaders decided to become more involved outside the congregation, and one joined another group. Then, as is the way of the imaginative capacity when a relationship system becomes less fused, they suddenly came up with a creative new idea. They conceived of another way of structuring the congregation that created a separate committee responsible for administration and that freed them up to do what they really wanted to do: focus on enriching programs.

Will leadership through self-differentiation always work? Of course not. What will? It cannot even be guaranteed to work better than charismatic or consensus approaches. But the real question is what does it mean "to work"? Effective family leadership is not simply a matter of leading people to a goal or to feeling good about their togetherness. It must also be judged by criteria such as the growth of the followers and the long-term survival of the family itself. Because leadership through self-differentiation is not focused on techniques for togetherness, it is more likely to take such other matters into account, and, as with a systems approach to marital counseling, it also gives us more comprehensive criteria for distinguishing fundamental change from the recycling of a symptom.

In summary, leadership through self-differentiation is less a technique than a way of thinking. Some of its advantages for any family (personal or congregational) are: It fosters independence without encouraging polarization and it allows interdependence without promoting cults. It seeks to promote togetherness but not at the cost of progress. It normalizes transition, and it is less susceptible to cut-offs. Most of all, perhaps, it reverses the pull and drain of dependents who normally gain power from the expectation (indeed, belief) that their demand to be included at their price and pace will always be satisfied. It also has advantages for the leader (or parent). It makes his or her job less complex, yet gives more leverage. Because the focus is on the development of the leader's own being, it requires less knowledge overload about other methods. It reduces enervating conflicts of wills (and triangles). Because it does not go in the direction of increasing interdependency, it fosters less guilt among followers, and because its primary focus is the leader's own position, it automatically answers questions about the distance a leader should try to maintain. Finally, because the approach is less load-bearing and more self-expressive, it minimizes the influence of the factors that contribute to burnout.

10

Leaving and Entering a Congregational Family

Shortly after World War II a new congregation in a developing urban area became sharply divided. The intensity generated by the opposing factions caused a dozen families to leave abruptly. As is the nature of cells that divide, a new colony was formed. They started their own congregation several miles away. The daughter congregation, imbued with a competitive spirit, grew rapidly. But in its 7th year, the "noise of this solemn assembly," hitherto muffled by its pioneering energy, drowned out its minister's message. Forty families that had become close in the unity of their "rejection" left the parish and created a third community. Emphasizing peace, harmony, and family togetherness, they found a naive seminary graduate to take the post.

Things went well for 2 years; then they turned him out unceremoniously and hired another to take his place. Again things went well for a while, but after 5 years history repeated itself once more. For their third match they selected a minister who was almost the opposite of all the previous ones. He was different in stature and, unlike his predecessors, not interested in social action or preaching. He saw himself primarily as a shepherd, and devoted all his time to his people's needs. It appeared that whatever "evil spirit" had troubled the members of this "family" for more than 15 years (for some it had been more than 20) finally had been laid to rest. Then, suddenly, with no warning, their saintly, devoted pastor committed suicide.

It has been emphasized that problems in a family can be the residue of emotional processes carried over from previous generations. The exact same transmission occurs with congregational families. Nor does the similarity end there. As with personal families, such processes tend to be perpetuated by, or originated during, transition periods. There is a great irony here because, as illustrated in Chapter 7, the major way to exorcise the demons that travel this multigenerational path falls within the clergy's own expertise, namely, rites of passage. Such nodal periods have the same natural therapeutic efficacy in the life of a church or synagogue, with potential long-range benefits for both the congregational family and its separating partner.

This chapter will apply the systems and ceremonies insights of Chapter 7 to the nodal events of a congregational family, in particular to the entering and leaving of its spiritual leader. As mentioned earlier, these moments are the one experience we can all relate to, and often they are the experience through which some of us are related. The manner in which each of us handles our separation from a given congregation goes far toward determining the kind of "family" our successor will "marry into."

THE LAME DUCK MYTH

In perhaps no other area of the clergy's emotional life has the emphasis on personality and psychodynamics created so much distraction from the natural healing power inherent in our community position. "Savvy" psychological advice is often given to ministers, priests and rabbis: "Once you are going to leave a congregation, don't be narcissistic; don't interfere in the selection process; stay out of the way; temper your ego; cut the cord; sever the bonds; what happens from now on in the future relationship of the congregation and your successor is none of your business; accept the reality of your 'lame duck' condition." But no member of the clergy would say that to a member of the congregation who is separating from his or her spouse, and who has been significantly involved in the raising of their children. Nor would this kind of advice to cut off be given to the relatives of someone who has a terminal illness, or the parents of a child (much less the child himself or herself) who has decided to leave home.

The notion that clergy become lame ducks, once it is known that they are leaving a post, is as short-sighted as are approaches to any terminal condition that urge physical distance or minimizing contact as the way to reduce emotional intensity. As in personal family situations, the effect of such all-or-nothing approaches to separation is far more likely to transfer the intensity of the experience than to reduce it. Obviously, as with a child leaving home to marry, it is better for the parent to stay away than to hang on. But it is not at all clear that staying away, particularly to the extent it approximates an emotional cut-off, is less pathogenic in the long run than hanging on.

That extreme forms of separation (cutting off and hanging on) are, in fact, connected is illustrated by the following tale: A rabbinical student quit his studies abruptly in the middle of the night. By the next morning he had left with all his belongings. He never made contact with anyone again. Years later, after a successful career in another field, he died while on a visit to another country. His family and his wife fought for years over who should have custody of his remains. In both types of separation, all or nothing was this family's style.

A SYSTEMS APPROACH TO SEPARATING

The family model offers a third alternative to these either/or choices. When the separation between a congregation and its clergyman or clergywoman can be handled in the manner emphasized throughout this work, the so-called lame duck periods can be among the most fruitful in the life of that family. Where the terminal period in our relationship with a congregation can be treated as an opportunity for emotional growth, rather than as a painful period to be shortened or avoided, the long-range benefits, for both the congregation and for ourselves, are numerous and fundamental; and more than the pastoral aspect of things is involved here. The nature of the separation can influence the lasting effects of all our *previous* years of effort.

Earlier it was mentioned that, in some uncanny time warp, how we function in a family before the death of a parishioner can do more for the ultimate grief work than the most sensitive counseling and eulogies after his or her demise. A similar time reversal occurs in separations. How we function during the end-stage of our relationships with our congregations can do more to prolong the message we had been spreading than how forcefully we articulated that message in the first place.

For the congregational family, the major benefit of a family sytems approach to separation is that it will enable more objectivity in the selection of a new partner. Also, the new relationship will have a fresher start. There will be less baggage. And the individual members of the congregation will learn something about separation that they can carry over into terminal situations in their own families. Indeed, members of the congregational family may be at that very moment going through some personal separation experience in their own families, such as terminal illness, divorce, or a child leaving home. In those situations, their reactions to the congregational family breakup will be sharper. But, as always, the emotional interlock between personal and congregational families also has the capacity to heighten understanding.

For the clergy, all the same benefits hold. We also will have a fresher start in our next professional relationship, and our personal families can also benefit from our increased capacity to deal with end-stage family situations. In addition, our future counseling of parishioner families suffering separation problems will be enriched by our own professional termination experience; each will inform the other, and out of that mutuality will develop a more integrated ministry and minister.

A SYSTEMS APPROACH TO ENTERING

But it is not just with regard to the rites of leaving that lessons can be learned from personal family emotional processes. Family theory can also be applied to the early stages of a relationship between a congregation and its minister. Analogies to so-called blended families, where one partner marries a spouse who already has children, are particularly apt. This kind of increasingly frequent family situation can teach us relevant strategies for how to function when we are first called to a post so as to minimize the effects of the residue left by the previous relationship. Also of benefit are analogies to the engagement period. For example, the manner in which we leave our previous system (here, seminary or congregation rather than parent or previous partner) can have a significant effect on our resiliency and objectivity in any new congregational relationship. In addition, as with personal marriage, a family history of our future congregational partner can provide many clues about the nature of its emotional system, when it is likely to be troubled, and how it is likely to function in crisis.

THE RELIGIOUS HIERARCHY AS AN EXTENDED SYSTEM

There is also a third dimension to the relationships of clergy and their congregations that is brought into sharper focus by the family model: the extended system of the religious hierarchy. Even as a full understanding of the joining or rending asunder of any personal marriage must be set against the background of the partners' extended families, so too in these professional marriages the extended system of the religious hierarchies affects and is affected by nodal events in the various nuclear families of which they are composed.

While the major focus of this chapter will be the clergy–congregational bond, it is first worth noting some of the emotional processes in these extended hierarchical systems. They always provide the larger context and as with any family of origin, often exert a very subtle influence. In addition, as with any extended family, a hierarchy often provides the continuous set of feedback loops through which unresolved issues in the faith system are transmitted from one congregation to another, and from one generation to another. Understanding how emotional process in these extended systems interlocks with emotional process in specific nuclear congregational–clergy groupings can help broaden the perspective on their "marriage problems."

HIERARCHICAL TRIANGLES

No matter what the denomination, religious hierarchies composed of district supervisors, directors, bishops, provincials, superiors, placement committees, etc., necessarily become involved in the upward, downward, and lateral movement of their members, sometimes excruciatingly so. In fact, a huge proportion of their time and energy is spent in matchmaking and mending. But since the members of these hierarchies are, together with the various congregational–clergy relationships, all part of some larger, extended emotional system, what often results is a broad, complex set of "in-law" issues.

Trapped in such a network of relations, those who occupy hierarchical positions are subject to endless, enervating triangulation. From the point of view of the front-line minister, priest, or rabbi, those over him or her may seem to have all the power, much as children tend to think that way about their elders (who think that way about their children). But, as in any family, those who supposedly have all this power often feel caught because of the perpetual juggling act they are expected to perform. The constantly revolving door, or game of musical chairs, as some have called it, can be extremely stressful for those who try to keep the entire system in balance.

In addition, the constant pulls from every direction make effective counseling within the system itself almost impossible. In religious hierarchies, the counselor must always be watching his or her own flank. It is difficult enough to try to help any congregational family and its minister work out their problems. It becomes much more difficult when there are various interlocking triangles that include the counselor's own boss in the extended system, or his or her own predecessor, or his or her boss's predecessor, not to mention the counselee minister's predecessor, who by now may have become the counselor's own boss. And this does not even begin to take into consideration the possibility that the people at the top of the hierarchy have alliances with members of the very parish that is experiencing trouble with their minister. This is like trying to do effective marriage counseling with your own brother and sister-in-law, who, along with your spouse, work for her father, who, in turn, is having an affair with your own father's sister, who is married to a man who was your father-in-law's chief business competitor. No wonder clergy in the hierarchy and clergy in

254

congregations are often suspicious of one another. As was said earlier, the manner in which clergy "parent" their parishioners affects the way the latter parent their children. Some similar effect exists with regard to the way members of a hierarchy parent the congregational clergy, thus grandparenting the members of the congregation.

The family model can be beneficial to the extended family of the hierarchy in several ways. It can lay the basis for setting up programs that teach ministers and congregations how to use transition periods creatively, and that will ultimately affect their own work and stress. The model could be used to establish guidelines to help foster the institutionalization of transitions, with rites of passage appropriate for that community. As with personal family marriage and divorce, the ceremonial focus is almost exclusively on joining. Religious communities tend to place far more emphasis on the installation ceremonies of a new minister than on appropriate terminal ceremonies for the outgoing spiritual leader. But once again, it is the "family" that is going through change, as well as the identified celebrant(s). Ceremonies marking the end of a given clergy–congregational relationship are often more important for the future of all the family members than those initiating a beginning for the new "couple."

A family systems understanding of entering and leaving congregations can also offer members of any hierarchy new ways to facilitate such changes through the realization that the entire passage comprises the year surrounding the event; using the concept of an emotional triangle enables one to coach without getting caught in the middle. Indeed, the concept of an emotional triangle almost appears to have been specifically created for these kinds of situations. The following is an illustration of triangles typically found in extended family hierarchies.

Coaching in the Hierarchy: A member of a hierarchy was called in because a church wanted a new minister. The latter was functioning in a very immature way, but the church also was displacing onto him their unresolved grief over their previous minister's abrupt resignation. It happened that the person who had been asked to mediate had above her in the hierarchy someone with relatives in that congregation. She was beside herself as to what approach or decisions would be best for the church, for the minister, or for herself. Adding to her stress was the fact that there was no one else available for the pulpit. It was suggested that she use the coaching model, and not take on personally such awesome responsibility for the congregation. As when a couple comes in to their minister and asks whether they should get divorced, she should try to facilitate a process in which the parties tell her what decisions *they* wanted to make. She should further this process by giving everyone choices. The congregation could be told, "If you really want him out, I can do that; but you will be without a replacement indefinitely." The minister, who was an "injustice collector," could be told, "If you really want to stay, that probably could be arranged; but you will have to be willing to face some interpersonal issues."

A lay leader had drawn up a list of grievances that he wanted to be read in secret session. It was suggested that the mediator tell the group, "If I am to be present, I have to be the judge of what should be reported back." The congregational committee agreed to let the minister be present. The list paralleled almost exactly the list of content charges congregational families usually bring against their clergy (see Chapter 8). Throughout the meeting, the mediator maintained a nonanxious presence with this "couple" in order to catalyze self-definition in the manner described in Chapter 3, detriangling after every complaint to her by asking each side its perception of another's grievance. Finally, one of the members of the congregational family got some distance, and joked that only an auto-de-fé would solve everything. At this point, the mediating minister suggested that the "marriage" might be continued on a trial basis for 6 months, after which a replacement would be available.

She continued during that period to use her extended family position in the triangle in order to keep both sides communicating. At the end of the 6 months, the congregation was ready to have the minister stay on, but he decided he would prefer to work on a college campus. They split up amicably, with genuine sorrow expressed on both sides.

The most important point is this: Far more than conflict resolution was accomplished. The process approach to resolution, rather than simply dealing with the content of the issues, managed to dissolve much of the emotional residue of the congregation's previous un-worked-out marriage. The next minister enjoyed a very harmonious union. No matter who that person would have been, no matter what his or her strengths, he or she would have found the job much more difficult had the residue from the un-worked-out previous breakup two generations back been heightened by its transmission through one more unresolved separation. This is exactly the kind of systemic healing that has been going on in personal families for centuries when marriages, births, bar mitzvahs, baptisms, deaths, and divorces, not handled in an uptight manner, are able to exorcise the spooks that entered the system during a previous uptight passage.

The remainder of this chapter will be divided into three parts: (1) a family-systems-based strategy for separating from a church or synagogue that is designed to leave the least amount of residue for each partner; (2) a description of my own efforts to put these principles into practice when, after 15 years of leadership, I left the congregation I had helped found; and (3) a family systems strategy for entering a post that reduces the likelihood of getting caught in the residue of our congregational partner's previous relationship(s).

A STRATEGY OF SEPARATION

There are four interconnecting elements to a family systems model for leaving congregational families in a manner that minimizes pathological residue: (1) regulating our own emotional reactivity to others; (2) permitting emotional reactivity in others; (3) nonanxiously being a part of the transition process; and (4) staying in touch after we have left, but continuing to detriangle.

EMOTIONAL REACTIVITY

The most important factor that affects the resolution of intense bonds is the degree of emotional reactivity between the partners. This is true during the course of a relationship itself, but is particularly true during its breakup. Reactivity, as compared to responsiveness, promotes fusion. It is a force for stuck-togetherness rather than an enabler of differentiation. Worse, reactivity inflames the wounds of separation rather than healing them. The idea is applicable to all kinds of leaving.

For example, the most intense forms of reactivity in marital divorce—battles over property visiting rights and support payments, kidnapping of children, refusal to let the other partner see the child, or no contact ever again—all are evidence that the couple had *failed* to separate. And the continuing struggle inhibits further separation. Property settlement struggles can also surface in a congregational–clergy split, of course, where the ruling lay committee says the minister is not entitled to a month's vacation, or the clergyman or clergywoman takes property from the "marriage," for example, books, furniture, ritual objects.

Similar symptoms indicating inability to separate surface after other kinds of separation as well, for example, property settlements after death, fights over the will, or the stealing of memorabilia; here too they lead to emotional cut-offs between survivors. However, as with divorce, it is the emotional reactivity already in the family and not the separation itself that promotes the bickering and the resulting cut-offs. And once again, continued reactivity inhibits resolution of the triangles between the relatives and the "separated" deceased.

Also similar is the conflict that can surround weddings (the separation of leaving home). As mentioned in Chapter 7, intense reactivity at these joyous events is almost always indicative of the difficulty parent and children are having separating from one another and, once more, the reactivity itself inhibits the separation necessary for the future marriage to prosper.

Naturally, in any relationship, the partner who is not initiating the separation will tend to be more reactive. It is, therefore, up to the initiating partner to be prepared for reactivity in the other, and to regulate his or her own reactivity in order to prevent reciprocal escalation. What adds to the difficulty is that, when any intense relationship breaks up, the first partner who succeeds in finding a new partner will receive a depressed or sabotaging reaction from the other. But even when the other partner, marital or congregational, is the "jilter," the capacity to commit ourselves to a course of regulating our own reactivity, although it can be more difficult in such circumstances, can go far to facilitate the type of separation necessary for both to get on with our future lives. This is also good for our children (charges), whether it is a marital or professional "split."

PERMITTING REACTIVITY IN THE OTHER

It is also important to allow reactivity in the other. As most family members would prefer that their relatives die in the middle of the night rather than through a slow process of deterioration, so most separating marriage partners would like to steal away nocturnally and never have to deal with their spouses again. In a similar way, most members of the clergy would like to have as little time as possible between the announcement of their resignation and the actual termination of their contract. This is also true of a congregation after it has refused to renew a minister's contract. During such periods, the avoidance responses of either party are usually misinterpreted as hostility rather than as the inability to face a terminal condition. Yet, in any kind of separation, it is that avoidance response during the passage that "spooks" the future. It is the middle-of-the-night departure that fosters "shades." Of course, it is true that the shorter the period of the interregnum, the less reactivity one has to deal with. But the ability to allow or even make room for reactivity in the other, without reciprocating, creates the best chance that both partners can go on to their next relationships with the least amount of emotional baggage.

Celebrating Early: A priest had been told he would be transferred after enjoying a deep, intimate relationship with his flock. He was having great difficulty with the separation, as was the congregation, as evidenced by the lack of enthusiasm for all programs. He began to put all his energies into one massive, terminal sermon that he would give just before he left at Christmas.

It was suggested that this was hit-and-run and that he give his "Christmas" sermon immediately so that people would have ample opportunity to respond. He took the suggestion, and the depression hovering over both "partners" lifted immediately. Each also did well with the next "spouse." (Allowing the other to react while committing oneself not to react is what "dying with dignity" may really be all about.)

ENGAGING ACTIVELY IN THE TRANSITION PROCESS

In Chapter 7 it was shown that parents often go to one of two extremes around the time of weddings of their children. Either they tend to become overinvolved and interfering, or they remove themselves from the process as much as possible. While interference in the future relationships of a relative hinders the separation process, extreme avoidance, as with a purely comfort approach to terminal illness, fails to make use of the opportunity. It was shown there that if parents can become part of the leaving home process without trying to influence its direction, more separation will be accomplished and the new bond will have more flexibility than if they had remained distant.

The same is true when leaving a post. Certainly, trying to influence the selection process of one's successor is "akin" to trying to choose a mate for one's child, or trying to nullify his or her choice. Either extreme will form pernicious triangles. But becoming involved in the creation of a selection process is another matter. For example, helping one's congregational partner to become more aware of how the relationship looks from the other side can heighten the congregation's objectivity in the selection process. Even though this "engages" outgoing clergy in more triangles at the time, ultimately it promotes more disengagement from them.

Depending on the faith group, the laity has varying degrees of say in the selection, but even when they have little choice during this rite of passage, members of any congregational family will be more open to appreciating the position of its spiritual leader if there is some involvement in the transition process. Where the laity is autonomous, helping them to find a successor—for example, by writing a job description based on our own expertise and experience—furthers the separation process in the same way as did the mother in Chapter 7, who helped with the wedding preparations but kept her personal preferences to herself.

One of the great ironies that clergy will find at such moments, analogous to personal divorce, is that their partner is at last making the changes they had sought to bring about for years. This is much like the marriage partner who finds his sexless or frugal spouse going in the opposite direction after the breakup.

But that is the way fusion and separation affect relationships. For clergy who are truly interested in their entire faith community, and whose commitment goes beyond gathering disciples, taking advantage of the separation from our disciples to achieve what we could not achieve while still their leaders is in everyone's best interests. It is one of the most mutually beneficial activities that the clergy of any faith family can perform for one another. It requires nonreactivity, but it also helps regulate it for both partners.

STAYING IN TOUCH AFTER THE DIVORCE

In the same way that postmortems after parties add to their satisfaction, that remaining together after climax can prolong sexual enjoyment, and that wakes or coming back to the house after funerals can deepen the parting, so continuing to relate to members of a former congregation in a detriangling manner *after* one has taken a new post can further facilitate the separation. Just as in personal marriage, where the other side of successful engagement is continued successful disengagement (from families of origin), so the capacity of any congregation or member of the clergy to make his or her next relationship "take" is somewhat dependent on a continuing disengagement process after the "divorce." Indeed, some forms of disengagement are only possible after the separation. (Cemetery visits may serve the same disengagement process. Ostensibly made to remember, they may really help us to forget better than when we try to carry our remembrances in our head.)

For example, members of a congregation, as former marriage partners, may feel squeamish about having their two "lovers" meet. Yet when they are alone with either, they will immediately triangle the two by telling the new one how bad the old partner was, or by telling the old partner how the new one does not measure up. (The former situation will be discussed below.) In the latter situation, if members of the clergy will keep up contact (a noninterfering contact) and comment upon such remarks in an uninvolved way, such moments can be opportunities to detriangle and to further more separation than if those remarks by former parishioners had never been given the opportunity to occur.

It is like a bride who comes back to mother attacking her husband.

If mother sides with her child, the future may be self-fulfilling because she will be keeping her daughter bound. But her daughter's very comments can be seen as an inability on her part to separate from mother. Thus, it is better that daughter make the comment and have mother detriangle, than for daughter never to bring the issue "home."

Where we allow former congregants to attack our successor, but refuse to conspire in an emotional alliance against him or her (not too much more difficult than resisting the wiles of Satan), we further disengagement with our separated partner and encourage the process of a less fused engagement in our partner's new relationship as well as in our own. Is there a danger in this process? Absolutely! But once again, as with all emotional and spiritual growth, the rewards of non-cloistered virtues are proportional to the risks. Playing it safe is more peaceful, but is avoiding challenge what responsible leadership is all about?

A PERSONAL EXAMPLE

The following story is about my own efforts to apply this four-fold strategy. It helped teach the teacher what separation was about.

My decision to leave my congregation was motivated primarily by a desire to devote more time to writing. I had agonized over it for several years but always put it off. Soon after my mother died, however, I found myself released to make this other separation. To whatever extent these nodal events in my life were related, I cannot be sure, but the correlation of such decisions with changes in family of origin is not unusual among the clergy. And, as I mentioned in Chapter 9, I do know that my mother's mother was the major influence on my own religious identity. (More will be mentioned about this type of connection in the next section on the clergy's family of origin.)

I had been the founding rabbi and the spiritual leader of the congregation throughout its first 15 years, and I knew that separation would not be easy for either of us. I therefore spent an entire summer planning how to go about it. My primary concern was to give my congregational partner as much time as possible to work through the separation. After all, I would be in the position of "jilter." I evolved the following plan: I decided to make the announcement at the beginning of the congregational year (September) in order to allow as much time as possible for working through the separation processes. I chose Yom Kippur evening since that was the occasion on which most of the congregation attended, and I thought it best that as much of the congregation as possible hear it at the same time and directly from me.

261

I had considered a letter, but in the end decided to do it personally. Because it was our custom to discuss all my sermons during the holy days on the last day, my announcement would come at a time when custom provided a time for congregational response.

I wanted to make the separation announcement on an upbeat note, if such a combination was possible. I therefore delivered a series of talks on the future of the congregational family, stressing its unique points and its strengths in a way that distinguished (differentiated?) the institution as an entity in its own right. I wanted to emphasize that the organism had grown to maturity, and was in no way my creation, foundling, or "dependent." Then in the next-to-last talk—the third of four—in a presentation that discussed all the changes we had seen over the years, I announced my intention to leave at the end of the contract year (June). I expressed the view that new leadership and new ideas were needed after a decade and a half (an argument I had often heard anyway).

In order not to get caught in the reactivity, I reminded myself that my watchword would be: "Go out with dignity." To help in this regard, I made a list of the type of comments that I thought I could expect, and jotted down some responses that I thought would help me stay non-reactive. For example, I was sure I would be asked "Rabbi, are you going to remain a member of the congregation?" Innocent on the face of it; but a direct answer, yes or no, could unduly influence their own decision to remain or leave, and I wanted each member to make his or her own commitment to the congregational family without my being part of the equation. I thought a serious response to the content of that question would inhibit the emotional separation. I therefore decided on a playful response, one designed to get at the process of separation: "Yes, if I like the new rabbi; but I hope you'll be fiscally responsible when it comes to his salary." Invariably, this response throughout the year provoked a double-take: a slow smile followed by good feelings.

The first responses to my announcement, however, were not at all in my preplanned repertoire. They were all related to the interlock. After the service I usually went behind the altar and derobed. This time I decided to stand there and see what would happen. The first person to greet me that evening told me that her husband was "terminal," and asked if I would be around for the funeral. She evidently had not heard me say I would be around until June. Her hearing had stopped with the realization that she was losing me also. Another woman had been told by her husband that very week that he was "leaving" her. Though she and I had been close personally and professionally for years, and she had been a founding member of the congregation, it took her 4 months to respond in any way to my announcement. I also immediately received a note from a member whose child had just left home. And—talk about interlocking emotional triangles—a lawyer and a psychiatrist, who had been members for years, told me months later that after that service they had looked at one another and said, "If Ed can do it why can't we?" Before the year was up, each had made plans for a professional change.

The next person to reach me after the service said that her daughter was engaged and asked if I could do the wedding; and a second said that her daughter wasn't engaged yet, in fact she still hadn't found a man, but would I be available for the wedding?

As I left the "sanctuary" that evening, I could see it was going to be far more difficult than I had realized. People just stared at me; some shook my hand and congratulated me for my courage; others turned away as I went by; a few had tears in their eyes; and one or two asked me if I were going to remain in the congregation.

The board of trustees immediately called an emergency meeting. I went, prepared with another portion of my plan: that I would not try to influence the selection processes of my successor in any way, but that I would be as helpful as I could be in teaching the congregation how to go about finding my successor. I could refer them to sources that had information about available rabbis, and I would meet with the various committees to help explain the details of my job so that they would know what questions to ask in an interview. I also thought that this process might help them modify their expectations.

At that meeting there was a great deal of looking the other way. This personal avoidance was to surface continually for a while. For example, at a bar mitzvah celebration the following month, I noticed something that recalled my teenage years when I went to a party and found that the girl I had just broken up with was there also. All night long, as I would turn in one direction or another, I realized that members of the congregation had evidently been staring at me. But if I inadvertently caught their eye, they immediately looked away, although one or two did come up and ask if I were going to remain in the congregation.

Over those first few weeks I also received several letters from members that ranged from anger to good wishes, the latter often from those who I never expected would care. The most interesting one came from that member of the board whom I would have counted as my bitterest enemy. He had fought me on issue after issue, had once organized a committee to investigate the role of the rabbi, and had polled the entire congregation with a 100-question questionnaire. In his letter he said that, while we had disagreed over the years, there were many aspects of our relationship that were important to him, and he was genuinely sorry to see me leave. My thoughts immediately flashed back to Castro after the Kennedy assassination. He was asked if he were not gloating to see his Bay-of-Pigs archenemy done in. He responded something like "No, I had kind of gotten used to him." I had learned still another form of symbiosis.

At that moment I wished that over the years I had been more consciously aware of what I had really known on some other level: that the most intensely negative members of a congregational family were as invested personally in their spiritual leaders as those who were most positive to him—not that I would have known how on earth to change the valence of the negative emotional charge. It was at this moment that I first realized how criticism is a form of pursuit.

At that first board meeting there had been a cloud of depression, but no panic. Most realized what had to be done and they set about establishing the proper mechanism for change. I announced my intention to be helpful in the selection process, and made clear that I would avoid trying to influence any final decision. The entire congregation, I soon learned, was also in a state of depression. Few showed up at weekly services, and the celebration of festivals was clearly shrouded in the pall of this terminal condition. At one point the congregational president called me and said I should do something to rescue the congregation from its sad state. I demurred, offering only to help with the selection procedures.

Naturally, there must have been some who would be overjoyed at my leaving, but it was hard to find them out. On the other hand, two members who had the most reason to be upset about my leaving turned out to be those who helped facilitate the process of separation best. These were individuals with whom I had done long-term family counseling, one in connection with an affair his spouse was having, the other with regard to problems with her grown children. The first came to me and said, "Why don't you repeat all your favorite sermons this year? Just do those you have liked best, the message you want to endure." I jumped at the opportunity. I managed, however, to fit into each some notions about universal problems in the human separation process, always talking generally and without too much pointed emphasis on the particular separation taking place. Once, however, I did say during a question-and-answer period that I thought if the congregation hired someone exactly like me or nothing at all like me, then they "hadn't worked it through." I was still thinking that "working it through" occurred during the separation process. I had not realized yet that the separation process only created the enabling factors that permitted or precluded the *ultimate* working through, a process that would take years, and maybe only could really begin after the official termination of the relationship.

The second helpful member came to me 4 months after the announcement with a decision of the board, which I think she herself had originally proposed to them. The congregation had decided to give me a goodbye luncheon. I was delighted that they had decided to do this on their own; I imagined that this decision meant the nadir of their depression had been reached, and that their spirits would be on the rise from here on.

Over the next 2 months the congregation became actively involved in the search for a new partner, polling themselves often on their priorities, and meeting with me periodically to discuss the requirements of the rabbinical profession and the nature of the interviewing process.

During that period I managed to stay on my course of going out with dignity, despite several provocations. The closest I came to blowing it was after a wedding when the father of the bride came up to me and said, "You know, Ed, over the years you really became a pretty good rabbi." It was one of those situations where you turned away knowing that a knife had been deftly sunk deep between your shoulders, and with such skill that even though you knew it was still in there, you felt no sharp pain. I had not prepared a response for this one. After I got my coat, I went over to him and said, "I want to thank you for your compliment and say in return that, as I think of it, over the years I believe you became a pretty good congregant." That was the closest, with one exception, that I came to being unable to regulate my reactivity that whole year.

The exception was something that happened the following month and that took me greatly by surprise. One evening as I was discussing some administrative matters with a member of the congregation, he said, almost parenthetically, "By the way, we've finally agreed on your successor." I immediately became depressed. In fact, I don't think I ever understood what depression was about until that moment. I thought I knew why I felt depressed, and yet I was still powerless to prevent it. It was the remarriage phenomenon I had noticed over the years wherein the first to reconnect is greeted by a sabotaging or dysfunctional reaction from the other. So my "partner" had reconnected first! Yet I was the one who had initiated the separation. Somewhat aware of what was happening, I sat down with my wife and talked about it. After a couple of hours, the depression lifted. It was, however, by far the deepest depression I had ever experienced in my life.

After the successor was chosen, my wife and I invited him to dinner. I did my best to make him comfortable. I tried to assure him that, for me, leaving meant not hanging on. I told him that in spite of the emotional investment I had always had in the congregation, I was into other things of equal importance for me. I felt content with what I had given the congregation over the years. I had gotten as much as I had given and in no way, therefore, felt any vested interest in my specific ideas and programs being retained. It was the truth, though I think he had some doubts. I also tried to convey that I would remain available for discussion and advice in any way he wanted as long as I remained in the community, but that I would not interfere. In other words, I would be receptive, but he would have to come to me. It was also my intention, I told him, to remain a member of the congregation (no matter how much they paid him).

That evening, after he had left, I received my insight into the universality of all separation experiences. Until then I had been thinking of the transition as a divorce. I was leaving my "partner" and my successor was marrying my former spouse. I realized now, however, that I felt more like a father who was turning his daughter over to a son-in-law. The two transition passages, I began to realize, were not that dissimilar. In both situations, the capacity of the new relationship to take hold successfully depended on the previous partner's being able to let go—but stay connected. I have worked at that process in my relationship with my former "partner" ever since.

Six weeks later at the farewell luncheon, they "roasted" me. Members of the congregation had found something from almost every significant part of my life. They decorated the room with these memorabilia and during the program had a lot of fun with my "character." They presented me with antique silver (Sabbath) candlesticks from Poland, where my grandmother had been raised, chosen by a member who was one of my closest personal friends, whom I had first met when I officiated at his wedding 17 years previously, and whom I had helped to deal with his furiously opposed mother (who had since been to my house many times). They also honored me with a plaque, personally calligraphed by a member, that noted my 15 years of service and straightforwardly thanked me for my "intelligence and wit."

Outstanding at the luncheon was one event. A member had taken one of my messages about interdependency and reinterpreted it in terms of the congregation and myself. (I had known him at my previous congregation, and our relationship went back 20 years through many dramatic events in his own personal life.) I had taken to writing parables that had begun as fantasies during my counseling practice. On several occasions I had interpolated these into a religious service, in place of the usual, formal sermon. The whole idea had proved very successful, even though it was "old-fashioned."

In one particular parable called "The Bridge," a man suddenly realizes what he wants out of life, but is told he must set out immediately or his opportunity will be lost forever. Hurrying on his way, he meets another while crossing a bridge. The other asks him if he will hold on to the end of a rope. The protagonist says, "Yes, but only for a moment," because he is on a very important journey. This man hands him one end of the rope, but the other end is tied around his own waist. And as soon as the protagonist takes hold of one end, the other man throws himself off the bridge. There then ensues a dialogue between the two in which the man holding the rope says he has to go, and the other just keeps answering passively, "I am your responsibility." Finally the one on the bridge says, "I can't pull you up because the rope is too long. If you will at least shorten it by twining more of it around your waist, perhaps I could obtain the leverage to get us both free." But the dangling one refuses to cooperate. After much soul searching, the one on the bridge finally "frees his hands." Congregants later said that they were up until 3 o'clock in the morning discussing various endings.

At the "roast," the parable was read dramatically by several members. This time, however, it was a rabbi, who finally had decided what he wanted to do, who meets a congregation "on the bridge." As in the original, the rabbi finally lets go of his parishioners who are still dangling at the end of the rope. But they added one last line: "And on the way down, the congregation called a general meeting and censured their spiritual leader." This recreation of my parable was for me the perfect homage and ending.

As June came to a close, I thought that my work at separating from the congregation had also finally ended. I was wrong. In the fall I decided that a parent does not go on the honeymoon, so I did not go back for the High Holidays. When I showed up at the new-member meeting a month later, however, I was immediately greeted by the head of the rabbi-selection committee who told me criticisms were already mounting about my successor. The specific issues were exactly the same faults they had always found in me. I told some of them that they had bad luck in selecting rabbis, and others, that all rabbis were probably cut from the same "cloth," and managed to stay out of it.

Much of my continued separation work, however, occurred outside the specific arena of synagogue activities. For as long as 2 years, I would continue to meet members of the congregation at social gatherings or in supermarkets, and they would tell me how much they missed me or my sermons. Often in passing they made invidious remarks about my successor. To each one I responded in a manner that conveyed to them there was no way I intended to return as rabbi ("Daughter, we can still visit one another, but you have made your bed"), and that I loved my new life. There were many therapists in the congregation, and I came to realize that how they handled the separation was a good basis for deciding on whom to recommend for referrals. During the next 2 years I also received an invitation to be the guest speaker one Sabbath. I accepted it and used the occasion to describe some of the ideas I had recently been working on. My successor introduced me, and he and a few members came over to the house for refreshments afterwards.

Five years later the state of things was as follows: The congregation had grown in size and changed in character. About 15 percent beyond the usual, annual 15 percent of transients had left. These were clearly members whose ties to the synagogue were mainly through me. They also tended to be older members whose children had been confirmed. My successor is still there after weathering some early storms. He has introduced new ideas. His personal style has begun to influence several important aspects of the congregation's style, and yet it is also clear that some of my own innovations over the years still form part of the fundamental framework. No parent could feel better about the marriage of an offspring.

STRATEGIES FOR ENTERING A CONGREGATIONAL FAMILY

There is, of course, no guarantee that our predecessors have handled their leaving well. Even if they have, there will always be some residue. Each of us inherits the un-worked-out part of our predecessors' relationships with our congregational partner. We must ask, therefore, what does family theory say about entering a congregational partnership? Two major variables contribute to residue. One is the length of the congregation's "marriages" previous to the most recent one, and the leadership styles of its partners. The second is the nature of the previous separations and how those "breakups" were handled. As pointed out earlier, congregations are organisms. Even though the laity may have changed over the years, the emotional system of a congregation tends to remain constant.

With any divorce, a highly emotional separation after a short-term relationship is more easily worked through than is a less intense separation in a relationship nurtured by long-term, deeply rooted, emotional interdependency. For example, a congregation had been totally unable to adjust to the loss of its leader after 25 years. It rapidly went through two ministers and was about to go through a third, who realized the problem had to do with the incomplete goodbye but had no idea what to do about it. Then it was discovered that the cremated remains of the former leader had been placed on some humble shelf in another part of town. It was suggested that, with all possible haste, they be buried with appropriate ceremony on the church grounds.

Sometimes, however, the nature of the separation is the more important influence. For example, if the congregational relationship had only lasted a year but the previous "partner" had been forced out or resigned after an intense struggle, perhaps around his or her efforts to change one of the congregation's major goals or practices, or if he or she had been divisive (a promoter of triangles), or if the reason for the "split" had been immoral or unethical behavior, under all such circumstances we can expect more unresolved residue than if the departing partner had been there many years. The worst possibility occurs when both conditions are satisfied: *the separation had been traumatic* and *the relationship had lasted many years* for example, when a charismatic leader who founded the church resigns without warning or commits suicide. For example, a deeply revered spiritual leader had killed himself. His successor found resistance to almost every program he initiated. The new leader knew it had to do with the mourning process, but he was getting fed up with everyone telling him how great his predecessor had been. It was suggested that he quote his predecessor in every sermon and talk and, since the departed had taped all his sermons, that a record be made of some of them and sold to the congregation so that the funds could be used for a memorial. Detriangling spirits can still be a very this-worldly matter!

Taking all of these factors into consideration, family systems theory creates a three-fold strategy for entering an established relationship system.

1. Avoid interfering with or rearranging the triangles in the established relationship system.
2. Be wary of efforts by members of the congregation to triangle you with the "departed" or with other members of the system.
3. Work at creating as many direct one-to-one relationships as possible with key members of the "family."

1. The model most applicable here is the phenomenon recently dubbed "blended families," where two previously married partners, at least one of whom has children, set up house together. In any second marriage, both partners will bring some baggage of unresolved issues from their first marriages in proportion to the previously mentioned interdependent variables of the length of the relationship, the nature of separation, and the degree of differentiation from their families of origin. In one sense, of course, all marriages are blended families because, from a family process point of view, it matters little whether the unresolved issues are from a previous marriage or from a previous symbiosis with our parents.

There is one important factor, however, that is unique about blended families: One of the partners usually marries into the established relationship system of the other partner. This also can be true in first marriages if one moves into the orbit or the house of the other partner's parents. The partner marrying into the other's system must never try to rearrange the established pattern of relationships. If a new husband, for example, tries to change the relationship of his bride and her daughter, the process will sponsor an infinite variety of problems from physical symptoms to conflict over sex and money. The partner entering the other's system has a right to individual relationships with the new spouse, as do each of them with the other's children, but efforts to change the relationship of any two of them will be ineffective at the very least, and most likely will get him or her expelled. (Witness the number of American presidents who have entered office with an enthusiastic resolve to change the Civil Service system, only to quietly give up by the end of their first year. Those most adamant about it will probably get the least cooperation on other issues.)

This does not mean a new idea cannot be introduced. On the contrary, sometimes a relationship system is far more open to change during a period of transition. But expressing ideas or suggesting changes is one thing; coming on as the fixer or the rearranger is another. It is also helpful to keep in mind that when there is a strong emotional reaction to an otherwise harmless suggestion for change, *the content of the suggestion is not the problem, but, rather, what the suggestion portends for change in the previously existing triangles of the relationship system.*

One woman who moved in with her new husband and his teenage daughters immediately went about changing the thermostat settings and the wattages of certain lamp fixtures. This "keeper of the thermostat" was out again in 6 months. Thus, also, when first entering a congregation, trying to change the "thermostat" settings too quickly can have similar results.

2. Be wary of the triangles that form immediately. In a blended personal family, for example, a man marrying into a system may take great care not to interfere with the set pattern of relationships already existing, but there is no guarantee that other members of the family will accept such noninterference. The children, for their part, may try to triangle him by complaining about their mother, or by criticizing him to her.

The analogy to congregational families is obvious. To the extent that a congregational family contains unresolved issues among the various "sibs," to the extent the new "daddy" or "mommy" is going to be greeted with remarks that try to get the new leader on one side or the other. The ambushes are various, subtle, and many. From a cynical, political point of view, we might try to convey that we have allowed ourselves to be triangled in an alliance, but take care not to become emotionally committed to one part of the family. The problem with that approach, however, is that, aside from the moral implications of such an attitude, to the extent that we form a new relationship based on the triangling out of a third party, that new relationship has been built on pseudo-intimacy, and later stresses will make the seams stand out. This is precisely what occurs in many second marriages where the couple gains an initial, calm togetherness by comparing the dastardliness of their respective ex-spouses. Sometimes, of course, the couple is fortunate enough to have an interfering "ex" for the rest of their marriage, in which case they can remain united till one of the three dies (and the same can be said regarding a first marriage and an interfering parent-in-law).

A related type of triangulation facing all clergy who enter a new system is the negative remarks members make, not about one another but about the congregation's "ex." These types of triangulations are generally more obvious, yet, at the same time, harder to resist because they usually are presented in a manner that praises the new minister by comparison.

All triangling remarks are residue. Because no relationship is ever totally worked through, there will always be such remarks. To the extent, however, that entering clergy can resist the flattery or the good feelings of togetherness that accompany such triangulation, the cleaner their own start with that congregation will be. This is true not only because they are then less likely to become a replacement in the old triangles, but also because, in refusing to become that replacement, they can force a resolution of the residue left over from the previous partner.

3. The third approach in family systems strategy for entering a new congregation is to work at individuating relationships with as many members as possible, particularly those in positions of influence. This third approach provides a concrete, positive approach for avoiding the pitfalls of the previously described separation dynamics. In many ways it feeds back to the concepts of "leadership through self-differentiation" described in the previous chapter. To become a leader of a new family, one must become its head. If it is an established family, then one will not emerge as its head through some natural process of that organism's growth. In such a "transplant," time must be allowed for the "graft" to take. In fact, if entering clergy would make this their main priority for the first year or two, rather than hurrying to introduce new programs, not only will they increase their chance of a long-lasting marriage, they are also more likely to see those program ideas accepted. And, to come full circle, to the extent the entering clergy can function according to these principles, when the relationship is ultimately dissolved, less multigenerational residue will be transmitted to the next relationship.

CHOOSING A NEW PARTNER

Finally, family systems theory has something to say about the courtship period between members of the clergy and their future congregational partners. It creates a paradigm for interviewing a congregation. While members of the clergy are experts in interviewing premarital couples, when it comes to their own professional marriages they spend far more time worrying about how they will appear in the eyes of their partner than in considering how they can use that premarital experience to learn more about that partner. For the most part, information about a future congregational partner is gathered through hearsay, what the previous minister(s) or others say. Imagine the outcome if people's expectations in a marriage, or their decision to enter a marriage, depended so much on the perceptions of others.

Family systems theory suggests that the same methods described earlier for interviewing premarital couples can be used to get a reading on a congregational partnership. Using the model of the genogram, whether or not one actually draws a schematic diagram, the following questions would seem important:

1. How and when was the congregation originally created? To what extent did it form out of the needs of the community or the natural coming together of the founders, and to what extent was it a splinter group from an established congregation?

2. To what extent are the founding members still in power or present in the congregation at all?

3. In what ways does the congregational charter (constitution) reflect the intensity of its origins?

4. How many different spiritual leaders has the congregation had, and is the average length of those partnerships significantly different from the overall average of one's faith group?

5. What has been the nature of the congregation's previous separations? To what extent have they been mutual; to what extent has the congregation been the initiator; and to what extent has the clergyman or clergywoman been the initiator?

6. If any of the previous separations have been stormy or traumatic, what has been the nature of subsequent separations or relationships?

7. What major homeostatic changes have occurred in the emotional system of the congregation recently, for example, geographical relocation, completion of new building (or a wing), major changes in lay leadership, recent leaving of other professionals who have been there a long time (including, espe-

cially, volunteer secretaries)? Have any other congregations of the same faith group been created nearby?

8. What is the relationship of the congregation to the local community and its faith community? What is its reputation in those extended systems and the extent of its involvement? Has there been any recent, abrupt change?

9. How do members of the congregation talk about their previous partner? To what extent is there clearly unresolved intensity (positive or negative), and to what extent do they immediately try to triangle you with him or her; for instance, how much and how do they mention him or her in the interview or early contacts?

10. Test the emotional system by taking some stands about what you believe and observing the response. To what extent do the interviewers respond with their own "I" positions; do what extent to they try to engage you argumentatively?

11. Listen for the triangles (factions) within. Do they seek a well-defined leader or just someone to keep the peace?

We obviously cannot say to an interviewing committee, "I want to interview you also. Will you please answer the following questions?" The above items are more a set of guidelines for what to ask at various stages of the meeting, and what to listen for. But a decision based on this information is probably more reliable in evaluating the emotional system we are about to enter than is the hearsay of our colleagues. At the very least, it will put that hearsay into perspective.

The reader may have noticed that this list is really based on two other listings that appeared earlier (see Chapter 8): the homeostatic changes most likely to spawn content issues, and the characteristics of a congregation most likely to burn out its leader. But this is consonant with life's emotional cycle—entering really has to do with leaving, and the nature of new connections is primarily a function of the nature of previous separations.

Finally, a foreshadowing comment regarding the next chapters on the clergy's own personal families. We saw earlier that sending marriage partners back to working at triangles in their families of origin can often increase their flexibility and resiliency in other important relationships. We will see shortly that a similar reciprocity exists for clergy between their families of origin and triangles in their congregations. The ability of members of the clergy to utilize the strategies just outlined for entering and leaving congregations is very much a function of their position in the triangles of their own personal family systems (nuclear and extended), as well as how separation issues are handled there.

THE PERSONAL FAMILIES
OF THE CLERGY

11

The Immediate Family: Conflict and Traps

Mr. Jones's wife had become increasingly isolated since the family's last move. Mr. Jones, on the other hand, found the new post exhilarating. It was a step up the ladder, and he had taken to his job with diligence and relish. As Mrs. Jones became more dysfunctional, he tried to be sympathetic, but the demands of his position made it difficult for him to be as helpful as he would have liked. The fact that they were new to the community and that Mr. Jones wanted to make a good impression made things worse. Mrs. Jones found she had no one to talk to and was reluctant to seek professional help out of concern for her husband's reputation. She began to feel increasing resentment at her husband's attention to his "other partner." The stress in the family finally erupted in severe marital discord, and, during this time, one of their children was picked up by the police for trying to steal a car.

Much has been written in recent years about the increasing number of problems in clergy families. The emphasis tends to be on the isolation, the "fish bowl" environment, the high expectations, the work load, the frequent moving that increases instability, and all of this compounded by the difficulty of developing lasting relationships or having friends one can really trust. But, in all these respects, clergy families are not that different. Frequent relocation is par for anyone in the corporation ladder; the wives of many husbands are too emotionally dependent, and too often they are encouraged to be so; the "fish bowl" environment exists for doctors, executives, military personnel, and politicians; many hardworking husbands are torn between the demands of family and the demands of work. And, as for problems related to closeness and trust, this is a very pervasive human dilemma.

PERSONAL FAMILIES OF THE CLERGY

Actually, the above story of the Joneses is not about a clergy family at all. Mr. Jones was an engineer who had switched to an administrative career and was being sent by his conglomorate corporation as a troubleshooter to various cities every few years.

Here is a story about a *clergy* nuclear family.

A Loving Minister: The Browns had lived in a suburban community for a decade. Mr. Brown was a highly respected minister known for his capacity to inspire young people. His wife was the "ideal" minister's wife, full of energy, always able to say the right thing, totally adaptable to his needs. In all outward appearances, they had a mature compatibility. (They had not engaged in sexual relations for 12 years since the birth of their youngest daughter.) Then a rumor began to circle that Mr. Brown had become a little too close to one of the teenage girls in the choir. He denied anything had happened. His wife was her usual polite self. Shortly after Christmas everything blew apart. Not only had Mr. Brown engaged in oral sex with this teenager, he had also been involved with other girls, and there was evidence he liked boys as well.

THE SIMILARITY OF CLERGY AND PARISHIONER FAMILIES

Emotional process operates the same way in all families. The notion that clergy families are different is myth. It is as misguided as assuming that, when it comes to the "laws" of emotional processes (see Chapters 1 and 2), Jewish families are different from Christian families, American families different from non-American families, modern families different from old-world families, or black families different from white families. Sociological studies would show some obvious differences; but when it comes to symptom location, triangles, and fundamental healing, *they are not the differences that count!*

Clergy families neither exceed nor lack their quota of the human family's problems with: closeness and distance; the capacity for flexible separation; the ability to maintain self in the context of intimacy; the binding quality of others' expectations; the persistence of misunderstanding, dissatisfaction, and resentment in human experience; or the displacement and projection of unresolved issues from one relationship to another, much less from one generation to another. They are not unique in the way they are affected by the forces of society: inflation, scarcity, the women's movement, inner city, or suburbia. Nor are they more immune to the unbalancing effects of extended family permutations.

Symptoms in clergy families can be both physical and emotional, and they surface in the exact same locations (husband, wife, child, marriage) as symptoms in secular families. Emotional interdependency will foster fusion to the same extent, and lack of differentiation from families of origin will create inflexibility in nuclear family functioning to the same extent. Even holier-than-thou attitudes among family members are hardly confined to the clergy. Many kids can't talk to their fathers, and most women are intimidated by their husbands. When those same attitudes and transactions surface in clergy families, we simply have a ready metaphor.

There is possibly one exception to this ecumenicity of the human dilemma: the intensity of the emotional interlock between work and home. For clergy, more than for any other professionals, work and / family system plug all too easily into one another and significant changes in either system may be quicker to unbalance the other. Yet even that difference does not really make the clergy family "different." Rather, it means that in order to insure its overall family health, differentiation of self is more imperative.

The emotional interlock between work and family can promote some particularly unhealthy double binds in a poorly differentiated clerical family. All parents double-bind their kids to some extent, and every family has its own particular style. But with clergy parents it tends to take one particular form. The minister (or rabbi) and spouse try to control their children in terms of the parent's congregational role. Not all clergy parents bind their kids in this way in order to keep them in line, but many do live in constant anxiety over how their children's behavior will affect the parents' image. Such comments, however, have more to do with the way the parents conceptualize togetherness in their "family unit." Nevertheless, a double bind can be a far more pernicious form of child abuse than smacking the kid around. In fact, the two types of abuse probably come from the same overall lack of family differentiation. The key to abuse is not the means but the displacement. In the better differentiated clergy families, the parents can relate to their children outside of the congregational family triangle, which often begins with a comment from a congregational member about the child. The innocent form is: "Your son is quite the preacher's kid, isn't he?" The more intense form is: "I think for the minister's child to behave that way is disgraceful."

The double bind comes when the clergy parent or spouse then triangles the child into such comments by making his or her own self-regard dependent on the child's functioning. Far better for the child is a direct, process response to the congregant (who is probably displacing something from his or her family anyway) that sidesteps the content of this emotional, triangling gambit.

279

PARISHIONER: Mrs. White, your children certainly are not setting a good example.

MRS. WHITE: You should see them when they're really acting out! [or] I guess you're going to have to see us as human after all.

The clergy spouse can also get caught in such binds, and, here too, the problem has less to do with the fact that she (or he) is a minister's spouse and more to do with the fusion in their marriage.

Out on a Limb: Mr. Paul was furious about the head of the ladies' auxiliary, who was doing everything she could to frustrate his plans for a youth project. He lamented nightly to his supportive wife who sympathized with all her being. For several months the tension between Mr. Paul and the lay leader was high. Mrs. Paul also found that this woman was cool toward her, and she responded in like kind. Then suddenly Mr. Paul and his parishioner sat down, had a good talk, and worked things out. And the triangle shifted. Mrs. Paul did not find it so easy to turn her feelings around. She remained cool far longer and almost came to resent her husband for not disliking that woman anymore.

There is no question that members of the congregational family make differentiation in the clergy nuclear family more difficult. Members of the congregational family tend to think about their minister and his or her family as one colony of cells in the congregation body (though the extent to which they do this depends on how they think about their own family). But such fusion in this kind of thinking works both ways; not only do such members of the congregational family have higher standards for their leader's own personal family than they do for their own, but also, the perceived holiness of the minister also rubs off on those related to him or her. Parishioners treat them more deferentially and go to them as quickly in time of need. For instance, one rabbi reported how he had gone on a quick errand just before High Holy Day services were to begin. In the meantime, a member of his congregation (a psychiatrist) called to say that her father had just died and that she was in need of comfort and advice. The rabbi's mother, who was down for the weekend, happened to answer the phone and had to listen to the psychiatrist for 30 minutes.

That type of ongoing emotional triangle certainly does not make it easier for the clergy family to maintain its own differentiation, either from the congregational family system or within its own set of relationships. This is again part of the emotional interlock and emphasizes once more the significance of self-differentiated leadership. It is the spiritual leader who must set the standard for self-definition in both systems, and he or she has to be able to do this without expecting too much cooperation from either family. To the extent that clergy are successful in this endeavor, however, they optimize health and healing in both emotional systems.

THE DISADVANTAGE OF THINKING WE'RE DIFFERENT

The myth that clergy nuclear families are essentially different from the families that comprise the congregation is a disadvantage to the clergy professionally and emotionally. First, it is a content focus rather than a process focus, and it hinders us from seeing the reciprocity among our three "families." This weakens our effectiveness in all three relationship systems and increases the likelihood of underestimating the power of their interconnectedness. Further, the emphasis on how clergy families are different sociologically allows members of those families to avoid seeing their own role in their own victimization. The blame can more easily be placed on situational (contextual) factors, and the failure to cope is more easily disguised by rationalizations based on traditional values (cultural camouflage). For example, ministers' wives who lead adaptive lives, as doctors' wives often do, frequently say that they gave up their "self" because their husband's job was so important to humanity. But most of those same women have been adaptive to a chimney sweep.

Another example of such displacement is the sociological camouflage employed when preachers' kids act out in an itinerant clergy family and the insecurity is blamed on the constant relocation. There is little clear evidence to show that children who grow up in families that move about frequently are automatically more insecure than children whose families stayed in one location. Similar "content" rationalizations exist among military and foreign service families when they have problems with their "military" or "foreign service brats." But many children from such families also reap the benefits of being "broadened." Similarly, sociological explanations of problemed children in clergy families always leave out the fact that the problemed child's siblings also are "theological offspring," yet they are not as affected by the same relocations. It is the problem child's position in the unresolved issues of the family, his or her identified patient position, rather than any constant relocations that is always the modulating factor.

And this leads to one other important way in which clergy families are disadvantaged by emphasis on how they differ from secular families rather than how they are similar. As we have seen, families are more likely to emphasize sociological differences when they want to deny family process, and they tend to emphasize them when they are focusing on pathology rather than strengths. But for every specific, sociological attribute of clergy families that is blamed for why they are troubled, there is always the other side that gets lost in the focus on pathology: the advantages to families that occupy such positions in society—for example, respect they receive from others, fluidity among class and caste, the chance to help our fellow beings, the opportunity for a more varied and enriched life, etc. It is quite likely that consideration of all these advantages was part of the motivation for every member of the clergy when he or she was originally thinking about taking the cloth. In other words, these aspects of clergy life fulfill important, basic emotional needs, none of which are necessarily neurotic. They all can be seen as evidence of sensitivity to self and others' needs, as well as a wish for a life on a higher, not merely biological, level. Thus, an approach to clergy families that emphasizes their similarity to families within the congregation in terms of human emotional process will tend to accent personal accountability rather than contextual or situational liabilities. It is also more likely to allow the *positive* differences to stand out and to become natural resources of inner strength.

THREE NUCLEAR FAMILIES

It will be the design of this chapter to view "typical" clergy family problems in the light of family systems theory rather than through the camouflage (excuse) of societal influence. Three case histories will be presented, drawn from the major religious denominations. All are composites, and because recognition of the specific family is more possible "among our own," possibly identifying characteristics, including the original faith setting, have been changed. The selected three were chosen because, together, they cover the various problem areas of a nuclear family in which symptoms can surface, and not because of the specific content of their symptoms. Also considered was the manner in which the clergy family system interlocks with the emotional system of the congregational family.

As the reader will see, this chapter (and the next) cannot help reviewing almost all of the major ideas discussed previously. This is the natural result of any effort to describe family process, which, by its nature, is always spiral rather than linear. As mentioned at the beginning, the book itself is isomorphic of feedback processes in any system and, therefore, can be read in any order, or tapped into at any level. The clergy nuclear family (or any family) can be a complete guide to relational, emotional processes.

IMMEDIATE FAMILY: CONFLICT AND TRAPS

THE MANNING FAMILY

This is a story of the "preacher's kid" syndrome. It is the story of a family of fundamentalist background, which tended to regard failure in raising children right as due to lack of values rather than to family emotional process that may have sabotaged those values. Change ultimately came about because of change made in the relationship system of the family, not because of change in their religious beliefs.

John and Helen Manning were the perfect ministerial couple. They were, in fact, referred to by their colleagues as Mr. and Mrs. Perfect. Both came from ministerial families. Mr. Manning, a good athlete, had signed a contract with a major league team, but after a year in the minors gave it up and went to a seminary. (Mrs. Manning's brother was also a minister.) Their life revolved totally around their church. They had three children, aged 15 to 22, who were also known for their "goodness." Each had done well in school, helped willingly around the house, and, as far as anyone knew, obeyed family rules with little disagreement.

The family prided itself on its togetherness. Mother and children could always be seen next to one another on Sunday morning, and Sunday meals were always taken together. Mr. Manning was neither the greatest preacher nor the greatest administrator in the world, but that was overlooked by a congregation that believed he was personally concerned. His wife, a tireless woman with an engaging smile, didn't hurt his ministry either. The congregation family mirrored that of their minister. The lives of many of the members also revolved around their church, which often served as the axis of their existence, whether their major interest was hymns, gardening, or basketball.

Then, suddenly, a shock wave hit the Mannings. First, their oldest, who was away at their demoninational college, was picked up by the police for flashing in the park. The following week their youngest was caught shoplifting. She had been selling the merchandise to get cash for drugs. Then Mrs. Manning learned she had diabetes.

At the first counseling session, they were polite, defensive, and, above all, serious. Mr. Manning kept repeating how close the family had always been, and Mrs. Manning listed all her efforts to bring her children up "proper." In the course of taking a family history, however, and as usually occurs, more information came out inadvertently. Both older children (boys), while obedient and good students at home, had had great difficulty with their studies when they went off to college. And this was not the first time the youngest, a girl (who like her

283

mother had a weight problem), had been in trouble with the police. When she was 14, she had "gotten in with the wrong crowd" and even then had been stealing to support her habit. Mrs. Manning thought that the drug issue was all over and was shocked to find it had reappeared.

Efforts to get the family to think in terms of relational factors rather than morality seemed almost impossible. Sin lurked behind every door. Since the devil demanded his due, his advocate was therefore summoned.

COUNSELOR: Mr. Manning, how would you account for all these problems? I mean, you're both intelligent, reasonable people, dedicated to the word of God.

MR. MANNING: I just don't know. We have tried so hard.

COUNSELOR: Maybe you didn't try hard enough.

MR. MANNING: I've thought of that, but I can't think of anything we failed to do.

COUNSELOR: Perhaps God is testing you.

MRS. MANNING: But it's not fair to use my children in this way.

COUNSELOR: Satan has many disguises.

MR. MANNING: We never ate without a prayer.

COUNSELOR: Do you pray for them a lot? I mean your kids.

MR. MANNING: Every morning and night.

COUNSELOR: Maybe you're using the wrong prayers.

MR. MANNING: Are you making fun of us?

COUNSELOR: No, I'm just trying to help. You're the second most serious couple I've ever met.

MR. MANNING: Life is a serious business.

COUNSELOR: It sure is rare to find such selfless dedication.

MRS. MANNING: Well, sometimes I wonder whether it's worth it.

COUNSELOR: Isn't that a little blasphemous?

MRS. MANNING: Yes, I guess it is. But you know, John, he is right about our seriousness.

COUNSELOR: I want to say something that may make you think I came straight from hell itself. But I think this family is too close.

MR. MANNING: Too close?

MRS. MANNING: You're not from our church. We all believe in the sanctity of the family.

COUNSELOR: To the point of making it a burnt offering? (*Laughter from family for the first time.*) Look, I'm not trying to change your values, but, well, Mr. Manning, you say you used to play baseball, so you know that the great fastball pitchers didn't make it unless they could also throw a change of pace or a curve; batters in a slump don't get out of it by swinging harder. I just want you to "change your stance."

MR. MANNING: I never fake a bunt.

COUNSELOR: I think it's going to get down to whether or not you want to be pure or effective.

MR. MANNING: My wife has said something similar over the years, but I've always felt we must not show weakness.

COUNSELOR: What has that got do do with being playful?

MRS. MANNING: John really does have a very good sense of humor, but he never shows it in public.

COUNSELOR: What's that all about?

MR. MANNING: I wasn't that way all my life. It began in the seminary. No, even there I had a reputation for wit. It was after I was ordained, after I received my first call.

COUNSELOR: Who died?

MR. MANNING: No one. The only member of my family who died back then was my mother's uncle.

The Mannings were seen first together and then separately. In the sessions together they were coached to stop "saving" their children and to try to challenge them instead. They understood the theory, but had difficulty putting it into practice. Mr. Manning was encouraged to consider the possibility that his replacement of his great-uncle, one of the first itinerant preachers in his state, had restricted his freedom to function in his profession. He made several visits home to his aged parents, where he discussed their expectations for him. Finally, he got his mother to take him to her parents' cemetery where, looking down on the grave of her uncle, he found he had his middle name.

Around this time Mr. Manning stopped asking his sons to phone home regularly, and took all advice-giving out of his letters. When the older one had an auto accident soon after, father refused him a loan, saying he would have to work it out himself. In the past he would have looked at the estimates and made suggestions for how to do it more cheaply. At the end of the year, the younger son said he wanted to drop out of school. Instead of warning him of the dangers of "idle hands," Mr. Manning encouraged him to do so. He didn't.

The work with Mrs. Manning concentrated on helping her daughter separate. The daughter's original problems had come during a period when mother had been deeply involved in the caretaking of her own dying parents. The notion of the addictive effects of maternal anxiety was explained to her, how if mother becomes deeply invested elsewhere, child will symptomatize to get a "fix." Asked what her own mother would have advised her to do if she were still alive, Mrs. Manning related that when she was 21, she had been considering marrying an older, divorced man, and her mother had been furious—despite the fact that her own father had been divorced. After having recalled this incident, she became less anxious about keeping up the "family standards."

Mrs. Manning's efforts not to get hooked by her favorite daughter were a challenge. At first the daughter became engaged to a ne'er-do-well from an entirely different background. Mrs. Manning stayed loose and the engagement broke up. The daughter tried all kinds of anxiety-provoking behaviors, such as not reporting where she was going in the evening and sometimes staying out all night. Mrs. Manning still managed to control her anxiety and reactivity.

But then daughter got to them both. The congregation had a nonordained minister who did most of the administrative coordination. Mr. Manning often said he did not know what he'd do without him. Six months previously, his wife had been diagnosed with cancer and, as she neared the end-stages of her fight, he had become despondent. In the midst of Christmas preparations it was revealed that their daughter was having an affair with him! For Mr. Manning, this was the last straw. He was ready to burn her in hell. Mrs. Manning anxiously called her counselor, worried that her husband would cut their daughter off. She was shown, however, that daughter always managed to land on her feet, and that the pain and destruction always lay in her wake, not her path. It was suggested that she try to keep the situation from getting too serious.

That night, as they both waited for daughter to return, Mr. Manning with the white fire of goodness flaring in his nostrils, Mrs. Manning turned to him and said, "You know, honey, if you do have to find another assistant, at least it will be easier to hire a replacement this time. Think of the fringe benefits you can offer." She admitted later that she was acting all the way. He, astounded, started to sermonize, deflated, laughed, and cursed for the first time in front of her.

They told their daughter that they were fed up with her irresponsibility and that she would have to leave their house and go on her own. He told the assistant that he could understand his loneliness, but that he had to make a choice between his job or his "needs." Daughter moved to another city and within 2 months was living with a man. The Mannings remained nonreactive. At the end of a year, daughter left this man because he was "too immature," took some aptitude tests, and decided to become a social worker!

One other change is worth noting. Mr. Manning reported that during the year he had made some modifications in his congregational functioning in the direction of less "dedication," such as taking a whole day off every week. He then noticed that many of the church leaders, who used to attend as "religiously" as he, had been missing more often, and he even had heard that one or two of the old regulars were considering leaving the congregation. At first, he became worried. But then he learned that, around the same time, the nominations committee, which always used to have difficulty recruiting members to serve, had found many newer members more receptive to positions of leadership.

THE LEVY FAMILY

In the previous situation, change in the clergy nuclear family effects change in the congregational family. Here, the nuclear family symptoms surface smack in the middle of the congregational family. The congregation's problem in succession and separation is a direct result of unresolved issues in both rabbis' marriages, as well as in their wives' own families of origin. It is the failure of these men to differentiate themselves in their respective marriages, and the failure of the women to have done likewise with their own families of origin, that shapes the problem in the congregation and prevents its resolution. This case also brings into high relief (1) the distinction between process and content in the conflicts of religious organizations and (2) how contemporary congregational problems can have multigenerational forces behind them.

Rabbi Levy was chosen to be the assistant in a large urban community. The senior man had only 2 years to go before retirement. With the call came the expectation that Rabbi Levy would succeed to the senior post. The first year went well. He was basically a friendly person and quickly ingratiated himself among the congregants. The senior, who had been there 30 years, also came to like him, though his own head was so much into editing his collections of sermons, it was not really clear whether he cared at all. Not so his wife. She had been a member of the congregation even before her husband came to town. Her family had belonged to another synagogue that had spawned this one in a split many years prior over an issue no one could remember. But some of the more "liberal" families had left to form this new congregation and had taken the younger rabbi with them. Not agreeing with her own parents' generally conservative attitudes, she had joined the new congregation as a sign of independence from her family.

That young rabbi soon left for another post, however, and the new rabbi who was to become her husband, recently widowed and with two young children, came to town. They met while working together at the synagogue and were married within a year. She was known to have once said, "When the young rabbi left and I realized the new congregation might collapse, I was in panic. It had been the scene of my independence and now it had to be the proof of my triumph." When her husband-to-be came to town, therefore, she became the force, the strength, the energy, and the spirit that enabled the congregation to survive. She introduced him to town society, gave him a rundown on city politics and congregational politics, told him whom he could trust, and shielded him from those she knew might turn his head. Over the years, she had raised his children, taken care of all his needs, and, frankly, had built the congregation. The week after their last daughter was married she began a virulent campaign against her husband's successor.

Rabbi Levy was totally taken aback by this turn of events. He had bided his time carefully, guarded his opinions when they differed sharply from his predecessor, avoided all gossip about his senior, and never allowed others to create alliances with him against the older man. As for the senior's wife, the old "battle ax" had never been particularly warm to him, but she had not previously vilified him either. He spoke to some of the lay leadership. They sympathized and said, "Just do your job. She'll run out of steam."

In December the senior and his wife went on a cruise, and stayed with their daughter for the winter. During this time Rabbi Levy was able to start some of his own programs in the Sunday School, and organize a new Social Services Committee that would involve the synagogue more with contemporary community issues.

When the senior returned, he called Rabbi Levy into his office and told him he had overstepped his bounds. Who was he to come in and undo all his hard work of the past quarter century? Rabbi Levy tried to reason with the older man, but to no avail. He quoted the old man's sermons to him, showed how his own innovations really were harmonious with the synagogue's philosophy. The senior rabbi, however, was adamant in his posture, unhearing of any logic, and so rigid in his opinions that it became apparent to Rabbi Levy that the man was either becoming senile, having trouble letting go, or most likely, was a puppet for someone else.

What he did not know was that this "someone else" was actively planning his ouster: He is "a fine young man, but is he really what this congregation is looking for?" The congregants had their own perceptions, but "Madame Defarge" had succeeded in convincing some of them whose head should roll.

That night Rabbi Levy told his wife that he had better start looking for another job. It would have been a great opportunity, but staying on would mean a terrific fight. Even if he won, it would hurt the congregation. It would be better to start again in a smaller place, even in a less exciting locale, than to pay the price of victory here.

His wife was appalled. She responded aggressively. "You're just going to give up like that? This congregation needs you! It's going through a bigger transition than just a change in rabbis. There's a whole contingent of younger people who want to see this place change in the directions you have started to go. Stand up for what you believe! She's forced your hand. You can't wait until after his retirement to start speaking your mind." "But I don't want to split the congregation," Rabbi Levy responded. "Besides, he's a very important person to many members. He's been here a long time." "I agree," said Mrs. Levy. "You must be above reproach. Let me talk to a few people. If I can say something in just the right way, they'll carry the ball."

Mrs. Levy was the elder of two sisters born early to a couple who had married late. Her sister, an artist, quit college after 1 year. Mrs. Levy was the achiever. She had been among the top five in both her high school and college graduation classes. She had edited the yearbook, organized a university committee for poor foreign students, and was working on her master's degree when she met her husband, who was an immediate success with her own mother. Her own grandfather had been a Jewish scholar in Europe, but he had neither sons nor grandsons. Mrs. Levy had planned to go into marketing but, after her husband's ordination, decided to devote herself to his career.

She knew just whom to contact. Two women with whom Mrs. Levy had found the most togetherness were married to up-and-coming men in town, one a professional and one a businessman. Both were the sons of founding members of the congregation, and both had become fed up with its stodginess. Both had absolutely detested the senior's wife from the time they were confirmed, and had often argued with their own parents about how false she was. One of those parents was her closest friend.

The lines were quickly drawn. Neither wife went to services if the other's husband were preaching; members of the congregation followed suit. The two rabbis also grew more distant, though Rabbi Levy continued to honor his senior in public and privately. But the senior grew more aloof, and never initiated any contact on his own.

Within the congregational family, discussions of the future rabbi dominated all conversations, before and after choir practice, before and after all committee meetings, before and especially after services. Voting lineups on other issues, such as fund raising and cooperation between other professionals in the congregational family, seemed to be determined more by where people stood on the rabbinical issue.

Then, a compromise committee came to Rabbi Levy with the suggestion that he be elected to stay on for a 2-year probation. He might have agreed, but his wife wouldn't hear of it. It was now down to a matter of honor.

That evening, Rabbi Levy awoke with severe chest pains. He survived but resigned and soon took an easier job in a warmer climate. Tension in the congregation immediately disappeared after the news of his illness. They decided to wait a year before choosing a successor. Eventually they hired someone who had resigned from his previous congregation in protest over the way they had treated his spouse. The following year the senior rabbi (now emeritus) died in his sleep, and his wife left town to live with her daughter.

FATHER HURLEY

The fact that Catholic clergy do not have personal nuclear systems in no way frees them from the emotional interlock between work and "family." Nor does it rob them of an important fund of learning. The intensity of emotional process in a rectory or an order can be just as severe and just as influential in their work system, or in their parishioner families for that matter. Once again, the symptoms are obviously content issues spawned by, and this time resolved by, "extended family" contact.

Father Frank Hurley went straight from the seminary to help with a parish that had been served by a seasoned pastor for 10 years. Energetic, bright, and enthusiastic, by the end of the first year he had clearly become accepted by the parish. His easy manner, in contrast to the pastor's gruff demeanor, gained him access to various parts of the community, and he soon had organized a coffee shop for young people and a thriving thrift store for charity, the space for which he had acquired rent-free.

His pastor's responses to his success were hardly enthusiastic, but he had heard through the grapevine not to expect much camaraderie with the older man. So what if the old guy never complimented him, so what if he were sour most of the time, Father Frank would just continue in his own direction. Soon, however, he found that not only could he not expect praise, but he also could expect criticism and sabotage.

The first blow-up came after a woman in the congregation, who had lost her husband and her child, came down with a virulent cancer that killed her in a matter of months. This was the first time Father Frank had lost someone he had become close to. He had visited her regularly in the hospital all during her decline, took her death almost as a personal failure, and gave a stirring eulogy on the shortness of life, which he had stayed up half the night composing. The congregation was duly impressed, and he received many comments about his sensitivity and his perspicacity for one so young.

IMMEDIATE FAMILY: CONFLICT AND TRAPS

The following day the pastor came to Father Frank and excoriated him for wasting so much time on one parishioner. He had other duties that he had let pile up, and he mustn't get too close to one member of the parish. Never being one to guard his opinions, Father Frank let the pastor have it in kind, told him that he was an insensitive old coot and that the congregation ridiculed him rather than revered him, and strongly defended his own position on the importance of personal relationships.

Later that week he was called into the office of the Superior who said that he had been given some bad reports. Father Frank explained his position to the Superior, but left feeling he had not been heard.

Several weeks later another incident occurred. The order was challenged to a baseball game by a different brotherhood. Father Frank saw this as an opportunity to do a little fund raising for his congregation and, at the same time, develop more of a sense of community in the parish. He suggested that they play the game before several congregations and charge admission. The funds could be used for buying baseball equipment for kids in one of the more impoverished parishes. Everyone thought it was a great idea. In addition, he invited his own team to have dinner with him at the church after the game. At home in the kitchen, he spent most of the previous day cooking a spaghetti dinner, used his own funds to supply the chianti, and got several women in the congregation to serve the meal. He also got two hits in the game. Trying to mend things, he went out of his way to invite the pastor. Not only did the latter not come, but later that week Father Frank received another personal sermon about how he had been neglecting some of his pastoral duties. There were also several parishioners in the local hospital, and one or two had come in troubled by marital difficulties. The pastor had had his hands full all week and had wanted to refer some of these responsibilities to Father Frank, but it appeared that baseball and spaghetti were more important than his pastoral commitments. Father Frank could not believe his ears. The previous month he had been chastised for paying too much attention to pastoral duties, now he was blamed for being insensitive. Once again he spoke his mind, told the pastor that he thought life required balance, and argued eloquently for the notion that the well-rounded priest made for a more spiritual priest. Father Frank's content response to the emotional process between them was as ineffective as any spouse responding that way to a partner's henpecking.

The following week he was again called on the carpet by the Superior, and this time he was told to stick to his duties. Again, his defense of his behavior seemed unheard by those above him.

Two months later a third incident occurred that so unnerved him he began to reconsider his vows. Father Frank had a deep interest in music. Before he had become a novice, he had played bass in a jazz quartet. Throughout his studies for the priesthood he had read about innovative liturgy being experimented with in the church. One day after choir practice he heard several members jazzing up some sacred strains. It was clear, however, that they were not making fun of the doxologies and, in fact, had modulated the melodies using the proper mode. He walked in on them, to their embarrassment, and told them of his interest; before long they were working on a creative service. Father Frank wrote a special introduction describing how, despite the changes in musical styles, certain basic concepts laid down long ago about mode and mood had been retained. The attendance was as high as it was at Christmas Mass, and everyone wanted to know when they could do it again.

Two weeks later Father Frank received a call from the Provincial asking him if he were ready to do the "will of God," which, it seemed, was to go to South America. At this point he asked, and received permission from his Superior, to get personal help outside of the Order. He was thoroughly disillusioned. All his life his dream had been to be a parish priest. He had wondered if he would be able to stick to his vows since he had so many interests, but in talking this over with older, experienced priests, all had urged him to stick it out. He would find it difficult at first, but if he could stick with it, they all said, he would be an important addition to the priesthood.

He had been feeling a genuine satisfaction with his work, his self, and his goals, and instead of being appreciated, he was being rejected. The sense of failure was so deep that he found himself questioning everything, and he was having a lot of fantasies about women. No matter how hard he had tried to get into the good "graces" of the older pastor, nothing worked. The old man was unwilling to have any personal relationship at all, and only initiated conversations with him around organizing of their responsibilities. It was suggested that perhaps there were some unseen triangles, some other unresolved issues in the order, local or extended, that were surfacing in this relationship. Father Frank was encouraged, therefore, to ask what might have been going on several years ago, either in the rectory or in the larger system, before the pastor became known for his grumpiness.

It did not take him long to find out. One of the older priests who had known the pastor "back when" spilled the beans. The pastor had never been known for his charm, but he had never been bitter either. He had always been a good, hardworking priest, a bit conservative perhaps, but basically kind. He had lived pretty much to himself in the rectory with his housekeeper who, as is sometimes the case, was *his* keeper as well. An old Irish widow with grown children and no family, she had cooked for him, washed for him, nursed him when he was sick, and protected him from demanding parishioners. Over the years, he had become more and more dependent on her functioning for all his personal needs and to some extent even his entertainment. His passion was backgammon, and they would sometimes be up until 2 o'clock in the morning finishing off a game.

About 6 years ago, the housekeeper's grown daughter had become paralyzed and she had had to leave the pastor to take care of her grandchildren. Since then, a series of housekeepers had come and fled, none lasting more than a few months. But there was more. That original housekeeper, after her grandchildren were in high school and she was not needed around as much, found another priest to care for. That other priest was a former acolyte of the pastor who in recent years had become the Provincial!

The suggestion was therefore made that Father Frank do something to rework the cut-off and try to detriangle himself from this system. First he talked with the pastor about it, but found him unresponsive. Then, since the town in which the former housekeeper now lived was on the way to his own home, on his way to visit his family at Christmas, he stopped by to see the lady, told her what was happening, and suggested that he take back a taped message to the pastor. She agreed, but broke off in the middle of the recording and said, "Let me write him." Father Frank left the parish later that year and went to a place more to his liking. His successor, unlike Father Frank and his three predecessors, found a much more cooperative pastor.

12

The Extended Family: Its Potential for Salvation

AN EXTENDED FAMILY EXPERIENCE

When my mother, whose condition had been deteriorating for several years, reached 79, she fell and broke her leg. With little circulation below her waist, the cast created a sore that was in danger of becoming gangrenous. The surgeon wanted to amputate. The decision was to be up to me because I was her only child, my father was dead, and she no longer understood what was happening. What complicated my own ability to think clearly was the incredible anxiety of my aunt, her overfunctioning, older sister who lived next door. Throughout those last 4 months of my mother's life, during which I was to become intensely involved in the daily lives of my closest kin for the first time in 30 years, she would constantly criticize me to everyone.

Remembering my mother as one who did not give up easily, for 6 weeks, and against medical opinion, I favored saving her leg. Finally, I told her directly I was giving up. To my surprise, her leg began to heal and she was able to return home. The visiting nurse, however, tied the bandage too tightly and my mother's leg immediately became gangrenous. At this point, positions switched, the surgeon now saying that my mother was so close to death that amputation would be a "heroic" act. Since I had done a lot of thinking about how unresolved attachment makes it difficult to let someone die, I had difficulty with this one. I made the decision for the amputation on the ground that I could not let my mother's body poison itself when that was preventable; she would have to die "naturally." My extended family was generally supportive. But my mother's sister and those closest to her went on

294

attacking me for my failure to put my mother in a nursing home where she(!) would have been more comfortable.

Then the same visiting nurse, severely chastened by the doctors for her previous mistake, wanted to put my mother back in the hospital. I said no. For 3 years I had fought, against family pressure, to keep her out of institutions. With great difficulty I made the decision not to have her go back and die in an institution, but to let ill-nature take its course. Within 5 days she was dead.

I called each relative and took advantage of the reminiscing typical of such moments to make notes of what they said. At the funeral I read a "family eulogy" that included my own thoughts and those of the other family members. After the funeral I felt an increased sense of ability to deal with acutely anxious crises. You could have come up to me and said, "We need someone to make a decision that, if it is wrong, will spin the Earth out of orbit," and I would have responded without flinching, "I'll take the job."

A week after the funeral I felt absolutely no residue of sadness. I was able to go back to work immediately, with enthusiasm and without depression. If anything, I found an increased sense of creativity in my work. But just then two interesting events occurred in my work system. Several families I had been counseling went into severe crisis. As I understood it, when I had learned to deal with the forces of anxiety that had made me "me," I inadvertently had pulled away some of the supports with which I had been buttressing these families in my anxiety over their anxiety. I managed not to get retriangled into their anxiety, however, and almost all of them made leaps of growth.

An analogous reaction occurred within my congregational family. Annually, at contract time, I had come to expect some attack from my "loyal opposition." In the past I had often become quite engaged with some of these members. This time, however, their criticisms seemed boring, and I did not take the complaints very seriously. The reactions to my disengagement escalated. Two members mounted a personal attack that was far more virulent than anything I had ever encountered in 20 years of congregational family life.

GENERATION TO GENERATION

A major theme of this work has been the significance of anyone's family of origin for his or her functioning in other systems. It has been emphasized throughout that not only does our position in our extended families affect how we function in other relationships, but also that efforts to gain better differentiation of self in that extended field will have corresponding effects at home, at work, and on our health. This is equally true for clergy and laity, and may be what we have most in common with the members of our congregations. The more we can understand our own origins, the more we can sympathize with theirs; the more we can define our own families, the more we can help them modify the influence of, or mobilize the strengths in, theirs. And the more we realize how difficult it can be to gain any measure of self-differentiation, the more humbly we can appreciate their plight.

But for rabbis, ministers, priests, and nuns, position in family of origin has additional consequences. It also affects our calling on the most fundamental levels of our being, for it also affects our beliefs.

PARTICULAR SIGNIFICANCE OF SELF-DIFFERENTIATION FOR THE CLERGY

Generally speaking, anyone who works to gain more differentiation of self in his or her family of origin will find that the way one thinks and functions within his or her vocation is affected. This is because in the process of becoming better defined, we become more clear about our life's goals. For the clergy, however, the connection is deeper and more direct. There is no other profession on this planet where the ideals, the values, the principles, and the professional commitment are so much part and parcel of one's work. Doctors, lawyers, and politicians are affected by their belief systems, but the work of the clergy *is* belief systems. Since beliefs are the essence of self, to the extent we work to gain differentiation in our families or origin, we directly affect the context of our professional existence.

This connection between our origins and our calling also affects us in two other ways. First, most decisions to enter the clergy are influenced by multigenerational forces. To the extent that we can obtain more differentiation within that transmission process, therefore, we will increase our flexibility to function within the parameters of our "calling," and that usually carries with it more latitude for facing crises, and provides satisfaction rather than stress. In other words, to the extent that we are able to understand those multigenerational forces, to that extent can we reacquire our profession for our own. Second, there is a connection between scruples, either their loss or their tyranny (scrupulousness), and our extended family positions. When we are troubled in either direction, by working at differentiation of self in families of origin we can often move away from such self-destructive extremes.

The significance of our extended family position also comes to the fore when we are called to serve "professionally" within our own personal families, because we are never just another family member. In addition, the same multigenerational forces that are contributing to the event at hand could also have contributed to our becoming the family's "identified clergyperson," with all the consequences such identifying process has for a fixed role. Thus, precisely when we are doing what any other parent, son, daughter, or spouse should do at such moments, and precisely when we are bringing to our own kin the essence of our expertise, there is always the danger that at precisely those moments we are locking ourselves into our family position even further. One result is that we can get professionalized right out of the intimacy. The way out of this bind is, on the one hand, not to be afraid to function as other family members would at such times, and not to be afraid to utilize our expertise and experience, but, on the other hand, to make sure to involve other family members in the process also. In other words, we should function in part as "coach" and never purely as "standard bearer." Where we can contribute in this way to our families, then the crisis of the moment becomes a further opportunity for our own differentiation.

This chapter will describe three situations in which members of the clergy were encouraged to deal with personal and professional dilemmas by reentering and modifying their position in the triangles of their families of origin. As in the previous chapter, personal details have been disguised and interchanged to protect privacy. The family emotional processes, however, and the course of the healing are presented as they occurred. Once again, the examples selected were chosen not because they exemplify typical "clergy" symptoms, but because they illustrate the most basic emotional triangles with which clergy struggle, as well as the range of family phenomena in which they surface.

THREE EXTENDED FAMILIES

SISTER MARY

Sister Mary comes back into contact with her family of origin and finds herself caught in the separation issue she had never resolved as an adolescent. Catholic clergy who enter an order before they have had time to work through such separation processes in their families often find that physical distance does not promote more separation. On the contrary, it freezes the process, keeps it from developing further, and transfers the unresolved issues to their new order.

The separation that should have been dealt with years ago is finally facilitated by having Sister Mary rework her position in the triangles of her family of origin (they have only been dormant, not absent, in her absence), and by enabling her to obtain a multigenerational perspective on the forces that led to her own manner of leaving and relating.

Sister Mary left home at 17 to join a convent. The oldest of six, and the only daughter, she had been a responsible, overly mature child who helped her mother with her crippled youngest brother and her ne'er-do-well, alcoholic father. Her relationship with her mother had been close, but it was more a closeness of administrative cooperation than intimacy. Her relationship with her father had been nil. The youngest of six, he had been nursed his whole life, first by his mother and older sisters, then by his wife. He had been absolutely no help in the raising of his children, and had developed over the years into the caricature of the beer-bellied, TV sports fan.

Sister Mary's interest in becoming a nun developed slowly. She had gone to parochial schools, and her brightness and energy kept her at the head of the class. Most of her teachers had thought she would be a good candidate. She did not remember her parents trying to influence her in either direction. She left immediately after high school graduation. At 41 she came back to her home town to obtain a graduate degree in education. During this period, she visited her family frequently, often staying for several days. Two years later, after completing her studies, when she was about to go back to her order, she found herself almost totally unable to separate from her family again. She sought help for her emotional dilemma.

Sister Mary belonged to a very liberal order. She had neither worn a habit nor lived in a convent for several years. Her own "liberality," however, went far beyond that. During the previous 10 years she had had several intense emotional affairs with married men whom she met in the course of her educational consulting. Her decision to obtain a degree was in part an effort to get distance from these men, but also to retrain herself in case she decided to abandon her vows completely. She had looked forward to being close to her family again, but was totally unprepared for the gravitational pull she found that system exerting on her.

She was back in the middle with her parents and her brother, but it was a far more intense situation this time. Dad, much older, was retired on a pension that barely kept her parents comfortable. Her crippled brother still lived at home, and her other brothers all gave financial support. Mother, still her overfunctioning self, continued to rescue Dad from the neighborhood pub, and put most of her emotional energy into her crippled son.

Mary said it was as if time had never passed.
Would she be willing to tell her father about her affairs?
Inconceivable.
How about mother? Could Mary ask her how to resist men?
More unthinkable.

The theory of an emotional triangle was explained to Mary, in particular, how her decision to become a nun could have been influenced by her position in her nuclear family, or her mother's position in her family of origin. If she were willing to work at obtaining better differentiation in those triangles, it was suggested, the resulting self-definition could have a positive effect on her religious commitment. She liked the concept, but was petrified. She just could not talk to her father. In fact, said Mary, she cried every time he came into the room. Would she be willing to talk with her parents, if not about the vow of chastity conflict, at least concerning her conflict about remaining a nun? Not possible.

For several months Sister Mary tried to get the courage to raise questions with her mother, but found herself too full of pity for the old woman to dare upset her.

The focus was then switched to mother's family of origin. Mary's mother, also the oldest of six, had taken primary responsibility for the raising of her own siblings. When she was 17, her father, Mary's grandfather, had simply vanished. She took care of the house while her own mother, Mary's grandmother, worked at odd jobs to support them. Further details showed an emerging pattern of anxiously energetic women and dependent husbands at almost every turn. In her own generation, Mary said, her brothers also had married "aggressive women" who "took over" their lives. She also realized that the seductive aspect in her affairs had been the great need of these men to be cared for.

The multigenerational pattern of overfunctioning wives and caretaking daughters enabled Mary to see that what was happening in her own nuclear family was almost a tradition. She still, however, was unable to "upset" her mother, though she did begin to suggest to Mom that the two "poor, unfortunate" men in her life might be able to do all right without her. Mother agreed that daughter was probably right, but seemed unable to let go.

As the spring arrived, the season for Mary's departure, a "fortuitous" event occurred. Mother suddenly began to develop sharp pains in her abdomen. The doctors weren't sure what it was, but Mary began to go home more and more to help. It was suggested that mother's symptoms could have something to do with Mary's preparations for leaving and that this could be the opportunity she was looking for to shift the triangle, that is, if she could get Dad to nurse Mom. A wonderful idea, she laughed, but knowing him, unimaginable.

Then, one night, Mary received a call from her father at 2 o'clock in the morning. Mother was in severe pain. But the light began to dawn: Why had he not called the emergency service himself? Resisting the impulse to make the call, she told father to take charge and said she'd meet him at the hospital. Father tried to outfumble Mary with excuses about his driving, his poor sense of direction, and his gout. Mary held firm. The diagnosis was gallstones; the recommendation, an immediate operation. Mary's instinctive reaction was to move in and take care of father and brother.

"Why not force father to take care of brother?"
"He wouldn't know what to do."
"Then offer advice if you must, but don't take over."

With the greatest of difficulty Mary agreed that this was the opportunity she had been afraid to create. Instead of moving in, she just kept in contact from a distance. To her complete shock, 2 days after mother's operation father called and asked if she would like to come to dinner. "Who's the chef?" she joked. "Come and find out," he said, with a lilt in his voice that Mary had never heard before.

The dinner was magnificent. Mary asked where had he learned to cook like that? Dad explained: "I never told you that I had once been a chef, learned it in the army. I'm a little rusty now. Your mother won't let me near the kitchen but we (*winking at her brother*) cook things up once in a while when she's not home."

With Mother in the hospital, Mary got to know her father for the first time in her life, and her brother too, who, it seemed, was far more functional when not under his mother's watchful eye. Emboldened by the evidence that what she had long observed in her nuclear family was systemic rather than characterological, Mary began to further her plans for going back to the order. But she decided to detriangle a little more beforehand.

On her hospital visits she started telling mother how she had better mend fast because father and brother were doing so well they might not need her when she returned. Then she started telling father that he shouldn't become so self-sufficient because everyone knew that if he didn't let mother take care of him she might get terribly depressed. She also "confided" in brother that his skill at getting mother to care for him was ingenious, but that since mother would not be around forever, he had better start finding another woman to take her place.

EXTENDED FAMILY: POTENTIAL FOR SALVATION

When Mary's mother returned from the hospital, father continued to look after her needs without having to ask Mary's help. Brother too helped his mother, wheeling his chair around like some private messenger service. Within a month Mary found herself looking forward to her new position enthusiastically. She also said she was able to pray comfortably again for the first time in years, and was sure that she would be able to stay committed to her vows. Then, the night before she left, when several of her "drinking sisters" came through town on their way to a conference, they all went out for a beer with Dad, who, as they skipped out the door, reminded his wife to have some warm tea before she went to bed.

RABBI BARUCH

Rabbi Baruch, like Sister Mary, has distanced from his family of origin. His relational symptom falls in a similar category (sexual acting out). In addition, he also has had a faith crisis. As he becomes more comfortable within his family of origin, however, those attitudes wither, thus revealing that they were content issues to begin with.

Rabbi Daniel Baruch had started or saved three congregations in three different communities over a 15-year period. Each time he had begun practically from scratch, assembled a small but loyal band around him, used his enormous reserves of energy to produce a vibrant committee structure, attracted new members with his dynamic preaching, and then, just as the congregation was beginning to feel established, left them in the lurch.

He had been with his most recent synagogue 6 years. This time he was considering leaving the rabbinate altogether, as well as his wife. Friends, sensing some connection between the two, suggested he seek professional help. He didn't think he needed it, but he decided to see a counselor anyway because the alternative profession he was considering was counseling. He had already applied to graduate school.

His parents, far more traditional than he, had not liked his becoming a liberal rabbi. In addition, his wife and mother did not get along. He had met his wife in Israel (she was from a poor Moroccan Jewish family), and she had had great difficulty adapting to the fast pace of American culture, no less than to American Jewish middle-class values. She treated her husband with utmost deference despite the fact that his boredom with her had become painfully obvious to everyone. Rabbi Baruch said his wife had "failed to grow," whereas he, facing challenge after challenge, naturally had continued to develop.

"What would your parents say if you left the rabbinate?"

"They probably would be ecstatic if it meant a move toward a more traditional posture."

"And if you left your wife?"

"My mother would have ten women lined up in a week. It's enough to make one stay married."

"Why leave something you're good at?"

"Because people today aren't interested in religion, just religious buildings. I quit each congregation because everyone was using me. They were thrilled at my eloquence, but they didn't change internally."

"Well, you're lucky to find out how disgusting humanity is while you're still young so that you can get on with something useful."

"And I'm having an affair with a non-Jewish woman."

"You really do want all the way out, don't you?"

"Met her at a community dance for the Jewish Family Service. She's a social worker, two kids, never met anyone so compatible. We can talk till 3 nonstop. Everything fits: our values, our views on raising kids, music, travel."

"Lucky for you religion isn't important."

"She said she'd convert."

"Does your wife know about it?"

"I think she suspects, but I'm on the run all the time anyway."

"Would you be willing to bring her in with you?"

"I don't know."

"Would you be willing to tell her?"

"I don't think she could take it."

"Wanna bet?"

"She's tough, in a way, but I'm afraid she'd break down."

At the next session Mrs. Baruch was present; she revealed that not only did she know that her husband was having an affair, but she also knew who the woman was.

"How do you know?"

"It happened before."

"You mean that's really why he's left these other congregations?"

"No. But when he gets like this, I know from experience that it's going to happen. The pattern is always the same."

"How come you've put up with it all this time?"

"I don't know. His mother thinks I should leave."

"His mother knows?"

"My mother knows?" (simultaneously)

"I told her last time, and she said he's just a spoiled brat."

"But she never said anything to him?"

"She's the same as me I guess. We're both afraid."

"He beats you?"

"No. He's really a very nice guy, but he's so sensitive, kind of fragile."

"Mrs. Baruch, he says you're boring."

"Well, I haven't had much opportunity to develop. As soon as we got to the United States I was pregnant. Then he started his first congregation. I felt I should help him get started, so I devoted all my efforts to his career. Twice I wanted to go back to school, but he kept asking me to wait. Then I got pregnant again. Then we moved to our next congregation and the whole cycle started over."

"I guess that's why he picked a Moroccan."

"What do you mean?"

"Well, women from Arab cultures know their place."

"That's one convention I'm about to change."

Rabbi and Mrs. Baruch were seen separately. Mrs. Baruch was encouraged to become more independent, to get closer to her family in Israel, and to some American cousins she had been wanting to look up. The doctrine that a self is more attractive than a no-self was described to her, and she came out of the Middle Ages overnight, much to the consternation, and admiration, of her husband.

Rabbi Baruch was meanwhile encouraged to move closer to his family, in particular, his father, whom he did not know at all. He should talk with him about his dilemma over whether to stay in the rabbinate or not. He was reluctant because father, an elderly man in his 80s, suffered from severe angina. In addition, he was sure his father would be critical and distant.

He was surprised by the closeness that did develop. His father talked about similar quandaries in his life when he himself had turned to his father. But he had received no support and had vowed that he would never turn away his own son like that. When Rabbi Baruch asked why it was, then, that his father hadn't been more available when Rabbi Baruch was younger, he replied, "I don't know. Too busy trying to make it, I guess."

During the course of their discussions, father told son how proud he was of him, that he had great ability, and that he should stop trying to save the world. It didn't matter to father at all if he remained a rabbi. He should just do what would make him feel fulfilled. What about the fact that he was a liberal rabbi? Didn't that bother him? No, it never bothered him. It was mother who found it so difficult. "Because of her great-grandfather," added his father. "You were named for him, I think."

It was far more than that. Great-grandfather was supposed to have been one of the *lamed-vav-nicks.* (*Lamed-vav* is the number 36 in Hebrew. Jewish folk tradition says the world is so wicked that it would have been destroyed but for the sake of 36 righteous in every generation—who, of course, don't know that they are the righteous ones.)

He then went to mother and asked why, if she thought he was such a spoiled brat, she had not raised him differently. Mother explained his importance to her own mother. As she talked about her own origins, he found that she softened on the religious issues, becoming more accepting of his choices, including his wife.

Over the next few months, Rabbi Baruch worked on individuating his relationships with both parents, with his older, very responsible sister, and with his younger, flaky, divorced sister, whom his parents supported along with her daughter, their grandchild.

A few months later, Rabbi Baruch's father died and his son conducted the funeral. Almost immediately afterwards he found himself triangled with the three remaining (female) members of his family of origin as each tried to give him advice on how to treat the other two. Recognizing the position he had inherited from his father, he began to appreciate some of his father's distance for the first time, and found an additional reason for his own tendency to distance. With additional coaching, however, he learned to keep detriangling by becoming a nonanxious relay between them. This enabled him to remain close to them and, at the same time, to reduce his emotional dependency on his other nuclear systems (marriage and congregation).

In the spring, when he was accepted at graduate school, he asked for a year's extension so that he could think things over. He used that year to try a less charismatic, less enervating style of leadership, which had positive effects on his congregation, his marriage, and his commitment. The following year he "forgot" to reapply for school.

MR. SANDERS

Mr. Sanders not only has followed in his father's footsteps professionally, but also has wound up in an identical family triangle between an overinvested mother, from whom he has distanced, and an adaptive wife who has conspired in the process to cut-off by becoming totally attached to her husband. Unlike his own mother, however, Mr. Sanders's wife tries to regain her sense of self. He responds to the loss of fusion by going into an emotional and physical deterioration that threatens his faith, his life, and his resolve to live.

We will see in this example not only the influence of multigenerational process, not only the influence of extended family from a distance, but also their availability and their power as a source for healing.

Joseph Sanders came from a missionary family. He and his older sisters spent their early years in China. Their father, a totally dedicated man, later served in Africa, where he died of cancer just when Joe was entering the seminary. Joe's mother and grandmother, a cantankerous "frontier" woman, one of his sisters, all his uncles and aunts, and several of his cousins still lived in the town where his mother had grown up. Joe, however, avoided the family like the plague. He had even less contact with his father's family, who lived in a nearby town.

Originally Joe also had planned to be a missionary himself, but dropped out of medical school in his third year after marrying his wife, and went straight to the seminary instead. Twenty years later, with kids on their own, his wife became very depressed, went into psychoanalysis, got Joe to go into couples therapy with her, and then left him with the house, the congregation, and the therapist. Joe immediately became despondent and had frequent thoughts of suicide, and for a while was almost totally unable to function in his post. She had been his soul mate, his constant companion, the one person he could trust, rely on, talk to. She was his best, if not his only, friend. Her complaint was that he was too rigid, too intellectual, never took initiative, and never showed feeling.

Joe was encouraged to reenter his family of origin so that his wife would become less important to him. He agreed with the idea but found that putting it into practice was all but impossible. During these months he talked mostly about his wife, whom he saw once a week.

About a half year after his wife had left, he was still despondent and heart-broken. One morning he found a small growth near the base of his spine. He called a doctor immediately, but even before he was examined, the former medical student expected what the diagnosis would be. His father had died of cancer, and so had his mother's father. In addition, he was sure one of father's surviving sisters now had cancer.

His wife came back to family therapy with her husband, her guilt only slightly less than if she had participated in the Crucifixion itself. It appeared, however, that Mr. Sanders would need no help with his own martyrdom. He considered resigning from his church. What was the point of starting new programs he couldn't finish? Let them begin afresh with someone who would be around. In an effort to encourage him to fight, the theory of survival in a hostile environment was explained, namely, that the response of the organism to the environment is a major factor, and could even modify the environment. He said he could buy that. But when the idea came back to reentering his family, he demurred once more.

Several weeks later he came in with his wife again. The opening question was: "What would you like to work on today?" (meaning the marriage or the extended family). His response was: "I can only focus on my death." The needle on the wife's guilt meter went right off the scale.

It was now clear that neither comfort, softness, encouragement, nor sensitivity would deliver this man from whatever spook was draining his spirit. An effort was therefore made to bypass the demon by challenging his soul directly.

"Well, a lot of people certainly will be sad when you die, but perhaps it will not be nearly as tragic as you think. Your kids have had you when they needed you most. Your wife is ready to start a new life anyway. Your mother does have two other children and several grandchildren to bring her comfort. Your congregation is already on notice to find someone else. While people will be sorry for a while, after some appropriate mourning they'll probably all be O.K."

"You bastard!"

"I'm just trying to help, but I'll not be tyrannized by your sensitivity."

Mr. and Mrs. Sanders were now seen separately. She was encouraged *not* to take all the credit for the malignancy and not to move back with her husband if she genuinely didn't want to, and furthermore to err on the side of challenge rather than sympathy. She was also seen with her own mother when the latter came for a visit. During that session the supersensitive overprotection in her family repeatedly came to the surface in discussions about how mother took care of her husband as well as all her married and unmarried children.

Since the day of the "exorcism," Mr. Sanders had stayed on a course for survival, and he finally agreed he had to do something about his cut-off with his family of origin. The first issue addressed was how to tell his family. His mother, he said, would come apart at the seams. First her father, then her husband, now him! He added: "Not only that, she'll be on the phone every week telling me all the new cures and doctors she's read about." It was suggested that he tell his 85-year-old mother first.

Granny took it in stride, called the American Cancer Society the next day and got all the material she could read on his type of cancer. He went over to his mother's and told her as straightforwardly as he could, and she reacted as he'd predicted.

For the first time in his life, Mr. Sanders said, he was able to keep himself from being overwhelmed by her feelings. "I don't know what you're getting so upset for. Your mother took it very well when I told her." "You told my mother!"

When his mother became less hysterical, Mr. Sanders invited her to visit his family counselor with him. During that session her general protectiveness of others was astounding. She never said a bad word about anyone. She was sweetness and light—despite the fact that Mr. Sanders implicitly blamed her and his father for all his problems. It also came out that, despite his passivity in his marriage, Mr. Sanders had grown up a very reactive and rebellious child. This preacher's kid had been arrested as a major leader of protest movements, was kicked out of school for refusing to shave his beard, and spent 6 months in a youth detention center when a search for his car revealed a cache of marijuana. Somewhat embarrassed, after each of these revelations Mr. Sanders was quick to remind his mother that he had been the innocent victim of larger forces.

At one point Mrs. Sanders lost her cool. Totally forgetting the circumstances, she told her son she was fed up with the fact that he never owned up to his own contributions to the problems. Then, stopping short, she turned and said, "That's the first time I've ever told him off."

After that session he still was reluctant to work at differentiating himself in his family of origin. But then an incident occurred that supplied the motivation. One day his estranged wife told him that she had been sleeping with another man. That night he woke up with all the symptoms of physiological shock. He realized that it could be related to his cancer treatments, but there was also no question in his mind that if the treatments had made his immunological system more vulnerable, the trigger was emotional. "My God," he reported saying to himself, "I'm having an unbelievably overreactive, autoimmune response!" Against his own better medical judgment, he did not go to the hospital, but sat quietly for 2 hours trying to control his reactivity.

The following week he began looking for employment, and the week after he began to work earnestly at differentiation in his extended family. Over the next 4 months, Mr. Sanders tried to learn as much as he could about his family's patterns of reactivity and his father's way of functioning in crisis. He also established direct relationships with members of his father's family, often to the disapproval of his mother, and he began to work at becoming less reactive to her anxiety. Throughout this period he also found himself less affected by the separation from his wife.

And then he happened to mention a fact never brought up before. He was encouraged to take his mother for a visit to his father's grave.

"That's almost impossible."
"Why? She won't go?"
"It's too expensive. Besides, we might not find it."

It turned out that father had died in Africa and was buried there. Mother had returned to the United States alone. No ceremony had

307

ever been conducted here to mark the occasion, and there was no grave site or funerary reminder of him in this country. Mr. Sanders's father, who also had spent his whole life avoiding his family of origin, had asked Joe's mother to leave him among his followers. He had been buried in the church's graveyard. Indeed, when they had gone on their last mission to Africa, he already knew he had cancer. Since his death, he had, in effect, been cut out of the family as effectively as he had cut himself off from them.

Joe was asked if he would be willing to bring him back into the system somehow. He said he had tried to do that at the time father died, but would just hear: "We don't need something material to bring him back to mind." It was strongly suggested that if some material reminder could be created for his father, it might affect his own material presence. He liked the idea. Joe wrote to people in Africa, obtained pictures of his father's grave and a memorial plaque he'd never known about. He was also sent personal reminiscences from some of those who had known him and who obviously still revered his memory. Joe had a similar marker erected over an unused plot in the family cemetery and asked everyone to a ceremony commemorating its unveiling.

Only a few came. His mother thought it was an unnecessary expense. After the ceremony, father's sister told Joe he was "doing the right thing" and mentioned how her mother (Joe's grandmother) would have been so happy to see this. She had died a year after this favorite son. The aunt added: "You know, she loved him so. But he really couldn't stand to be around her." Joe reported afterwards that his family, who never used to mention his father, was now including the absent saint in their conversations.

A few months later, his doctors told him that his cancer was in remission. He took a new post, where he met a woman he had known before he had married. He stopped longing for his wife, allowed her to divorce him without any struggle, and later wrote: "Things are going fairly well. I keep telling my congregation we're all in remission. It helps my survival. But the biggest change is in my preaching. I used to live in perpetual dread of of not being able to come up with material for my next sermon. I anxiously looked for topics in everything I read, from newspapers to novels, everything I saw, movies, plays, or TV. No longer! The self is an inexhaustible supply of sermons."

FULL CIRCLE

And so we have come full circle. Here is the ultimate reciprocity among all our families. To the extent that we can learn to define

ourselves within the emotional triangles of our families of origin, to
that same extent will we have the increased capacity to do this in any of ✓
our other relationship systems. And in the process of doing so, our
position in that set of interlocking triangles will become converted from
a source of stress to a source of strength and survival. It is at this point,
also, that we can see most clearly how leadership can become a more
fundamental healing modality than expertise, both for others and
ourselves. Increased self-differentiation in a family leader, in particular
the ability to treat his or her own personal crises and transitions as
opportunities for growth (rather than as hostile environments that
victimize or which must be escaped), has immediate ramifications
throughout all interlocking family systems. This is true for any leader
of course, but for members of the clergy, because of the special entrée
afforded by virtue of our community position, such effect on our
followers is a "natural" process. In other words, it works this way not
because we consciously "model a role" for others to emulate, but
because of the nature of our connectedness.

AUTHOR'S BIBLIOGRAPHY

Numbers in parentheses indicate relevant chapters in this volume.

"The Birthday Party: An Experiment in Obtaining Change in One's Own Extended Family," *Family Process*, Vol. 10, No. 3, September 1971. Describes my own personal efforts to bring about change in my family of origin centered around the occasion of a surprise party for my mother on her 70th birthday. (1, 12)

"Systems and Ceremonies," in *The Family Life Cycle: A Framework for Family Therapy*, edited by E. Carter and M. McGoldrick, Gardner Press, New York, 1980. The original basis for Chapter 7 containing, in addition, a section on how clergy can use their knowledge of family process to heighten the spirituality of the occasion by involving family members in life-cycle ceremonies, while remaining within the parameters of their tradition. (7)

"Bar Mitzva When the Parents Are No Longer Partners," *Journal of Reform Judaism*, Vol. 28, No. 2, Spring 1981. Discusses how clergy become triangled into unresolved family issues during life-cycle celebrations and end up bearing the stress for the entire system. (1, 7, 8)

"The Myth of the Shiksa," in *Ethnicity and Family Therapy*, edited by M. McGoldrick, J. K. Pearce, and J. Giordano, Guilford Press, New York, 1982. Describes the family dynamics involved in cross-cultural marriages, and how all families use their cultural background to avoid taking personal responsibility for their behavior. (3, 7)

"Theater and Therapy," *The Family Therapy Networker*, Vol. 8, No. 1, January–February 1984. A comparison of the efforts of great dramatists and therapists in their attempts to overcome resistance in the process of increasing awareness. (2)

"Family Therapy and the Spirit of Adventure," *Newsletter of the American Family Therapy Association*, May 1984. Compares the present difficulty the healing establishment is having in accepting the family model to the difficulty

311

AUTHOR'S BIBLIOGRAPHY

Europe had in assimiliating the discovery of the "New World" into their established world view. (1, 2)

"Synagogues and Churches," in *Practicing Family Therapy in Diverse Settings*, edited by M. Berger and G. Jerkovic, Jossey-Bass, San Francisco, 1984. A systems approach to premarital counseling. Illustrates how helping courting couples to understand the emotional heritage of their families of origin, and working at unresolved issues there, can be used as a general approach to premarital counseling, and for dealing with specific problems in their own relationship. (3)

"Emotional Process in the Market Place: The Family Therapist as Consultant to Work Systems," in *The Family Therapist as Consultant: New Applications of Systems Theory*, edited by L. C. Wynne, T. Weber, and S. H. McDaniel, Guilford Press, New York, in press. Applies the concepts of Section III to nonreligious (i.e., general work) systems. (8, 9, 10)

"Family Resources for Healing and Survival," in *Family Resources*, edited by M. Karpel, Guilford Press, New York, in press. Develops in depth the concepts introduced in Chapter 2, rule 10, that describe how victim-thinking, variability of response, and the presence of a nonanxious leader affect a family's role in its own survival. (2)

INDEX

INDEX

Disease
  linear model of, 123, 124
  psychosomatic, 123
  systems model of, 124, 125
Disengagement process, 260, 261
Divorce, 189

E

Ecumenicity, 1
  of family systems theory, 19
Emotion
  health and, 121
  polarity of, *see* Symmetry
  in separation process, 257–259
  spirituality and, 7
  unresolved, aging and, 152
Emotional coordinates, 180
Emotional distance, 41, 42
Emotional field
  physiological systems connected
    with, 125–129
  and systems model of disease, 124
Emotional interdependency, 25, 26
Emotional triangle, 35, 36
  laws of, 36–39
Endocrine system, 126, 127
Entering
  strategies for, 268–271
  systems approach to, 253
Esalen, 14
Exorcism, 146, 306
  and abortion, 186, 187
  life-cycle ceremony as, 162
Expertise
  counseling, 4–6
  multiple, 3, 4
  versus self-definition, 2, 3
Extended family, 31–34
  of clergy, 290–293
    case histories of, 294, 295, 297–
      308
  health of marriage in, 69, 70
  self-differentiation and, 32, 34, 35,
    295, 296
  symmetry in, 61
  see also Family of origin

F

Faith crisis, 301–304
Faith healing, 5
Family
  as unit of treatment, 20, 21
  blended, 269
  child-focused, *see* Child focus
  of clergy, *see* Clergy family
  congregational, *see* Congregational
    family
  extended, *see* Extended family
  individual member symmetry, 60
  life-cycle events in, *see* Rites of
    passage
  marriage in, case example of, 11–
    13
  nuclear, *see* Nuclear family
  overlapping forms, 1
  projection process in, 21, 22
  systems thinking and, 17
Family counseling, and family
    therapy, distinction between,
    122
Family model, and religion, 6, 7
Family of origin
  self-differentiation and, 32, 34, 35
    case history of, 304–308
  sibling position in, 54, 55
  see also Extended family
Family process, 40
  chronic conditions in, 45–47
  diagnosis and, 56–58
  emotional distance in, 41, 42
  and human response, 63, 64
  loss and replacement in, 42–45
  medical model in, 123–125
  pain and responsibility in, 47–50
  paradoxical intervention in, 50–52
  resistance in, *see* Resistance
  secrets and communication
    systems in, 52–54
  sibling position in, 54, 55
  and survival, 62, 63
  symmetry of, 58–62
Family systems theory
  congregational family and, 194,
    195
  and differentiation of self, 27–31

315

INDEX

Toman, W., 54
Toxicity, 64
Transactional Analysis, 14
Triangle
  and detriangling, 75–78
  emotional, 35–39
  and entrance into congregational
    family, 269–271
  hierarchical, 254–257
  interlocking, 88–91
  of nuclear and extended family,
    133, 134
  in religious organizations, 212
    and life-cycle events, 214, 215
    between parishioners, 213, 214
    between staff, 213
  of resistance, 223, 224

  self-differentiation and, 231–234
  responsibility, 49, 50

V

Vicious circle, 131
Visitation, family systems approach
  to, 136–146

W

Walden II, 13
Weddings, 179, 182, 183
  preparation for, 184
Work systems, 197–202
  see also Religious organizations

319